Practical Reason

Philosophical Papers of Georg Henrik von Wright

Practical Reason

GEORG HENRIK VON WRIGHT

Philosophical Papers
Volume I

Cornell University Press
Ithaca, New York

First published 1983 by Cornell University Press

International Standard Book Number 0-8014-1673-6
Library of Congress Catalog Card Number 83-71775

Printed in Great Britain

Contents

Introduction

The first six studies published in this collection have their point of departure in my book *The Varieties of Goodness*, the remaining two in *Norm and Action*. Both works were based on my Gifford Lectures in the University of St Andrews and published by Routledge & Kegan Paul, London, in 1963. The first had no ancestor worth mention in my earlier literary output. The second had grown out of my preoccupation, since 1951, with "deontic logic" which was in origin a by-product of my inquiries into the logic of modal concepts.

The two works mentioned, although simultaneously written and published, are different in method and spirit. My contributions to the logic of actions and norms are straightforward "philosophical logic" in the sense that they use methods and techniques of formal logic for the purpose of clarifying the structure of actionist and normative discourse. The discussion of the same kind of discourse in *The Varieties of Goodness* can perhaps be labelled "logical analysis" but it is decidedly not "formal". I always had the feeling that formal methods simply are not applicable to this second approach. I mention this because others who are working in the same field may not share with me the impression of opposition and maybe irreconcilability between the two types of approach.

At the time of writing *The Varieties of Goodness* I had been much influenced by Elizabeth Anscombe's book *Intention* and her revival of the Aristotelian theme of "practical reasoning (inference, syllogism)". Anscombe also drew my attention to Charles Taylor's book *The Explanation of Behavior* (1965). It impressed me deeply. After reading it, my interest in practical inference became an interest in action-*explanation*—and this interest led me to consider the relationship between the (predominantly) "nomothetic" natural sciences and the (typically) "hermeneutic" sciences of man. The outcome was a book, *Explanation and Understanding* (Cornell University Press, Ithaca, N.Y./Routledge & Kegan Paul, London, 1971) in which I tried to give a new twist to a classic debate in the theory and philosophy of science, the so-called *Erklären—Verstehen* controversy.

The type of practical inference which I have studied can, in rough outline, be described as follows: An action is being related as "conclusion" to an aim or end of a given agent and an opinion of his concerning the means to its attainment as "premisses". When the action is a *fait accompli* the inference schema provides an explanation of the action. The structure of the schema and the nature of the connection between premisses and conclusion in it is, however, very much of a problem.

Dissatisfaction with my earlier attempts to deal with practical inference urged me to return to the topic time and time again. The first attempt—simultaneous with the publication of *The Varieties of Goodness*—and three "returns" to the subject are published in this collection. They testify, I hope, to some progress towards a better understanding of the subject-matter—but they also represent essential shifts in the angle under which the problems are being attacked. These changes seemed to me important enough to justify republication of the papers in spite of minor inconsistencies between the author's successive positions.

In *Explanation and Understanding* (here echoed in the essay "On so-called Practical Inference") I claimed that the practical inference pattern holds a position in the human and social sciences similar to that of the deductive–nomological inference pattern ("the covering law model") in the natural sciences. This is an exaggeration. Far from all explanation in the human sciences is explanation of *action*—either individual or collective. And far from all explanation of action conforms to a practical inference pattern. Moreover, though action is, primarily, *intentional* behaviour not all forms of intentional action spring from the *intentions* of agents. The much wider range of the intentional has only gradually become clear to me. Yet the type of teleological schema which I have discussed under the heading "practical inference", linking intentions with actions, still seems to me to hold a pivotal position in the field of action explanation. Of this I have tried to give a fuller and more balanced picture in the essays "Determinism and the Study of Man" and "Explanation and Understanding of Action", printed in this volume, and also in a monograph with the title *Freedom and Determination* (North-Holland Publishing Company, Amsterdam, 1980).

The two papers "The Foundation of Norms and Normative Statements" and "On Promises" also belong in the orbit of *The Varieties of Goodness*. They reflect efforts to show how normative requirements may be given a foundation (justification) in the practical necessities under given ends or basic valuations. I think it is of the essence of norms (norm-giving activity) that there is a connection between what might be called the "deontic" and the "technical" aspects of norms—or between genuine (categorical or conditional) norms and that which Kant and others have called "hypothetical imperatives".

This connection does not mean reduction of the deontic "ought" to an anankastic "must". Nor does it establish a one-to-one correlation between norms and means–end relationships. The connection is reflected in phenomena of a more "global" nature which might be described as an *"aura of normative pressure"* surrounding an efficacious code (order, system) of norms. (See below, pp. 39 and 55.)

Ever since the appearance of my first paper on deontic logic in *Mind* in 1951 I felt that there was some philosophically essential aspect of norms (normative concepts and discourse) which the formal system I had constructed either did not capture at all or tried to capture in the wrong way. In the 30 years which have passed I have again and again returned to the topic—often with a new idea which I thought would at last put things essentially right. But always, so far, to be disappointed. When writing a survey paper[1] on the subject for a conference in Rome in 1977 I had again some ideas leading in a hitherto unexplored direction which seemed to me promising. They eventually found embodiment in a longish study "On the Logic of Norms and Actions", first published in an anthology *New Studies in Deontic Logic* (ed. by Risto Hilpinen; D. Reidel Publishing Co., Dordrecht, Holland, 1981) and republished here with minor revisions. A feature of this new approach is a dualistic conception of the basic deontic notions. Under the one conception these notions are *operators* on some proposition-like entities; under the other they are *predicates* of (actions regarded as) logical individuals. The two conceptions supplement and depend logically on each other. This approach here stands side by side with another, rather different one, which is attempted in the concluding study of the present volume. How the two approaches are related and what may be fruitful about each of them will have to be disclosed by future research.

For my part, I regard my passage through the wilderness of deontic logic as terminated. I hope the feeling I now have will last, that the new essay "Norms, Truth and Logic" has eventually removed the uneasiness I felt about advancing with the instruments of logic beyond the frontiers of truth and falsehood. The approach in the concluding essay is, incidentally, not in a, for me, new direction but is rather a continuation and refinement of the (formal) approach taken in *Norm and Action*. If I am not mistaken this work has had a certain amount of influence on recent action and norm theory; but it has surprised me that what in *it* was a *new* approach to deontic logic has seemingly gone unnoted by later research.

Georg Henrik von Wright

---

[1] "Problems and Prospects of Deontic Logic—A Survey", in *Modern Logic—A Survey*, ed. by E. Agazzi; D. Reidel Publishing Co., Dordrecht, Holland, 1980.

Acknowledgements

Those of the papers in this volume which have been previously published originally appeared as follows:

"Practical Inference", *The Philosophical Review*, **72** (1963), 159–79.

"On so-called Practical Inference", *Acta Sociologica*, **15** (1972), 39–53.

"Determinism and the Study of Man", in *Essays on Explanation and Understanding*, ed. by J. Manninen and R. Tuomela, © 1976; D. Reidel Publishing Company, Dordrecht, Holland, pp. 415–35.

"Explanation and Understanding of Action", *Revue Internationale de Philosophie*, **35** (1981), 127–42.

"The Foundation of Norms and Normative Statements", in *The Foundations of Statements and Decisions*, ed. by K. Ajdukiewicz; Polish Scientific Publishers, Warszawa, 1965, pp. 351–67.

"On Promises", *Theoria*, **28** (1962), 276–97.

"On the Logic of Norms and Actions", in *New Studies in Deontic Logic*, ed. by R. Hilpinen, © 1981; D. Reidel Publishing Company, Dordrecht, Holland, pp. 3–35.

A preliminary version of the first part of the essay "Norms, Truth, and Logic" appeared in *Deontic Logic, Computational Linguistics and Legal Information Systems*, ed. by A.A. Martino, North-Holland Publishing Company, Amsterdam, 1982.

The papers are here republished with the kind permission of the copyright-holders.

Practical Inference

I

In this paper I shall be dealing with a type of logical argument, which I propose to call *practical inference*.

Aristotle distinguished between theoretical and practical syllogisms. His treatment of the latter is very scanty and unsystematic. The examples, of which he gives hints without elaborating them in detail, are a rather mixed bunch. Some of his general remarks on practical syllogisms, however, are of great interest. They show that Aristotle was aware of the peculiar character of a type of reasoning which logicians after him have tended either to ignore or to misrepresent.

The nearest Aristotle comes to giving a full example of a practical syllogism is in the third chapter of the seventh book of the *Ethica Nicomachea*. The two premisses are "All sweet things ought to be tasted" and "That thing is sweet." Then, instead of stating the conclusion in words—"That thing ought to be tasted"—Aristotle goes on to say that you are bound, if able and not prevented, to taste the thing immediately. The practical syllogism thus leads up to or ends in action. "When the two premisses are combined, just as in theoretical reasoning the mind is compelled to affirm the resulting conclusion, so in the case of practical premisses you are forced at once to *do* it", he says.[1] And in another place Aristotle calls the conclusion of a practical syllogism an *action*.[2]

Aristotle seems throughout to be thinking of practical inference in terms of the subsumption of an individual act under a general rule of action by the intermediary of a particular fact-stating premiss.[3] I shall not in the present paper be dealing, directly, with this type of inference.

The type of argument which we shall here be primarily studying is concerned with (necessary) means to an end. Although the notions of means and end are prominent in Aristotle's ethics, Aristotle seems not to have had this type of argument in mind when speaking of practical syllogisms. Yet the chief peculiarity, as I see it, of Aristotle's practical syllogisms—namely, their relation to *action*—is characteristic also of practical inference of the type which is here studied. It is this common feature which justifies us in calling both types of argument "practical" and in contrasting them with various types of "theoretical" reasoning.

---

[1] *Ethica Nicomachea*, 1147a 26–30. Quoted from the Loeb Classical Library translation by H. Rackham.

[2] *De Motu Animalium*, 701a 12–14.

[3] Cf. *Ethica Nicomachea*, 1147a 25–6.

II

Consider the following inference:

(1) One wants to make the hut habitable.
Unless the hut is heated, it will not become habitable.
Therefore the hut must be heated.

The first premiss is a want statement. The thing wanted is that the hut be habitable. This I shall call an *end*. The end, moreover, is an end of *action*. This means that we want to attain the end as a result or consequence of something which we do. That the end has this character is indicated in our example by the use of the phrase "one wants to make".

The second premiss may be said to rest upon a causal relationship. This is a relationship between temperature and habitability (of a hut). That there should be this relation is a causal fact about the living conditions of men. Essential to the above inference is the assumption that the temperature does not rise "of itself", that is independently of human interference with "the course of nature". Something has to be done in order to make the temperature rise. "Heating" is a word for (actively) raising the temperature. A rise in temperature may serve (favour, further) the ends of a person, as a favourable wind may further the ends of a sailor. But we do not ordinarily call it a "means" to an end. Raising the temperature, however—that is, producing a rise through action—may quite appropriately be called a means to some end. The action which is mentioned in the second premiss is thus a means to the end which is mentioned in the first premiss.

Of the conclusion I shall say that it expresses a *practical necessity*, namely the practical necessity of using the means mentioned in the second premiss in order to attain the end mentioned in the first premiss. I deliberately use the word "must" in the conclusion and not the word "ought". (Instead of "must" we could also say "has to".) Ordinary usage does not maintain a sharp distinction between the meanings of "must" and "ought". But it may be said to hint at distinctions, which the logician has reason to observe. "Must" is somehow stronger than "ought". To say "I ought to do this, but I am not going to do it" can make sense. To say "I must do this, but I am not going to do it" has the ring of a contradiction.

The inference (1) may be regarded as an instantiation of the following general pattern of inference:

(2) One wants to attain *x*.
Unless *y* is done, *x* will not be attained.
Therefore *y* must be done.

I shall call an inference of this form a *primary* practical inference. There are a number of related patterns, which will also be called primary; compare

(8), (11), and (24) below. I shall not here attempt a systematic description and study of all such patterns.

Is an inference of the above form *logically conclusive*?

I think that many logicians and philosophers would answer this question in the negative. Some of them would perhaps support their view with the following argument: The two premisses of the inference are *descriptive*. They state what is the case. The conclusion, however, is *normative* or *prescriptive*. And, it is said, one cannot draw a normative conclusion from (only) factual premisses.

The normative "look" of the conclusion is even more striking if one uses "ought" here instead of "must". It is a well-known and widely accepted idea that one cannot deduce an "ought" from an "is". I do not deny that there is an important truth hidden in this idea. But I would deny that it constitutes a counterargument to the logically conclusive character of the pattern of inference which we are here studying.

III

We have so far formulated in only an impersonal way the pattern of inference which we are discussing, using such phrases as "one wants to attain" and "must be done". An end, however, is necessarily somebody's end. And an act is necessarily done by some agent or agents.

The impersonal formulation of the inference may be said to cover a number of personal formulations of it. I shall here distinguish between two such personal formulations. I shall refer to them as the *third-person* and the *first-person* pattern of inference.

An example of an inference in the third person would be:

(3) *A* wants to make the hut habitable.
Unless *A* heats the hut, it will not become habitable.
Therefore *A* must heat the hut.

A here stands for the name of some agent (person). The corresponding inference in the first person would run:

(4) I want to make the hut habitable.
Unless I heat the hut, it will not become habitable.
Therefore I must heat the hut.

The question may be raised whether the person who figures in the premisses and the conclusion must be the same throughout the whole argument. Consider the following pattern:

A wants to make the hut (have the hut made) habitable.
Unless *B* heats the hut, it will not become habitable.
Therefore *B* must heat the hut.

This, obviously, is not a logically conclusive argument. But what shall we say of the following?

> *A* wants to make the hut habitable.
> Unless *B* heats the hut, it will not become habitable.
> Therefore *A* must make *B* heat the hut.

This last is analogous to the following inference:

> *A* wants to make the hut habitable.
> Unless the temperature rises, the hut will not become habitable.
> Therefore *A* must make the temperature rise.

Assume that the temperature rises "of itself," that is independently of anything which *A* does. Then it was not necessary for *A* to *make* the temperature rise. Similarly, it may happen that *B* heats the hut "on his own initiative", that is independently of any steps which *A* takes. Then it was not necessary for *A* to *make B* heat the hut (or to see to it that *B* heats the hut). We shall not here stop to discuss the question whether a person can be correctly said to have attained his end of action if the wanted thing comes about independently of anything he does. But we may note that the inference with the conclusion that *A* must make *B* heat the hut is not valid in the form which we gave it. It becomes valid, however, if we amend it as follows:

> (5) *A* wants to make the hut habitable.
> Unless *A* makes *B* heat the hut, it will not become habitable.
> Therefore *A* must make *B* heat the hut.

The answer to our above question of identity of persons is that the agent who is in pursuit of the end and the agent upon whom the practical necessity is incumbent must be the same. But, as also seen from the case which we were discussing, it is quite possible that another person beside the one whose end and practical necessity of action are concerned may be "involved" in the inference. We shall presently return to the discussion of some such cases. First, however, we must settle the question which was raised at the end of Section II, namely that of the logical conclusiveness of primary practical inferences.

IV

There is an important difference with regard to the second premiss to be noted between the inference in the third person and the inference in the first person. This difference is relevant to the problem of logical conclusiveness.

A can be ignorant of the causal relationship between his end of action and various necessary means towards its attainment. *A* wants to make the hut habitable. It is a fact that the hut will not become habitable unless *A* heats it. *A*, however, does not realize this. Perhaps he thinks he can make the house habitable by some different means, for example by repairing a broken window.

It seems obvious that the inference nevertheless is valid *of him* (of his case). Its validity is independent of whether *A* knows or believes anything at all about the causal relationship. Thus its validity is also independent of whether *A* himself acknowledges the practical necessity for him of acting in a certain manner.

But is this true? Is it really the case that, *if A* wants to make the hut habitable and *if* the hut will not become habitable, unless he heats it, *then A must heat the hut*—even though he is unaware of the necessity?

The answer depends upon how we interpret the "must". If we understand the phrase "*A* must heat the hut" to mean the same as "unless *A* heats the hut, he will fail to attain some end of his action" or to mean the same as "there is something *A* wants but will not get, unless he heats the hut", then the answer is affirmative. For the following, undeniably, is a logically conclusive argument:

(6) *A* wants to make the hut habitable.
Unless *A* heats the hut, it will not become habitable.
Therefore there is something *A* wants but will not get, unless he heats the hut.

Or, to put it in more general terms, this is logically conclusive:

(7) *A* wants to attain *x*.
Unless *A* does *y*, he will not attain *x*.
Therefore there is something *A* wants but will not get, unless he does *y*.

Is the interpretation plausible which we have given to the "must" in the conclusion of a practical inference in the third person? It seems to me that it is. Suppose we were asked what we mean by saying of a person that he *must* do a certain thing. We should sometimes answer, I think, that we mean that, unless he does this thing, he will not be successful in the pursuit of some end of his. We sometimes dispute whether a person must, or need not, do a certain thing, in this very sense of "must". (But there are other senses of "must" beside this one.)

On the view which I have here suggested, it is logically or necessarily true that, if *A* wants to attain *x* and will not attain it unless he does *y*, then he *must* do *y*. But it does not follow that he *will* do *y*.

The logical peculiarity, noted by Aristotle, that practical inference leads to action is thus not a characteristic of such inference in the third person. This peculiarity, as we shall show below, belongs to the first-person case. One could mark the fundamental difference between the two cases by saying that only practical inference in the first person is truly "practical", whereas the argument in the third person is actually "theoretical". One could also use the terms "subjective" and "objective" to stress the difference. I shall do this and say that the conclusion of a practical inference in the third person states an *objective* practical necessity.

V

An inference in the first person is necessarily conducted or performed by the same subject, of whom (of whose case) it is valid. As a consequence of this, the subject will necessarily know or believe the truth of the second premiss.

Is it (logically) possible that a man should *want* to attain a certain end and should *understand* (know or believe) that a certain action on his part is necessary if he is to attain his end, and yet should not act accordingly?

It is of course possible that a person who wants to attain x may *revise* his end, when he comes to understand that unless he does y he will not attain x. He no longer wants to attain x. The two premisses fail to *combine*, as it were, to form a practical inference. The inference, one could also say, fails to materialize. (Compare Section IX below.) Then the subject does not act according to "the dictate of practical necessity", because there is no such necessity incumbent on him.

It is also possible that a person wants to attain x and understands that unless he does y he will not attain x—and then *tries* to do y, but fails or is prevented. Did he then "act accordingly"? The answer depends upon how we interpret the phrase. If to act accordingly means to accomplish the necessary feat, he did not act accordingly. If, however, to act accordingly is to set oneself to do (try to do, go on to do) the necessary act, then he did act accordingly.

I shall here understand "act accordingly" in the second of the two senses. And I shall maintain that, if a man can truly be said both to want to attain a certain end and to combine with this will a knowledge or belief that unless he does a certain act, he will not attain his end, then he will act accordingly.

Instead of saying "he will act" I could also have said "he will necessarily act". This, moreover, is *logical* necessity. For, if action does not follow, we should have to describe the subject's case by saying either that he did not in fact *want*[4] his professed object of desire or did not, after all, *think it necessary* to do the act in order to get the wanted thing.

---

[4] The English word "want" is both ambiguous and vague. (Cf. below p. 9, fn. 7.) One could make a distinction between wanting something *actively* which entails "going after" the thing in question and wanting something *passively*—which means merely wishing for this thing to come. Active wanting, moreover, presupposes an intention or resolve on the part of the agent to do something which he thinks is in his power to accomplish. (1983)

A practical inference in the first person thus necessarily leads up to or terminates in action. Wanting the end and understanding the causal requirements for attaining it put the subject in motion. One could also say that want is what *moves* and understanding (of causal connections) is what *steers* the movement. The two together *determine* the subject's course of action.

I shall call the determination of action through a practical inference in the first person *subjective* practical necessity. It seems to me that Aristotle must have been thinking of this peculiar kind of necessitation when he insisted that the conclusion of a practical syllogism is an act.

Subjective practical necessity shows that there is a sense in which human action can be, at the same time, voluntary and strictly determined.

VI

Sometimes action must follow immediately, or else the subject will not attain his end. Sometimes, however, action need not take place immediately, but perhaps only by tomorrow afternoon or within a week from now, or "sooner or later".

When action need not follow immediately, the subject may revise his end in the meantime—not only under the impression of his insight into the necessary requirements, but also for other reasons. He may come to aspire after different things. It may also happen that he comes to think he was mistaken in believing that he will not get x if he does not do y. But unless he changes his attitude to either the first or the second premiss of the argument, he is bound to act in accordance with these premisses. In this sense his future action is (pre)determined by his present want and insight.

Would it not, someone may suggest, in view of the fact that the (necessary) action may become delayed, be more to the point to say that a practical inference in the first person terminates in a *decision* or *resolve* to act than to say that it terminates in *action*? It does not seem to me that this would be more to the point.

A decision is normally the outcome of deliberation. There are at least two entirely different senses in which deliberation may be said to concern the means to a given end. A man can deliberate as to what the means to the end *are*. Or he can deliberate which means to the end he should *choose*— assuming that there are several means productive of the end without being (individually) necessary for its attainment. In the first case the outcome of deliberation is not a decision to act. In the second case the outcome of deliberation may be a decision to act (in a certain way). But the course of action which has been decided upon is not a practical necessity, since it is but one of several possibilities. When action is a practical necessity, there is no room for choice.

VII

A few words should be said about the case in which the subject cannot perform the necessary act, the reason being that he has not learned or does not know how to do the thing in question. Then, necessarily, he will not do the thing.

If the subject does not know that he cannot do y, he may try to do it and find out that he cannot. Then his practical inference ended in action. This case does not differ in principle from the one which we have been discussing.

If, however, the subject *knows* that he cannot do y, then, I would say, he cannot correctly apply to himself the phrase "unless (now) I do y".[5] He will then have to modify his argument as follows:

> (8) I want to attain x.
> Unless I learn (how) to do y, I shall not attain x.
> Therefore I must learn to do y.

This is, in fact, how we often infer when we aspire after things which are beyond our present abilities of action. And having thus inferred, we take some steps to acquire the needed ability—unless at once we relinquish the end.

VIII

It is important to see *how* different the inference in the first person is from the inference in the third person. The difference is concealed, not only by the use of the impersonal inference schema (1) to cover the two personal inference patterns (3) and (4), but also by our linguistic presentation of the two last patterns themselves. Let the question be raised: what *are* (is the nature of) the premisses and the conclusion of the two types of inference? They are not sentences which stand printed on paper. In the case of the inference in the third person the correct answer, I should think, is this: the premisses are the *propositions* that a certain person pursues a certain end of action and that a certain thing is a necessary means to this end. The conclusion is a third proposition, namely that the person will fail to reach some end of his action unless he does this thing. In the case of the inference in the first person the correct answer seems to be this: the premisses are a person's *want* and his *state of knowing or believing* a certain condition to be necessary for the fulfilment of that want. The conclusion

---

[5] A thing which is not *now* possible cannot *now* be a necessary condition of anything. To say "Unless I do y (which, however, I cannot do), I shall not attain x" is not to state a necessary condition of my attaining x. But to say "Unless in future I do y (which at present I cannot do), I shall never attain x" is to state a necessary condition of something—even if, in fact, I never learn to do y.

is an *act*, something that this person does. Wants, states of knowing or believing, and acts are not only mutually rather different from each other. They are all of them entities of a radically different sort from propositions. It is of the essence of propositions that they are expressed by sentences. (Some philosophers would say that a proposition is the meaning or the sense of a type of sentence.) Wants, states of knowing or believing, and acts have no analogous essential connection with *language*. Therefore the relation to language of a practical inference in the first person is in principle different from the relation to language of a practical inference in the third person.[6]

IX

An end of action is something, which one can be said to *want to attain*. Kant, in a celebrated passage, expressed the opinion that whoever wants to attain an end is bound also to want to use the necessary means towards its attainment.[7] Kant thought, moreover, that this was an analytic principle of the will. Properly interpreted the principle is, I think, analytic. But then it is important to see what its "proper interpretation" is.

It is plausible to think that, if one wants to attain an end and realizes the necessity of doing a certain thing in order to attain that end, then one also wants to do that thing *for the sake of* (attaining) *the end*. But normally one does not want to do this thing *for its own sake*. It may, moreover, happen that this thing is something which one shuns doing or which one does reluctantly or which one would rather leave undone, if it were not necessary to do it for the sake of something else. When this is the case, our will to attain the end can be said to fight against our unwillingness to use the necessary means.

There are several possible outcomes of such a struggle. One is a "compromise". One sets oneself to do the thing, but half-heartedly. As a

---

[6] I am indebted to Mr Lars Fröström of Lund University for his having drawn my attention to this difference between the two patterns of inference.

[7] *Grundlegung zur Metaphysik der Sitten* (2nd ed.), pp. 44–5: "Wer den Zweck will, will (sofern die Vernunft auf seine Handlungen entscheidenden Einfluss hat,) auch das dazu unentbehrlich notwendige Mittel, das in seiner Gewalt ist." In the translation by H.J. Paton (*The Moral Law*, Hutchinson, London, 1956, pp. 84–5): "Who wills the end, wills (so far as reason has decisive influence on his actions) also the means which are indispensably necessary and in his power." The peculiarities of meaning of the words "want" and "will" in English make adequate translation difficult. To say that who *wills* an end *wills* also the necessary means to it sounds to me somewhat artificial and calls for a "translation" into more colloquial English. To say that who *wants* an end also *wants* the necessary means to it suggests a meaning which makes the statement appear plainly false. But to say that whoever wants *to attain* an end wants also *to use* the necessary means to its attainment seems unobjectionable from the point of view of language and not wholly implausible from the point of view of truth.

consequence of this, one perhaps fails to accomplish the act. One could then say that the will which, in accordance with Kant's principle, has been "transferred" from the end to the necessary means is weakened by our ("natural") impulse against the use of these means. This is one aspect, among many, of the phenomenon known in moral philosophy under the name of *akrasia* or weakness of will.

Another possible outcome of the struggle is that the unwillingness to use the means gains the upper hand, conquers the will to attain the end. Then, I think, can we no longer be said to *want* to attain it. The practical inference "collapses". We may still wish that the thing which we wanted to attain as a result or consequence of our action will happen, "of itself" or thanks to the action of some other agent. We should welcome it if it were to happen. Perhaps we can still be said to want it to happen. But we can no longer be said to want to *make* it happen.

A third possibility is that the will to attain the end conquers the impulse against the use of the means without "compromising" with it. Of such cases we sometimes say that the subject *forces* or *compels* himself to action. We can also say that the subject then *makes himself do* the action.

The case in which a subject makes himself do a certain thing by thwarting an impulse to the contrary exhibits an interesting analogy to the case in which a person commands or orders another person to do something. To command others is "heteronomous" commanding. To make oneself do something may, by analogy, be called "autonomous" commanding. Autonomous commanding does not reflect the practical necessity, as such, of action. It reflects the practical necessity of making oneself act.

I think we are here in the neighbourhood of the Kantian notion of an autonomous command (norm, rule). Perhaps one could say that we have arrived at the Kantian concept, stripped of its moral connotations. But then it should be remembered that, on Kant's view, a conceptual separation of the notion of autonomy from that of moral duty is not possible.[8]

X

Consider once again the inference mentioned at the end of Section III:

---

[8] It seems to me that there are (at least) two entirely different notions of "autonomy" involved in Kant's discussion of the moral law. The first notion is that of a man commanding (giving laws unto) *himself*. This notion corresponds fairly closely to our notion here of autonomous commanding. The second notion is that of a man's will being affected by any (subjective) *ends* of his action. On Kant's view that which I here call practical necessity of action is not an instance of autonomy at all, but of heteronomy (although not of heteronomous commanding). The two notions of autonomy should be kept apart. The second is closely related to the Kantian idea of "duty for duty's sake".

(5) *A* wants to make the hut habitable.
   Unless *A* makes *B* heat the hut, it will not become habitable.
   Therefore *A* must make *B* heat the hut.

Assume that *A* himself conducts this argument in the first person. The conclusion will then be that he sets himself to make *B* heat the hut. How does *A* do this? There are many ways of making or trying to make people do things: asking them, telling them, requesting them, commanding them, persuading them; threatening them with some evil, if they do not comply with our wish; holding forth some reward or promising a service in return if they comply.

The above inference rests on the assumption that *B* does not heat the hut on his own initiative, but has to be *moved* to do this. *A* has to *make* him heat the hut, *see to it* that he does this.

Assume next that *A* can heat the hut himself and that there is in fact nobody who could do it in his place. Then it is necessary for *A* to do the heating himself. Assume, however, that he does not do the job willingly, but has to conquer his laziness or reluctance. He can then, as it were, "identify" himself with *B* in the above example and conduct the following argument about his own case:

(9) I want to make the hut habitable.
   Unless I make myself heat the hut, it will not become habitable.
   Therefore I must make myself heat the hut.

How does one make oneself do a thing? And how does making oneself do a thing differ from simply doing it? (One does not very often use the phrase "make oneself do".) Literally, I would say, to make oneself do a thing is to set oneself to do it in spite of an impulse to the contrary, for example, under the impact of a practical necessity. One cannot literally (in a primary sense) command or persuade or promise or threaten oneself to do any of the acts whereby one makes or tries to make others do things. But in an analogical or secondary sense, making oneself do a thing (by conquering a contrary impulse) may sometimes aptly be called commanding oneself (and sometimes perhaps rather persuading or threatening oneself). It is aptly called commanding when we think of the movement to action and the conquest of the contrary impulse as a victory of reason over blind passion or of our rational self over our animal nature.

XI

Compare these two patterns of inference:

(10) *A* wants to attain *x*.
   Unless *A* does *y*, he will not attain *x*.
   Therefore *A* must do *y*.

and:

    (11) *A* wants to attain *x*.
          Unless *A* makes *B* do *y*, he will not attain *x*.
          Therefore *A* must make *B* do *y*.

The conclusions of these two inferences are *logically independent* of one another. It can be true both that *A* must do *y* (himself) and that he must make *B* do it (as well). Or one of the propositions may be true and the other false. Or they may both be false. (The case when they are both true has peculiar problems of its own, which will not be discussed here.)

(10) is the pattern of a primary practical inference. (Compare Sections II and III above.) (11) I shall also call a pattern of a primary practical inference (though of a more complex form). (11) can be obtained from (10) if we substitute "makes *B* do *y*" for "does *y*" in the second premiss and "make *B* do *y*" for "do *y*" in the conclusion.

Compare next (10) with the schema:

    (12) *A* wants to attain *x*.
          Unless *A* makes himself do *y*, he will not attain *x*.
          Therefore *A* must make himself do *y*.

The conclusions of (10) and (12) are not logically independent. The conclusion of the second argument entails the conclusion of the first. For if it is true that an agent will not attain a certain end of his unless he makes himself do a certain act (which he is reluctant to do), then it is also true that he will not attain this end unless he does that act.

An inference with the conclusion "*A* must make himself do *y*" therefore *presupposes* an inference with the conclusion "*A* must do *y*". An agent can be under a practical necessity to make himself do something (to compel or force himself to do something against inclination) only when he is (already) under a practical necessity to do that same thing. For this reason I shall say that the inference pattern (12) above is secondary to the pattern (10).

XII

It follows from what has been said in Section XI that, if the premisses of a practical inference which ends in the conclusion "*A* must make himself do *y*" are affirmed, then the premisses of an inference of the following form are also affirmed:

    (13) *A* must do *y*.
          Unless *A* makes himself do *y*, he will not do *y*.
          Therefore *A* must make himself do *y*.

This pattern may be regarded as a derivative case of a more general pattern:

(14) *A* must do *x*.
Unless *A* does *y*, he cannot do *x*.
Therefore *A* must do *y*.

(13) is obtained from (14) through substitution and by weakening the second premiss of (14) to "Unless *A* does *y*, he will not do *x*". If it is true that unless *A* does *y* he *cannot* do *x*, then it is also true that unless *A* does *y* he *will not* do *x*.

I shall call (14) the pattern of a secondary practical inference (in the third person). The secondary practical inference has its "starting point" (first premiss) in a practical necessity, and it ends in a further practical necessity. The logical conclusiveness of a secondary practical inference can be seen from the following expansion of its pattern:

(15) There is something *A* wants but will not get unless he does *x*.
Unless *A* does *y*, he cannot do *x*.
Therefore there is something *A* wants but will not get unless he does *y*.

XIII

I shall next discuss some patterns of practical inference with "ought". Consider the following example:

(16) The hut ought to be made habitable.
Unless the hut is heated, it cannot be made habitable.
Therefore the hut ought to be heated.

This impersonal formulation of the inference may be said to cover a third-person and a first-person variant of it:

(17) *A* ought to make the hut habitable.
Unless *A* heats the hut, he cannot make it habitable.
Therefore *A* ought to heat the hut.

and:

(18) I ought to make the hut habitable.
Unless I heat the hut, I cannot make it habitable.
Therefore I ought to heat the hut.

Are these arguments logically conclusive? Someone may think that the question of their conclusiveness is less problematic than the question of the conclusiveness of primary practical inferences. For the above inference schemas contain an ought-sentence among the premisses. Thus the idea that one cannot draw normative conclusions from factual premisses cannot be adduced against the logical conclusiveness of the inferences. I do not know how much weight should be attached to this argumentation. It seems to me that the question of logical conclusiveness is more, rather than less, problematic in the case of the inference patterns (16) through (18) than it is in the case of inferences from ends and causal connections to practical necessities of action.

The question of conclusiveness essentially depends upon how we understand the crucial word "ought" in the context. "Ought" is commonly used when we talk about duties or obligations (legal or moral, as the case may be). Duties and obligations are not, by themselves, practical necessities of action. Sometimes, however, doing one's duty or fulfilling one's obligation may become a practical necessity.

Let "ought" be translated by "it is duty", and consider the following inference in the third person:

(19) It is A's duty to make the hut habitable.
Unless A heats the hut, he cannot make it habitable.
Therefore it is A's duty to heat the hut.

The duty mentioned in the conclusion I shall call a *derived duty* or a *derived obligation*. And a derived obligation I propose to define (interpret, understand) in the following way: a derived obligation is something which *must* be done in order that we may be able to fulfil another (derived or primary) obligation. A derived obligation, one could also say, is something which *must* be done for the sake of doing one's duty. The "must" here is the "must" of practical necessity. The derived obligation to do a certain thing is a practical necessity of action, *relative* to some other obligation.

Under this interpretation of the duty mentioned in the conclusion of (19), the above schema can also be cast in the following form:

(20) It is A's duty to make the hut habitable.
Unless A heats the hut, he cannot make it habitable.
Therefore A must heat the hut.

Is this a logically conclusive argument? The answer is that it is conclusive, if we take "A must heat the hut" to mean the same as "unless A heats the hut, he cannot do (what is) his duty". For the following, indubitably, is conclusive:

(21) It is A's duty to make the hut habitable.
Unless A heats the hut, he cannot make it habitable.
Therefore, unless A heats the hut, he cannot do his duty.

(The first and the second "cannot", or the second alone, may become weakened into "will not".)

Derived obligations, in the above sense of the term, play a prominent role in the lives of most people. The law prescribes what our legal obligations are. But it leaves to the individual citizen to consider the various measures and steps which he must take in order to fulfil his legal obligations. This is convenient, since the nature of these necessary steps may vary with the particular circumstances of the individuals concerned. For example: I am under a legal obligation to make an income tax return to the proper authorities. In order to fulfil this obligation I must do various other things, of which the law, however, says nothing. I must keep some records of my earnings, I must procure for myself the needed forms to be filled in, ascertain to whom and before what date they should be returned, and return them. These are "derived obligations", practical necessities of action relative to "primary obligations".

XIV

Consider an inference in the first person which terminates in a derived obligation:

(22) It is my duty to do x.
      Unless I do y, I cannot do x.
      Therefore I must do y.

This sort of argument can be, and very often is, I think, no more than reasoning about one's own case. A man can be aware of the fact that something or other is his duty, realize that, unless he does a certain thing, he cannot do his duty—and yet not go on to do it. Then the inference is on a level with "theoretical" reasoning; that is, its conclusion states an objective practical necessity of action. (Compare Section IV above.)

But cannot the argument also terminate in a subjective practical necessity of action, which will ensure that the subject actually sets himself to do his duty? (Compare Section V above.)

One could make a distinction between *being aware of the fact that* something or other is duty (for example, under the law) and *acknowledging* something as duty. Then the question may be raised: is it (logically) possible to acknowledge something as being one's duty, realize that, unless one does a certain (other) thing, one cannot do what is one's duty—and yet not set oneself to do this other thing? We are here in the neighbourhood of a problem which is familiar from the ethical thought of Plato and Aristotle.

The answer to the question essentially depends upon what it is to acknowledge something as duty, that is upon how one understands the meaning of the phrase "acknowledge something as duty".

It is easy to see that, *if* to acknowledge it as one's duty to do x entailed that one wants to do x for its own sake, then the logical conclusiveness of the schema:

(23) I acknowledge it as my duty to do x.
      Unless I do y, I cannot do x.
      Therefore I must do y

would be a consequence of the logical conclusiveness of:

(24) I want to do x.
Unless I do y, I cannot do x.
Therefore I must do y.

(For, if p entails q, and if q and r jointly entail s, then p and r jointly entail s, too.)

The last pattern, although slightly different from (2) and the variations of it which we have been discussing earlier in this essay, I shall call a primary practical inference, too. There need not be any doubt that the conclusion of (24) can be a subjective practical necessity, that is, can consist in the subject's setting himself to do y under the impact of his will to do x and his knowledge or belief that it is necessary to do y in order to be(come) able to do x.

There is, however, a grave objection to regarding the subjective practical necessity of fulfilling one's derived obligation as the conclusion of a primary practical inference. The objection is that it is not plausible to think of the primary obligations, which a man acknowledges to be his, as things which he can necessarily be said to *want* to do for their own sake.

Another possibility of making duty-bound action subjective practical necessity would be to let the logical conclusiveness of (23) depend upon the logical conclusiveness of the pattern:

(25) I must do x.
Unless I do y, I cannot do x.
Therefore I must do y.

To let the logical conclusiveness of (23) depend on the logical conclusiveness of (25) is to take the view that derived obligations are subjective practical necessities of action, if and only if acknowledgement of the primary obligations themselves constitutes such necessities. The pattern (25) we recognize as that of a secondary practical inference. (Compare Section XII above.) If a derived obligation emerges as the conclusion of a secondary practical inference, it follows that the practical necessity, which is the first premiss of the inference, will also be the conclusion of another practical inference. This other inference can be secondary or primary. If it is secondary we shall, by tracing the chain of obligations further back, after a finite number of steps reach a primary obligation, which is the conclusion of a primary practical inference from ends and causal connections.

On the suggested view, the things which we acknowledge it to be our duty to do are things which we *must* do—since otherwise some end which we pursue will not be attained. This is, of course, not to suggest that we should call everything "duty" which we are under a practical necessity of doing for the sake of some end. We call it duty only when this end is of a peculiar nature—for example, has some peculiar connection with ideas of good and evil or of justice. The question of the nature of these ends falls outside the scope of the present essay and has no immediate bearing on the problem of practical inference.

To do one's duty for duty's sake can be a (subjective or objective) practical necessity of action, if this is understood to mean that one has to fulfil one's derived duty for the sake of fulfilling one's primary duty. But to do one's primary duty can be *a practical necessity* only if one has to do it for the sake of some end "beyond duty". On this point Kant, I think, was in serious error.

On So-called Practical Inference

I

Since the publication of Anscombe's *Intention* (Basil Blackwell, Oxford, 1957) practical inference has been a live topic in philosophy. There can be little doubt that the topic is important. I would claim, for example, that practical inference as a schema of explanation plays a comparable role in the human sciences to that of nomological deductive explanation in the natural sciences.[1] To vindicate this claim is difficult, however. This is so, for one thing, because the logical nature of practical reasoning is much more obscure than that of deductive and other forms of "theoretical" argument.

The division of inferences ("syllogisms") into theoretical and practical stems from Aristotle. The most exciting thing which Aristotle has to say about the topic is that a practical inference leads up to or ends in action, that its conclusion is an action.[2] About the premisses he is not very clear. The example he gives of the major premiss often mentions something generic which is good or ought to be done, e.g. that dry food suits every man or that sweet things ought to be tasted.[3] The minor premiss mentions some particular thing which "falls under" the generic label, e.g. that this particular dish is dry or this particular lump of white stuff is sweet. In these examples the conclusion would be that the person who argues proceeds to eat the stuff.

According to Anscombe the first premiss of a practical inference mentions something wanted.[4] This characterization, it seems, does not fit Aristotle's version of practical inference very well. It fits better another type of inference. This is an inference in which the first premiss mentions an end of action and the second premiss some means to this end. The "practical" conclusion which results from the premisses would consist in using the means to secure the end.

Aristotelian practical inferences, one could say, subsume a particular thing or action under some general principle or rule about what is good for us or is our duty. The study of reasoning of this kind is relevant to the question—central not least to Plato's and Aristotle's thinking—how knowing the good is related to being good and to right action.

The second type of practical inference is not concerned so much with

---

[1] On my attitude to this claim see above Introduction, p. viii. (1983)

[2] *De Motu Animalium*, 701a 12—14.

[3] *Ethica Nicomachea*, 1147a 6—7 and 1147a 28—30.

[4] *Intention*, Sect. 35.

right conduct as with purposive behaviour and intentional action generally. Its study is relevant above all to the problems of explaining and understanding conduct—both of individuals and of groups of men.

Of both types of practical inference it is right to say, with Anscombe, that their study has been much neglected. But perhaps not as thoroughly neglected as she seems to have thought. In his *Logic*, Hegel construed purposive action as an inference, leading from the subjective setting of an end through insight into the objective connections of natural facts to the objectivation of the end in action.[5] (This is a very summary description of a complex and perhaps not very clear idea.) And in his lectures on the philosophy of history Hegel applied the same schema to the historical process as a realization, through the actions of individual and collective agents, of the "aims" immanent in the absolute mind. The Hegelian conceptualization of action as inference also left an impact on Marx and Marxist thinking.[6]

In this paper I shall discuss only practical inference which views actions as the use of means to attain ends.

II

Let it be assumed that the premisses of a practical argument, when conducted in the first person, are:

I want to attain the end *E* (e.g. make this hut habitable).
Unless I do action *A* (e.g. heat the hut) I shall not attain *E*.

It may very well be the case that, if I have this end in view in combination with that opinion of the means to its realization, then I shall actually proceed to act in the appropriate way. But what sort of *connection* would this signify between want and thought on the one hand and action on the other? Can I say that wanting and opining *make* me act? If so, would this be a form of causal efficacy? Or would it be more like a logical compulsion?

Before we proceed to answering these questions we must consider the following "objection" to the first person premiss as stated above. Cannot a person at the same time want to attain several ends? And can it not then happen that some of his ends (wants) are mutually incompatible? For example, that in order to attain one of the ends, he thinks he must forbear doing something which he thinks he must do in order to attain another end of his? Then there are two practical arguments for him. He may act in accordance with the premisses of one of them. But could he then, in any sense, be said to have been compelled to act in the way he acted?

---

[5] *Wissenschaft der Logik*, Bk. II, Sect. iii, Ch. 2B.
[6] As shown by Juha Manninen in "Praktisen päättelyn mukaisista ajatusmalleista Hegelillä ja Marxilla" ("On Practical Inference Models in Hegel and Marx"), *Psykologia* 5, 1970.

Suppose we change the word "want" in the first premiss to "intend". One does not normally speak of intending to attain ends. Some further change in the first premiss will therefore be required here.

One speaks of pursuing ends. Pursuit of ends is intentional action. The phrases "pursue an end intentionally" and "pursue an end" I shall regard as synonymous. To speak of intending to pursue an end points to the future. It is like saying that one is planning or has resolved to go after something later on. But an agent in pursuit of an end can rightly be said to intend to make the end-state, i.e. the state which obtains when the end is attained, materialize or come true.

It may now be suggested that, if one pursues an end E, then one cannot, for conceptual reasons, at the same time pursue another end E' the pursuit of which one considers (causally or logically) incompatible with pursuit of E. I shall accept this as a valid point about "the logic of intention".

It seems obvious that "I pursue the end E" is a logically stronger statement than "I want to attain the end E". The first entails the second, but not *vice versa*. A plausible way of coping with the difficulty caused by possibly conflicting ends would therefore be to replace the first premiss in the practical argument under consideration by

I intend to make it true that E (e.g. that this hut is habitable).

and the second premiss by

Unless I do A, I shall not achieve this.

Is there a conclusion which can be said to follow logically from the two premisses thus reformulated?

I think there is one for which this claim can be made. It is the conclusion:

I will do A.

This is what we call a *declaration of intention*. An inference is normally thought to be between true or false propositions. But it is doubtful whether a declaration of intention could qualify as a proposition. The logical nature of the argument therefore is obscure.

In order to see things in a clearer light, let us shift the argument from the first person to the third person. What we then get is, in the first place:

X intends to make it true that E.
Unless he does A, he will not achieve this.
Therefore X will do A.

Here all three components of the inference are clearly propositions. The conclusion is a prediction about a certain agent's conduct.

It is quite clear, however, that this argument *is not* logically conclusive. There are several reasons why this is so. For one thing, both premisses may be true but X himself need not know or think that the second is true, i.e. he need not realize that he will not attain his end unless he does A. And then there is, of course, no guarantee whatsoever that he will do A. (I shall not here take up for separate discussion the possibility that X is not aware (conscious) of his intention and whether this would affect the conclusiveness of the inference.)

We might now try to make the argument approach conclusiveness by expanding the second premiss to something like

X thinks that unless he does A, he will not bring about that E comes true.

It should be noted that the same expansion may be said to be implicit in the premiss in the first person. For, if I argue to myself "Unless I do A, I shall not achieve this or that", then I also subscribe to the *truth* of the statement. Perhaps I do not claim to *know* it to be true, but at least I believe it or consider it highly probable.

In the case of the premiss in the third person, however, its expansion is not merely to make explicit a concealed presupposition. It adds something substantial to the statement. We shift from a statement about "objective facts" to a statement about a person's "epistemic attitudes".

It may be suggested that in order to make the argument in the first and the third person run completely parallel we must not only add the above epistemic clause to the second premiss of the argument in the third person, but also change the conclusion of the argument in the first person to

I shall do A.

When cast in this form the conclusion is a prediction about my own future behaviour. This would turn the first person argument into a special case of the third person argument. Such a "reifying" move is possible, but it misses what is specifically "first person" about the first person argument.

III

There is, however, also another course to be tried in order to make the argument in the third person conclusive. We leave the premisses as they (originally) stand and change the conclusion to:

Therefore X has to (must) do A.

Whether this conclusion follows logically from the premisses depends upon how one interprets the meaning of "has to" or "must" here. The following seems to me a reasonable view to take: A must-do-statement (in the third person) is elliptic. It says that an action is a necessary condition for the attainment of some end which is left unspecified in the statement. On this view the statement "X must do A" would be short for "X is in the pursuit of some end of action of his which he will not attain unless he does A". And *this* follows logically from the premisses (by application of the principle *fa* → *(Ex)fx* and assuming that an agent's intending to make a state of affairs come true entails that this state is an, intermediate or ultimate, end of his action).

Consider this variation of the argument:

X intends to make it true that *E*.
Unless *Y* does *A*, he (i.e. *X*) will not achieve this.
Therefore *Y* must do *A*.

Shall we call this a valid argument? The answer again depends upon our understanding of the "must" here. The argument is conclusive, if "*Y* must do *A*" is short for "*Someone* is in pursuit of an end of action which he will not attain unless *Y* does *A*". Is this a feasible interpretation? Perhaps must-statements are sometimes thus understood. But why not then take an even more "liberal" attitude and say that sometimes "*Y* must do *A*" means simply "Unless *Y* does *A*, something or other will not happen (be the case)"? Here the necessity of action need not be related to any end at all, nor to anybody's intentions.

Consider finally the following variant:

X intends to make it true that *E*.
Unless *Y* does *A*, he (i.e. *X*) will not achieve this.
Therefore he must make *Y* do *A*.

But must he? Assume that we (or *X* himself) know that he cannot make *Y* do *A*, that nothing he does will move *Y* to this. Then we should perhaps say that *X* must give up pursuing *E* as an end. And if pressed about the meaning of this last "must" we might say: *X* must do this, or else he will suffer frustration. But maybe *X* is so keen on his end that giving it up involves a still bigger frustration for him. Then we might conclude that *X* *must learn* how to make *Y* do *A* (which may or may not involve teaching *Y* how to do *A*). And this conclusion would follow, logically, if we change the second premiss to "unless *X* learns how to make *Y* do *A*, he will not make it true that *E*". We are back at the first pattern.

Generally speaking: If there is something which an agent cannot do and which is such that, unless he does it, he will not attain a certain end of his, then he must *learn* how to do it or else he will not attain this end. Learning how to do something can be a practical necessity in much the same sense as is doing something. Furthermore, that somebody else does something can be necessary (causally or logically), if an agent is to attain his ends in much the same sense in which it may be necessary for this that something should happen. These last two are comparable cases. I propose, however, that the term *practical necessity* be reserved for the first pair of cases. Practical necessity is the necessity of doing something under which an agent is, if he is to attain some end *of his own*.

An agent thus is under a practical necessity of doing everything which it is necessary that he should do, if he is to attain the ends he pursues. But can an agent intend to do anything (make it true that E, for example) without being able (generically) to do this?[7] Does intention presuppose ability—pursuit of ends ability to obtain them? I would answer as follows:

One can intend to do only such things which one either thinks one can do or realizes that one cannot do but intends to learn to do and thinks one can learn to do.[8] (This is not a psychological observation about intending, but a rule about the logical grammar of the concept.)

Sometimes an agent thinks he can do something which, in fact, he cannot generically do. By trying to do this thing but failing to accomplish it he may come to realize his inability—and, if the action was a practical necessity for him, the practical necessity of acquiring the ability. But it may also happen that when the agent realizes his inability to do the required thing, he "changes his mind", i.e. gives up the pursuit of his original end.

IV

Let us again shift back to the first person case. Consider this inference:

I intend to make it true that E.
Unless I do A, I shall not achieve this.
Therefore I must do A.

Can I be mistaken about my own intentions, think that I intend to do something which, in fact, I do not intend to do? Without prejudging an answer to this question, let us just lay it aside.

The second premiss can surely, "objectively speaking", be false. Then the conclusion too will normally be false. (It will be false, unless I also pursue some end which is different from E and for the attainment of which the doing of A is required.)

When the second premiss is false, it may still be the case that I (mistakenly) *think* it true. And then I will also think of the conclusion as true, i.e. I will think of the doing of A as a practical necessity incumbent upon me. Thus arguing from the two premisses above makes the conclusion *valid for me*, even though the second premiss may be false and therewith the conclusion false too. This is a peculiarity of a practical inference in the first person.

If the second premiss of a practical inference in the first person is true,

---

[7] That an agent is (generically) able to do something shall mean that on most occasions, when there is an opportunity for doing this thing and he sets himself to do it, he will also accomplish it. He has the necessary "know how". This he may, but need not, possess as a result of learning.

[8] My position here differs slightly from the one which I took in *Explanation and Understanding*. There (pp. 101–3) I suggested that an intention to do something necessarily involves an opinion on the agent's part that he can do the thing.

then the agent who conducts the argument will *rightly* consider himself to be under the practical necessity of acting which is stated in the conclusion. If it is false, however, he (normally) will *mistakenly* consider himself to be so. The practical necessities under which an agent (rightly or mistakenly) considers himself to be we may call his *subjective* practical necessities. And we can distinguish them from the *objective* practical necessities under which he is, as a matter of objective truth. There can be a discrepancy between the groups, either because the first one does not embrace all the members of the second, or because it contains members which are not members of the second. Each source of discrepancy is a source of frustration for an agent in pursuit of ends.

                                   V

We now leave the "must do" case. The arguments henceforth to be discussed are:

> *First person case*
> I intend to make it true that *E*.
> Unless I do *A*, I shall not achieve this.
> Therefore I will do *A*.

> *Third person case*
> *X* intends to make it true that *E*.
> He thinks that, unless he does *A*, he will not achieve this.
> Therefore he will do *A*.

The conclusion of the first person inference, we said, is a declaration of intention. This intention may not have been formed until we realized the practical necessities involved in our aiming at a certain end. So its formation may come later, after the first intention was already formed. We can speak of a *primary* and a *secondary* intention here.

The connection between the two intentions is, moreover, a kind of logically necessary connection. The second (epistemic) premiss can be said to "mediate" between the primary intention of the first premiss and the secondary intention of the conclusion. One can also speak of a transfer or *transmission of intention*. The "will" to attain an end is being transmitted to (use of) the means deemed necessary for its attainment.

This principle of "transmission of intention from ends to means" is basically identical, it seems, with a principle which Kant thought analytically (logically) true and which he expressed in the following words: "Who wills the end, wills (so far as reason has decisive influence on his actions) also the means which are indispensably necessary and in his power."[9]

------

[9] *The Moral Law*, Hutchinson, London, 1956, transl. by H.J. Paton, pp. 84–5. Cf. above, p. 9.

I said there was "a kind of" logical connection here. For, although I think it obvious that the conclusion of our first person argument follows logically from the premisses, this "following" has a peculiar nature: A declaration of intention is not a true or false proposition. Whether an argument which is actually conducted from premisses of the kind under consideration will terminate in a declaration of intention is, in a certain sense, contingent and not logically necessary. Perhaps such arguments as often as not terminate in a *change* of intention on the agent's part. Realizing what is necessary for him to do, and perhaps feeling a strong aversion against doing this, he changes his mind and gives up pursuit of the original good (cf. above p. 23). And even if the agent does not change his primary intention, he need not *declare* his secondary intention, not even to himself, "in thought". He can nevertheless be said to *have* it and, moreover, to have it necessarily. If he declares his intention, he only "reveals" to the world, or admits to himself, something about himself which is already there.

So what is logically necessary is something which holds between true and false propositions and which is best expressed in the form of a third person inference of the following type:

X intends to make it true that *E*.
He thinks that, unless he does *A*, he will not achieve this.
Therefore *X intends to do A*.

This argument, however, moves wholly on the level of intentions and epistemic attitudes. *It* does not, it seems, link intention with action. Or does it, after all? We shall return to this question presently (in Section VII).

VI

Even after we have added the epistemic clause "*X* thinks that" to its second premiss the argument in the third person, ending in a prediction, remains inconclusive. This is due to the existence of a time gap, separating the premisses from the conclusion. The premisses may be true, but the agent has not yet performed the action. This leaves open the truth-value of the conclusion.

Assume that the premisses are true at a certain time. Normally, they will then remain true for some time. Unless *X* does *A within this time span*, we shall have to say that the prediction failed to come true. For, if *X* does *A*, but only after the end of the time span, his action is irrelevant to the argument. So is it also, if after the lapse of time he does *not* do *A*.

It can happen that we wait for the prediction to come true and, having waited for some time, begin to doubt whether the premisses still obtain. Suppose we find that they do no longer obtain. Does it follow that the conclusion was invalidly drawn from the premisses? Not necessarily. For assume that what X intends to achieve is the result of a "long time project" and that the doing of A has to be done at a late stage of it, or that the doing of A can be postponed to a late stage. There is in any case *a latest time* when A will have to be done. Suppose now the agent "gives up" his project before this time arrives. Then it could still be true that, had he not given up, he would have done A before the time was up.

So in order to show that the conclusion "he will do A" was falsely drawn from the premises, we should have to show that the agent failed to do A *at the latest time* when he thought the time was up for him to do it and the premises were still valid. This observation makes it possible for us to eliminate considerations relating to the time gap from considerations relating to the logical conclusiveness of the inference schema here. The problem can be reduced to a question about a given moment in time, we shall call it "now", and the argument reformulated as follows:

> X intends (now) to make it true that E.
> He thinks that, unless he does A now, he will not achieve this.
> Therefore he will do A now.

The mere fact therefore that in ever so many cases an agent will never do what he considers himself under a practical necessity of doing, if he is to attain some end of his, is by itself quite irrelevant to our problem. For in many of those cases the agent had changed his mind before the time was up in which he had to do the thing he never did.

Is the statement that an agent *will* do a certain thing *now* a "prediction"? The answer depends upon what we think of the "now". Is "now" the present *instant*? Very often we conceive of the "now" as having duration, extension in time; sometimes we mean by it to-day or even this year. So what is "now" supposed to mean in the argument we are discussing here? Not necessarily an instant in time, but rather a *temporal location* of some duration. Of this "location", however, the following must hold true: We cannot slice it up into an earlier part of which it is true that the agent did not even *begin* to do A then and a later part of which it is true that he then did A. The "now" of which we are here speaking covers what may be called the *specious present* of the performance of an action. Most actions take some time to perform. Only when the action is one which can be performed at an instant ("in an inkling") does the specious present of its performance, the "now", shrink to a point. (Whether there are such actions, I do not know.)

Under the above conception of the "now", *will do A now* "reduces" to *does A now*. One could also say that "will do" has no proper application to the "now" case—and that the conclusion to match the two premises must be reformulated "Therefore he does A now". In any case, the conclusion is no longer a prediction. It is a description of what an agent does, is engaged in doing, now.[10] ("He will accomplish the doing of *A* now" would be a prediction which is compatible with the present tense description "he does *A* now".) So, in non-linguistic terms, the conclusion is an action. This is exactly what Aristotle said it should be.

But what remains open to debate is, whether this conclusion *follows*, i.e. whether an agent's present intentions and awareness of what he has to do right now in order to make them effective will of logical necessity lead, "compel", "prompt" him to action.

VII

From what was said before about "transmission of intention" we should from the two premisses

X intends to make it true that *E*.

He thinks that, unless he does *A* now, he will not achieve this.

be able to conclude:

Therefore *X* intends to do *A* now.

The problematic conclusion was

Therefore *X* does *A* now.

Our next task will be to compare the two conclusions.

If an agent does *A*, is it then also true to say that he intends to do *A*?

Sometimes a man is said to have done various things which he never intended but which happened to be consequences of his action. (He may even have foreseen that they were going to happen.) Perhaps one could call this "accidental doing" and distinguish it from "intentional doing". Here we understand by "doing" only intentional doing. Thus the practical argument would be invalidated, if it could be shown that on some occasion its (above) premisses were true and that the agent did *A*, though only accidentally, by mistake or as an unintended consequence of his acting.

So our question must be given this more precise formulation: Does it follow that an agent intends to do *A*, if he intentionally does *A*?

It is important to distinguish between intentional doing and intention(s) to do. "Intend to do" normally refers to the future. If "now" designates the specious present of the action, then under this normal use "intend to do now" is a self-contradictory phrase of a sort. (Not to be confused with

---

[10] If instead of "now" we had put in a reference to an arbitrary moment of time "at *t*" in our inference schema, the conclusion "He will do *A* at *t*" or "He does *A* at *t*" can be a prediction relative to the station in time where *we* happen to be. But this is irrelevant. What matters is that the conclusion is not a prediction *relative to the premisses*—in this case that the agent, at *t*, intends something and considers the doing at that very moment of some action necessary.

"intend now to do" which is logically in order.) "Intend to do", like "will do", has no proper application to the "now"-case. But what happens then to a persisting intention to do, when the moment of action is there? A suggestion would be that it "matures" and emerges on the behavioural level as intentional action.

Shall we say then that the two conclusions which we are comparing are identical? Shall we say that when the transmission of intention argument is applied to the present moment, then the conclusion which emerges is that *X* does *A* now?

The answer to the first question is, I think, affirmative. To answering the second affirmatively there is an objection, however. This objection may appear so grave that, in fact, it shows that action cannot possibly follow logically from premisses about intentions and epistemic attitudes.

VIII

Something happens which *prevents X* from doing *A*. He stumbles or has a stroke or someone seizes him and keeps him immobile.

If intention is for the future and the preventive interference occurs before the agent makes the intention effective, he will normally either change his intention or evaluate the practical requirements of the situation differently. This case therefore does not affect the problem of the validity of the inference schema which we are discussing.

If the preventive interference occurs within the specious present of the action but after the agent has commenced acting (set himself to act, embarked upon the road to the end), then we usually describe the case by saying that he *tried* but failed to accomplish the thing. Failure to accomplish can also be due to a change of intention within the specious present of the action. Then we say that the agent began or tried, but gave up. Failure can finally be due to the agent's not knowing, how to accomplish the thing. This can be called failure of ability. The agent had misjudged his powers. He intended to make it true that *E*. He realized that doing *A* was a practical necessity for this. He thought he could do *A*. But he was mistaken. Learning how to do *A*, or at least perfecting his ability, was a prior practical necessity for him (cf. above p. 22). Since he did not understand this, he proceeded to do things in the wrong order, so to speak. He set himself to do *A* but found that he could not accomplish it. This is another case of trying but failing.

It is a common feature of all these cases of failure to do *A* that the agent *embarks* on the action and that the failure is one of *accomplishing* the action. Embarking on an action involves some physical effort and therefore some behaviour or conduct aiming at the (completed) action. If the agent's embarking on the action is, moreover, a logical necessity under the premisses, we could still say that Aristotle was substantially right in thinking that a practical argument terminates in (some) action.

But we have also to consider the case, at least as a theoretical possibility, that the preventive interference occurs exactly at the same time as the specious present for the action begins. Then the agent cannot be said to have embarked upon the action. There was no time for doing this. At most we could then say that he *would* have embarked upon it, had he not been prevented.

If we understand "prevented" to mean either prevented right at the beginning of the action or prevented in the course of an attempt to perform it, we can state the conclusion which finally emerges from our considerations of the form of a practical inference as follows:

> Therefore *X* does *A* now, unless he is prevented or else cannot accomplish the action.

IX

In order to show that an agent *does* a certain thing *A*, it is not enough to show that *A*, the result of the action, happens as a causal consequence of some movements in the agent's body (rising of arms, twisting of hands, etc.). We must also show that what took place was *intentional*, i.e. was a case of an agent's *doing A* as distinct from merely bringing it about without intending it.

To establish that the agent's causing *A* to come about is a case of his doing *A* is not to establish, in addition to the happening of *A*, a different event which so to speak occurs "inside the agent". It is to *understand* (the meaning of) the agent's conduct, i.e. to see that by certain changes in his body or changes causally connected with changes in his body the agent is *aiming* at this result. If he aims at it without achieving it, we shall have to say that the agent tried but failed—either because of insufficient ability or because he was prevented.

Now we can see more clearly, I think, wherein the claim to logical validity of the practical inference consists. Given the premisses

> *X* now intends to make it true that *E*.
> He thinks that, unless he does *A* now, he will not achieve this.

and excluding, hypothetically or on the basis of investigations, that he is prevented, then his actual conduct, whatever it may "look like", either is an act of doing *A* or aims, though unsuccessfully, at being this. Any description of his behaviour which is logically inconsistent with this is also logically inconsistent with the premisses. Accepting the premisses thus forces on us this understanding of his conduct—unless for some reason we think that a preventive interference occurred right at the beginning of his action.

X

What *uses* has the type of argument which I here call practical inference?

One can distinguish between a *retrospective* and a *prospective* use.

When the argument is used retrospectively we start from the conclusion and so to speak reconstruct a set of premisses to match it. Then the "conclusion" normally is the established or hypothetically assumed proposition that an agent has done a certain thing, performed an action *A*. (But it can also be the proposition that he set himself to do a certain thing which he failed to accomplish, either because he changed his mind, or was prevented, or did not possess the needed ability. Here I shall consider only the "normal" case.)

An agent did *A*. *Why* did he do it? We *explain* his action by placing it in the "teleological perspective" of his aiming at some end and his epistemic attitude to the requirements of the situation, i.e. his judging the action a practical necessity under this end. This is a prototype case of what is usually called *teleological explanation*.[11]

I did *A*. Someone challenges me: Why did I do this? I may *justify* my conduct by reference to what I was after and that I thought my doing of *A* a practical necessity for me. (This, however, is not the only sense in which a man is said to "justify" his actions.)

When the argument is used prospectively we set out from the premisses and "extract" from them a conclusion. In the first person case the argument ends in a *declaration* (formation) *of intention* to do a certain thing. I *commit* myself to doing it. Such use of the argument takes place particularly in situations where I *ponder* what I have to do in order to attain some already set aim of mine.

In the third person case the prospective (forward-looking) argument produces a *prediction*. Since so and so is the agent's aim and he evidently considers the doing of *A* necessary for its attainment, he will (probably) do *A*.

Is there, in addition to the retrospective and prospective uses of practical inference also something which might be called an "instantaneous" use of it? Is there explanation of action only on the basis of what is *now* the case—and is there intentional action which is *simultaneous* with the construction of a justification for it?

I think the answer to these questions is No. When practical inference functions as an argument it either looks to the past for the reasons or to

---

[11] The term "teleological explanation" has a multitude of rather different uses. For explanations which set human actions in a "teleological" perspective of intentions and epistemic attitudes I would now prefer the term *intentionalist* explanation. Cf. my book *Freedom and Determination*, North-Holland Publishing Company, Amsterdam 1980, p. 28 and *passim*.

the future for an action. So in any use of the argument there is a time gap involved between premisses and conclusion and with this gap there is also a rift in the logical connection between the intention and epistemic attitude on the one hand and the action on the other hand.

When therefore, in Section VI, we closed this time gap, we thereby also obliterated the character of an argument or an inference from the propositional connections which we were investigating. What happened to our "practical inference" was in the end (Section IX) that we turned it into a set of conditions under which the conduct of an agent has to be interpreted or understood in a certain way, *viz.* as the doing of *A* or as aiming at this result. The premisses of the practical inference became the description of a teleological perspective in which conduct is being understood as intentional.

What then will be our final position on the question of conclusiveness of practical arguments?

When the argument is used retrospectively to explain or, in the first person, to justify action, the clause "unless prevented or else cannot accomplish the action" does not appear in it. That the agent did or tried to do *A* is not called into question and is, moreover, something that was logically bound to happen, assuming that the teleological frame, the intention and the epistemic attitude which the premisses attribute to him, lasted up to the moment of action. For, granting the truth of this assumption, the premisses then set the conditions for *interpreting* what happened.

When the argument is used prospectively in the first person, the clause "unless prevented or else cannot accomplish the action" likewise is no part of the argument. Therefore we have no logical guarantee here concerning that which the agent will in fact do. But this is not what the argument purports to give either. Its binding nature stems from the fact that its conclusion declares the intention which an agent is logically bound to have within the teleological frame which in the premisses he acknowledges for his prospective action.

Only when the argument is used prospectively in the third person, is the unless-clause a part of it. We know that if this clause is satisfied and if the teleological frame attributed to the agent in the premisses remains stable up to the moment of action, then conduct of the predicted character is logically bound to follow. (Since this is how the situation will then have to be understood by us.) But whether the clause will be satisfied and whether the teleological frame will remain stable, we cannot know in advance. It is therefore contingent, whether the prediction will be fulfilled or not.

Postscript on Understanding

The "logical core" of the propositional connections which I have been discussing in this essay can be called a schema of interpretation or of understanding conduct as being intentional (action). This schema is what a practical inference "becomes" when it is applied to the moment of action, the "now"-case—and ceases to be an inference. I tried to show how the validity of this schema is relevant to the validity of the inference.

This schema also has an independent use, namely for purposes of *understanding* what an agent is doing—as distinct from the (third person) uses of the inference which is to *explain* why an agent did what he did or to *predict* what he is going to do. But here a warning is in place.

On no account must it be thought that the understanding of behaviour as action is always based on an interpretation of an agent's conduct in the light of some intentions and cognitions which we attribute to him. To think thus would be to distort the logic of the situation seriously. It would, moreover, be a similar distortion to the one of which philosophers make themselves guilty, when they say that any statement about physical objects is the result of interpreting certain sense-data.

In the normal cases we say off-hand of the way we see people behave that they perform such and such actions—raise their arms, walk or run, open key-locks or hand things over to one another. Many of these actions we ourselves know how to perform; those, and others which *we* cannot do, have a familiar "look" or "physiognomy" which we recognize. We are further acquainted with innumerable ends for the sake of which these actions may be performed (when not "done for their own sake"). Therefore we need not first seek for the agent's end of action in order to be able to tell *what* he is doing. Only when we are curious, *why* he is doing what we already think we know he is doing, do we look for a specific object of intention with him. (Explanation of action follows *after* understanding behaviour as action.)

These are the normal cases. But there are others. There are first of all the abortive cases, when an agent fails to accomplish the action. Even then we can usually say what, in fact, he did. He, for example, grabbed a handle and pulled, twisted his hand, etc. and in doing these things he was trying, though unsuccessfully, to do a certain thing which one normally does by doing just those things (and perhaps something else beside). In what he *did* we see at once what he was *aiming* at—and therefore we say that he *tried* to do so and so. On the whole only when failure to accomplish is due to insufficient know-how, or to quite false conceptions of how to achieve the result (of the action), may it be necessary to "interpret" what we witness in the light of hypothetical aims and cognitions of the agent. We then say some such thing as: "Evidently he is trying to open the safe but has no idea of how to do it."

Secondly, there are cases when we are unfamiliar with the (kind of) action and therefore do not understand *what* the agent is doing. Perhaps he performs some strange ceremony. Even then we can usually describe various things which he is doing in the course of doing this strange thing. We, e.g., *see him move* his legs and arms in certain ways and not only see *his legs and arms move.* When we nevertheless say we do not understand what he is doing, this is because we feel reluctant to say that what he primarily intends to do is to make those movements with his limbs but suspect that the object of his primary intention is something which is done *by* moving legs and arms in a certain way. (Perhaps he is saluting or dancing.) We must learn what the new action "looks like", become acquainted with its "physiognomy" before we can understand what a man is doing, who behaves in this way. We can learn this by being told what the agent is doing, sometimes by just being told the *name* of the action. (I can learn to recognize when a man is saluting without having any idea why people salute.)

So not even in the cases of unfamiliar actions is a practical inference always or normally needed to understand what is being done. Only in some, rather exceptional, situations will the construction of a practical argument be helpful here. We see a person go through some movements, the significance of which we do not understand "in themselves"—but we have a strong hunch that he evidently intends to do a certain thing in behaving thus, e.g. that he is saluting somebody in the street. (But then we must also know, not just the name of the action, but also something about the occasions on which it is appropriate to perform it.) "So this is how these people salute", is our guess. Here a practical inference can be said to guide our understanding.

Sometimes we mistake behaviour for action when in fact it is not. A person's arm goes up and I say I see him raise his arm. Then I learn that what I witnessed was a physiological experiment and that the person's neural system was being stimulated in a way which made his arm go up. (Perhaps the experimenter had even told him not to raise his arm "himself".) Then I must withdraw the claim, implicit in what first I said, that the person raised his arm. I can redescribe what I saw in a way which does not carry that claim with it by saying that I saw his arm rise. When thus I modify my original description, it is tempting to speak, *post hoc*, of a false interpretation of what I saw. We say: I interpreted what I *really saw*, *viz.* his arm rise, as a case of seeing him raise his arm—but this was premature. This is like the case, when we withdraw a physical object statement and replace it by a sense-data statement, because it turned out that the object we saw was only illusory—say a column very skilfully drawn on the wall. In both cases, however, is it misleading to say that we interpreted what we saw in the wrong way. For we did not *interpret* what we saw at all.

I can understand something as an action and be mistaken in thus understanding it. I can see something as a physical object and be mistaken in thus seeing it. But this is not to say that what I really *saw* was, e.g., his arm rising and not him raising his arm—or a painting on the wall and not a column. Understanding is compatible with misunderstanding, one could say. Only when we are on our guard against misunderstanding or confused about the nature of the case, do we *interpret* what we immediately witness. And if what we witness are the movements of some living beings, the interpretation normally consists in the construction of a practical inference to match the case.

Determinism and the Study of Man

By determinism I shall understand ideas according to which that which *is* also (somehow) *had to be*. Such ideas play an important role both in the natural and in the human sciences. Whatever the ultimate answer may be to the question as to how these two types of sciences are related, the following difference between them is striking on the surface:

In the natural sciences, deterministic ideas are connected with such other ideas as those of universal regularity, repeatability, and experimental control. In the human sciences the immediate connections are with ideas such as motivation and social pressure, goal-directedness and intentionality. In the natural sciences determinism serves in a large measure the forward looking aims of prediction; in the human sciences there is a relatively much stronger emphasis on retrospective explanation, or understanding, of what is already a *fait accompli*.

These differences between naturalistic and humanistic study in relation to determinism I would attribute to the following source—well aware that what I say may sound provocative: Natural science can be characterized as a study of phenomena under the "reign" of natural law. Human science again is primarily a study of phenomena under the "reign" of social institutions and rules. I shall argue for what may be termed a "methodological parallelism" between laws of nature and rules of society. That is, I shall argue that deterministic ideas in the human sciences have a relation to societal rules which is *analogous* to the relation in the natural sciences between deterministic ideas and natural laws. I am not, of course, saying that laws of the state and other social rules are, in themselves, like laws of nature. They are, on the contrary, very different. The former are normative, the latter descriptive, as we say. And from this profound difference between the two types of law it follows that, if the "methodological parallelism" I am making is at all correct, determinism in the study of man means something utterly different from determinism in the study of nature.

I can foresee immediate objections. The theoretical aim of the human sciences, it will be said, is to discover laws which state, not regulations and rules of conduct, but factual regularities of individual and collective behaviour and of institutional change. Such laws, if there are any, will "determine" or "govern" the life of men and of society in a similar way to that in which the laws of nature "determine" or "govern" natural phenomena. On this view, determinism in the study of man would mean essentially the same thing as determinism in natural science.

Deterministic claims of this character have often been made for the human sciences. Sometimes with the qualification that the laws of behaviour are not as "rigid" as the laws, say, of classical mechanics, but are rather of a probabilistic than of a "strictly" causal nature. Or it is said that it has not yet been possible to formulate them exactly. The social sciences are still young and we must not expect too much of them in their infancy.

To view matters in this light is, I think, to be guilty of a serious "methodological misunderstanding". It is symptomatic of an illegitimate transfer of conceptions and ideals from the natural to the human sciences. To say this is not to deny legitimacy to a study which ascertains factual regularities in human and social behaviour. Nor is it to exclude the possibility of relying on such regularities for successful predictions. But it is an invitation to view in a new light the study of man and all theorizing and philosophizing in the social sciences.

This shift in point of view will also have consequences for the age-old philosophic problem of "the freedom of the will". This is, roughly, the question of the relation between the actions of an individual and various forces working from within him: his will, his wants, his passions and sentiments, and his deliberations. There is a deep-rooted tendency to wed this question to the further question of the relation between neural processes and macroscopic reactions in the individual's body. This "internalization" of the problem is another illegitimate transfer to a sphere where it does not belong of an attitude appropriate to the natural sciences, in this case physiology. The way to a solution is what I propose to call an "externalization" of the problem. This consists in working one's way from considerations of individual action to considerations of the factors which influence ("determine") the individual's conduct as a member of a community, in the context of institutionalized human relationships. It would be a slight, but still useful, exaggeration to say that the problem of the freedom of the will, like the problem of freedom generally, is essentially a question of social philosophy.

II

As a basis and starting point I shall present and briefly discuss two patterns of explanation of action.

The first explanatory pattern I shall call *intentionalist* explanation. It is related to a type of reasoning sometimes called "the practical syllogism". In its simplest form this reasoning goes as follows:

A intends to p (e.g. go to the theatre tomorrow).
A thinks that unless he q's (e.g. reserves a ticket in advance), he will not
    be able to p.
Therefore: A takes steps to q.

The inference remains valid, if for "intends" we substitute "has decided" or "is resolved" or "is determined", perhaps also "is anxious". For "thinks" in the second premiss one can also put "considers", "realizes", "knows", or "believes".

It is easy to see what practical reasoning has to do with action explanation. Assume A, as a matter of fact, q's. We are curious to know *why*. It would be a satisfactory answer to this question to point out that he intends to p and considers q'ing necessary to this end. And the same answer would explain, why he tried to q in a situation when he failed.

It is quite natural to say here that A's behaviour was *determined* by his intention and epistemic attitude. Given them, he had to do what in fact he did. We can speak of the intention and epistemic attitude as *determinants* of the agent's action and say that they jointly constitute a (sufficient) ground or *reason* for q'ing. The thing for the sake of which A undertook to q I shall call A's *object of intention*, and the q'ing itself, I shall say, was part of the *requirements of the situation*, as A saw it, upon his action.

Suppose that A considers q'ing sufficient, though not necessary, for attaining the object of his intention. He intends to go to town and knows he will have to use a public conveyance to get there—say, either take a bus or a train. He takes steps to catch the bus. Should we here too say that his actual choice of the bus is fully explained, determined, by what he intends to do and knows about the means of making his intention effective?

Obviously we should *not* say this. The behaviour which we can explain on the basis of the facts, as I presented them, is the "disjunctive action" which consists in the agent's taking a bus *or* taking the train. This action he can perform in one of two ways, *viz.* by taking a bus and, alternatively, by taking a train. So, if now he chooses the bus, he performs the disjunctive action. *This* action is then fully determined by the agent's intentions and beliefs—but not his actual choice of alternative.

But could not his choice be determined too? Certainly it could. Various *reasons* might have existed for his choosing to go by bus: perhaps it is safer or cheaper or quicker than going by train. If his choice of means of transportation can be attributed to some such reason, then it is also true to speak of the *choice* as determined. But it is important to note that, although a man's choices between alternative courses of action *can* be in this sense determined, they *need not* be. To insist that they must would be sheer deterministic dogmatism. Choice *can* be completely "fortuitous".

III

Many actions are performed in response to a verbal (or other symbolic) challenge. The challenge can be, for example, an order which I obey, or a request with which I comply, or a question which I answer—or a traffic light to which I respond. Why did I reach out for the salt on the table and hand it to my neighbour?[1] Because he asked for it. This can be a complete explanation. His request determined my action, constituted for me a sufficient ground or reason for doing what I did.

Normally, when I respond to a challenge of this kind, I cannot rightly be said to *intend to* respond. I simply *respond*.

Assume, however, that the saltcellar had slipped from my grip and the salt poured out on the table. I hear people cry out: "What are you doing?" Then I could quite truthfully reply: "I intend*ed* ('I meant') to hand the salt to X, who asked for it". The fact that I can give this reply, when I fail in the performance, shows that complying with a request is intentional action—and not just a conditioned response to a stimulus.

In our example the object of intention was to hand the salt to my neighbour. This object was, so to speak, set by the request, and only reconstituted by me in retrospect. For this reason I shall call it externally set—and contrast it with the internally set objects of intention which are there when I can say, before proceeding to act, what I intend to achieve.

Similarly, we can divide the determinants of action into internal and external ones. Intentions and epistemic attitudes are of the former, symbolic challenges of the latter kind.

Response to verbal and other symbolic challenges is participation in various *institutionalized* forms of behaviour or *practices*. That the practices are "institutionalized" means that they are shared by a community into which we are reared by being taught to participate.

Response to symbolic challenge is only one form of participation in an institutionalized practice. Another is behaviour in conformity with rules such as the laws of the state or the codes of morality and good manners or customs and traditions. "Why don't you park your car here?" (It would perhaps be convenient.) The answer might be "It is not allowed". Here a traffic regulating rule functions as a determinant of my behaviour. Obedience to it is an externally set object of my intentional acting.

The proportion of our actions which are determined internally and externally respectively, is not fixed. It varies from society to society, and it varies with the position of the individual agent in society. In a social order with many taboos and ritualized ways of life external determinants can steer the actions of men in the minutest details. In such societies the margins of individual freedom are very narrow.

IV

External determinants of our actions are given to us like stimuli to which we react. Such responses have to be learnt—as is the case with conditioned reflexes. Learning to participate in institutionalized forms of behaviour is

---

[1] I owe this example to Professor Frederick Stoutland.

connected with a characteristic motivation. I shall call this motivational mechanism *normative pressure.*

Non-conformity to legal and moral and other rules of conduct and good manners is likely to have unpleasant consequences for the agent. In the case of legal norms the "administering" of these consequences is itself institutionalized and consists in various coercive measures against the agent. In the case of moral norms the consequences are disapproval, ostracism, loss of esteem or confidence—things which make a man ill at ease in society.

I think it is essential to the idea of participating in institutionalized patterns of behaviour that it should be surrounded by this "aura" of normative pressure. This does not mean that the answer to the question why people participate or conform to rule, is always or even normally teleological. People do not usually conform *in order to* escape the unpleasant consequences of non-conformity. But sometimes they do this—e.g., when participation or conformity is against their personal interests or connected with discomfort or when it seems pointless. Then the answer to the question: Why did you do *x*? could be: Had I not done *x*, *y* would have happened to me and this I am anxious to avoid. Here the determinant of my action is not the invitation to participate—but the internal determinant constituted by my intention to avoid a certain thing which I consider likely to happen to me, if I do not participate.

In educating people, particularly children, to participate in practices and obey rules, rewards also play a characteristic role. When reward is merely an alternative to punishment in making people conform, I shall call reward external. On the whole external reward seems to play a subordinate role in the institutionalization of patterns of behaviour. Philosophers have noted and tried to give an account of this fact. I think the explanation should be sought along the following lines:

Institutionalization of behaviour normally serves a purpose. Institutions have what we call a social function. Without traffic regulations there would be chaos on the roads. This nobody wants. Participation in the practice, by everybody concerned, is therefore supposed to be in the "public interest", i.e., something which will be in the interest of each individual participant, bring him some good. This good can be thought of as a "reward" connected intrinsically with the practice, i.e., with the idea of having it. Therefore it is a further feature essentially connected with the institutionalization of behaviour that the reason for conforming to the set patterns should, on the whole, *not* be the impact of normative pressure, but simply acceptance of the rule. When rules function in this way, they are also said to be *internalized* with the members of the society in question. The more often normative pressure determines behaviour, the more strongly is the coercive force of society felt and the less "free", in a subjective sense, are the individual agents. But internalization is also a loss of freedom of a kind. For it means that externally given stimuli are allowed to determine the actions. It is on these two forms of non-freedom that social critics play. They question the fact of internalization, e.g., raise and make people reflect on the question whether various institutions and practices *are* in the "public interest" or whether they perhaps only serve to cement interests not at all "public" but, say, those of a ruling class. Thus their criticism contributes to an increase in the normative pressure felt within the society. The society becomes more and more coercive and its institutions malfunctioning. Hereby the ground is prepared for institutional changes.

V

Assume that it were true that A q'ed *because* he intended to p and thought q'ing necessary for this. What sort of connection does this "because" establish between an intention and epistemic attitude on the one hand and action on the other hand? This is a question on which philosophers violently disagree.

Some hold that the connection is causal. This position can be understood in two ways. I shall call them the trivial and the non-trivial.

The trivial understanding of the causalist position stresses the fact that intentions are quite commonly *called* "causes of actions". This is in order, and we should not attempt to reform language here. The only objection which one can have to this kind of talk is that it obscures the difference between the sense in which intentions can uncontroversially be called causes of actions and some other important senses in which things are said to be causally related. One of these other senses is often called "Humean". The existence of a Humean causal relation entails that there is a general law connecting instances of logically independent generic phenomena as cause and effect.

The non-trivial interpretation of the causalist position in action theory holds that a specific combination of intention and epistemic attitude is a Humean cause of a specific kind of action.

Defenders of this position sometimes think that it requires a reinterpretation of intentions and cognitive states in neurological terms. The causal relation is then in the first place between certain brain events and certain movements of limbs and other parts of the body. Of this view I shall here only say the following:

We need not doubt that there are causal relations of the kind just mentioned. But the neurological interpretation of volitional and epistemic attitudes is, at best, only a contingent correlation of them with equivalents in the brain and not a necessary connection. And whether the movements caused by those brain events are actions or not is again a contingent matter, depending upon other facts about the agent than movements of his body and processes in his nervous system. These observations, when more fully substantiated, suffice, in my opinion, to wreck the non-trivial causalist thesis about the relation between intentions and actions. But I cannot argue the point at length here.[2]

The contrasting opinion holds that there is a conceptual or logical connection between an action and its grounds in an intention and epistemic attitude. This opinion is sometimes called the Logical Connection Argument or the intentionalist view. I think it comes nearer the truth than the causalist view. But it is difficult to argue for it correctly.

Thus I think it is a mistake—of which I myself[3] and others have been guilty—to understand the intentionalist view to mean that there is a relation of logical *entailment* between the premisses and the conclusion of a practical argument.

Consider the following example.[4]—A man is firmly resolved to assassinate a tyrant. He has access to his room, aims at him with a loaded revolver —but cannot bring himself to pull the trigger. Nothing which we later find out about him would make us think that he had changed his intention or come to a different opinion about the things required of him to make it effective. Is this conceivable, i.e., logically possible?

It should be noted that we do not assume here that the assassin *in spe* forbore to pull the trigger. Had he done so, it would be, I should think, a contradiction to say that the man (still) intended to shoot the tyrant and knew what he had to do. (It would be a contradiction reminiscent of the so-called Moore paradox.) What is assumed is simply that he did not do anything at all just then which was relevantly related to his resolve to shoot the tyrant. He was "paralysed"—but neither physically nor mentally in a way which would make us revise the description of his intentions and cognitions.

In view of this example I think we should say the following about the nature of the relation between intentions and actions:

An intention and an opinion of what is required for it to become effective, constitute, as was already said, *a sufficient* ground or *reason* for acting accordingly. If the agent then acts accordingly, we understand completely why he is doing what he is doing, e.g., trying to kill the tyrant by firing at him. No further information can help us understand *this* better. (We may, of course, wonder why he should have had the intention he had or how it was that he thought as he did—quite wrongly perhaps—about the requirements of making his intention effective. But these questions do not concern the determinants of his action but the determinants, if there are any, of these determinants.) If again the agent fails to "act accordingly"

---

[2] Cf. *Freedom and Determination*, especially pp. 57–61.
[3] Cf. *Explanation and Understanding*, pp. 97–118.
[4] *Ibid.*, pp. 116f.

we do not understand him at all. His behaviour is incomprehensible to us and in this sense *irrational* or, considering that he had sufficient grounds for acting in a certain way, anti-rational.

The relation between what I have called internal determinants of an action and the action itself is thus neither a relation of entailment nor a causal relation. We must resist the temptation to reduce it to something which it is *not*. But there is a sense in which we can call the relation *conceptual*—and something remains to be said about this before we have a full understanding of its nature.

VI

What is action? One could answer: Action is normally behaviour understood, "seen", or described under the aspect of intentionality, i.e., as meaning something or as goal-directed.

Intentionality can quite rightly be said to be in the behaviour. But not like a "quality" inherent in the movements of limbs and other parts of the body. For these movements we can describe completely without mentioning intentionality. So what then is the intentionality of behaviour?

To understand behaviour as intentional, I shall say, is to fit it into a "story" about an agent. We see a person walking in the street, carrying a parcel in his hand. He drops it and bends to pick it up. We should normally think of his picking it up as intentional. Why?

We may not know at all why he picked it up. But we can name hundreds of reasons why he might have done this, reasons which are such that had they been his at the time, they would explain his action completely. Perhaps the parcel contained something he was anxious not to lose; or a gift which he had bought for somebody. Or perhaps he took care not to litter the street or maybe was just following an existing regulation requesting one not to do this. We are, in other words, familiar with a number of possible, internal and external, determinants of his action here. We think it likely that some such determinant will be at work. This is what it is to "see his behaviour as intentional".

There are on the whole reliable ways of coming to know, of verifying, what a person intends to do, what he thinks are the requirements of the situation, and whether he acts accordingly. Verification may not always be conclusive, and ascertaining one of the three things mentioned may sometimes have to rely upon the accepted verification of one or both of the other two. But normally the verificational procedures here are applicable independently of one another.

A standard way of ascertaining a person's intentions and epistemic attitudes is by asking him. If we doubt whether his answers are reliable, there are usually other checks available. Ascertaining what a person does again, is usually a matter of simple observation. We literally *see* him do various actions, i.e., we can describe his perceived behaviour under an appropriate aspect of intentionality. We may be mistaken, but normally we take what we see to be conclusive.

Relying on these verificational procedures we can establish a predictive correlation between the premises and the conclusion of practical inferences. Having verified the premises, we expect the conclusion to turn out to be true. The reliability of the prediction is in the following sense a function of *time* here:

When a person intends to do something, the object of his intention is in the future. This is so also when he intends to do something "right now"— for "now" then means the time immediately ahead of him. For this reason a person will normally have time to change his intention, and also his opinion of how he has to act, before he proceeds to making the intention effective. The more time he has to change his mind, the greater the risk that he will actually do so. If he does, the prediction may fail.

It is essential, however, that for short time intervals the reliability of the predictions should be high. This seems to be a feature of the way in which the *concepts* of intention, of the various epistemic attitudes, and of action are related to one another. If it were normally the case with a given person that he did not act in conformity with his shortly before professed intention and understanding of the situation, we should doubt either the veracity of his reports or doubt whether *he* knew what it *is* to intend and to believe something. And if this were the case with people generally, it would modify our view of what intentions and beliefs are. We could no longer be taught nor teach to others the present use of the words and therefore we should not *have* the concepts either, at least not in their present form. One could say that the language-games we now play with action-words and with epistemic and volitional terms rest on (presuppose) a high degree of correlation between intention and action in accordance with the understood requirements of a situation.

The prediction of actions from a background of intentions has a certain resemblance with the prediction of effects from knowledge of their causes. But there are also important differences to be noted.

One difference is this. The prediction of action is subject to a clause that no change occurs in the volitional and epistemic background before action is supposed to take place. The frequency of the failure of the prediction, with a given agent—assuming that his intentions and epistemic attitudes are known for certain—is therefore a measure of the degree to which he is, as we say, "capricious" or "unreliable" or even "irrational". The only *hypothetical* element involved in the prediction is, in other words, that a certain volitional and epistemic attitude of the agent should remain constant in an individual case and that the agent should not act "irrationally". This is different from a typical causal context in the natural sciences. Here the failure of a prediction can always in principle recoil back also on a hypothetical *law* relating the cause to the effect.

In the case of predictions of actions there simply are no such "covering laws" to be confirmed or refuted. To say that such and such intentions and beliefs, assuming they do not change, will normally result in such and such behaviour is not to state an empirical generalization based on observations or experiments. It is to state a necessary truth to which anybody familiar with the concepts involved will agree off-hand. And therefore this truth is very seldom stated—except, perhaps, in philosophic debates.

VII

What is the nature of the relation between actions and their external determinants?

Assume that it were true that *A q*'ed *because* he had been ordered to do so. It is quite obvious that the connection between the determinant and the action cannot here be a relation of logical entailment. For, it would then be selfcontradictory ("unthinkable") that *A* had been given the order, had understood it and was able to carry it into effect, and yet did not do so. This, however, is far from unthinkable. Is the connection then causal? (Here it may be worth noting that it is much *less* natural to call an order a "cause" of action than to call an intention by this name.)

If the connection were one of Humean causation, there should exist a *law* connecting cause and effect. This law cannot be that *A* always obeys when he is ordered to *q*. Perhaps this is true of *A*. But most probably it is not true of everybody who has learnt to obey orders. It may, for example, not be true of *B*. Still it could very well be the case that *B* too, on some occasion, *q*'ed *because* he had been ordered to do so. So whether the agent concerned happens to be one who always obeys orders to *q*, or not, is quite irrelevant to the question of the nature of the connection, in an individual case, between the order and the action.

As far as I can see, the "because" does not rest on any law at all here. And if this is so, then the relation between the determinant and the action is not one of Humean causation. What then is it? I propose to call it a relation of *justification*.

Let it be that *A* answers when asked why he *q*'ed: "Because I was ordered". May he not be lying or even mistaken about his own motives? When pressed with further questions, he may admit that really he *q*'ed because he feared the anger of the order-giver, i.e., acted under the influence of normative pressure, and not just in response to the order. But if he does not admit any such other motive—not even "to himself", "in his heart"— then we must take him at his word and say that he *q*'ed because he was ordered. There is no "external" way of deciding the truth of the "because"-

statement to which we could concede ultimate authority here.[5] The connection between the external determinant and the action is, as I have said, not intrinsic in the sense that it were a logical entailment. But it is in a characteristic sense an "internal" relation, dependent upon the agent's judgement of why he acted as he did. Therefore it is not, in any good sense of the word, a "causal" relation.

Just as one can, within limits, predict the actions of an agent from antecedent knowledge of internal determinants, one can make predictions on the basis of knowledge of external determinants. The degree of reliability of such predictions may vary with the agents concerned and also with the society under consideration. One can use this degree as a measure of the responsiveness of an individual to external determinants (of one sort or another, or generally). For example, one could use it as a measure of his obedience to the law or to his superiors. One can also use it to measure the degree of internalization and of normative "cohesion" of a given society. The characteristics thus measured do not explain predictability. Predictability is their criterion. Nor is there any other general law besides a rough statistical correlation which connects the determinants with the actions.

It is of some interest to ponder why we do not willingly speak of such correlations as "laws". Is it because of their unprecise and statistical nature? Or because of their dependence upon individual agents and individual societies? An even weightier reason for not calling them "laws" is, I think, their dependence upon factors, *viz.* norms and institutionalized patterns of behaviour, which are themselves susceptible to change in the course of history as a result of human action. "Scientific laws", we tend to think, must not for their validity be dependent upon historical contingencies. They should hold true *semper et ubique*.

VIII

Determinants of action, I have said, are either internally set or externally given. By referring to their determinants we explain the actions, i.e., answer questions why agents acted as they did.

Such answers, however, are only explanations "in the short perspective". They give rise to further questions. For example: Why do people have the intentions they have?

Sometimes the answer to that question is given in the terms of a further intention. Why did *A* intend to go to the concert tomorrow? The answer could be that he intends, is resolved, to acquire some education in music. Going to concerts here serves as a means to an end. But why should he be

---

[5] On this question I have later come to change my opinion. See the essay "Explanation and Understanding of Action", below, pp. 64f.

resolved to pursue this remoter end? The answer in terms of intentions will ultimately take us, I suggest, to one of two main types of determinants of intentions. I shall call them *wants* and *duties*.[6]

Let us first consider wants. Why did *A* intend to go to the concert? A frequent type of answer could be: Because he wanted to hear *B* perform or because he wanted to hear symphony *S* again or simply because he wanted to hear some music. Such answers are normally complete explanations. One wanted *just this*, and there is no further thing for the sake of which one wanted it, as a means to an end.

If the further question is raised as to why one wants what one wants, the answer sometimes is: Because it pleases or one likes it or because it is thought fine or nice or amusing. But such answers do not point to determinants of the want. They merely specify it by setting it against a background which is there independently of my present intention to reach out for the wanted thing. If, for example, I like to listen to music, I shall, given an opportunity and in the absence of any other determinant already at work on my intentions or actions, listen to music. On such an occasion I might say "I want to hear some music, I like music." My liking of music is, so to speak, a latent want which manifests itself in my intention, say, to hear some music now or to go to the concert tomorrow.

One cannot ask why people should want things they like or take pleasure in. It is, one could say, "in the nature" of pleasant and liked things that they should be wanted—as it is "in the nature" of unpleasant and hurtful things, such as illnesses or punishment, that they should be shunned. Shunning things is wanting not to have them or wanting to get rid of them. When we intend (decide) to follow a rule or order because we are anxious not to risk punishment, it is our shunning of something intrinsically unwanted that determines our intention.

A person says: "I intend (have decided) to go to the Canary Islands during my vacation." "Why do you want to go there?", we ask. We are anxious to know the *want* behind his intention. He answers: "Oh, I just want to see the place, it is supposed to be nice." This could be his sole motive force (want) here. But assume he answers: "I think it will do me good, I have been very tired and run down lately." Then the planned action is seen as a means to an end, the end being one's health or well-being generally. This is what one wants to promote.

Health, well-being, and happiness are "natural" objects of want. Other things being equal we pursue them of necessity, for their own sake. In this they resemble the things we like or which give us pleasure. It makes no sense to ask "Why do you want to be healthy?" But it does not follow that a person will necessarily care for his health, or pursue his pleasures or happiness. There can be overriding considerations. He may have "no time"

---

[6] For a fuller discussion, see *Freedom and Determination*, Ch. IV.

for his pleasures or "be forced" to neglect or even to ruin his health. The determinants which can override the influence on our intentions and actions even of things which are "by nature" objects of wants, have the character of *duties*.

IX

The word "duty" should here be taken in a broad and somewhat loose sense.[7] The range of things which I have in mind can be roughly characterized as follows:

As a member of a society any man usually holds one or several positions in which he is expected, or sometimes even obliged, to do various things. Some such position a man can be said to hold "by nature", such as the position of a parent; others he holds, e.g., by appointment or by election. But in either case the actions or types of action expected of him are defined by the explicit or implicit rules (laws, customs, conventions) of the society to which he belongs. I shall call such positions *roles* and the things expected of a *role*-holder *duties*. (The etymology of the word then suggests that they are things which he "owes" to the rest of the society by virtue of his position in it.)

Thus a head of state is expected to care for his country's prestige, its power and prosperity. This will make him form intentions and take decisions which, as a "private citizen", he neither could nor would contemplate. The objects of these intentions form part of what he and others consider his duties. Failure to perform need not have legal implications for him, but will surely have consequences which it is in *his* ("personal") interest to shun, such as loss of popularity or an unfavourable "verdict of history". So, failing a motive "from duty", there will be a motive "from want" ("self-interest") to make him have the action-guiding intentions which are appropriate to his role.

A policeman is seen jumping into a car and speeding away. Why this behaviour? We are told that he intends to catch the thief who was seen running in the street. Why should he intend this? As a private citizen he may even have felt inclined to let the poor man escape. But his role as policeman "imposes" this intention on him with all the actions following upon considerations about the means of making the intention effective. If he does not realize this and act accordingly, he runs the risk of being fired or even punished.

Similar considerations apply, *mutatis mutandis*, to all holders of roles. It is an essential part of the picture here that roles should be surrounded by an aura of normative pressure which, when needed, makes people

---

[7] For a different notion of "duty", cf. *The Varieties of Goodness*, Routledge & Kegan Paul, London, 1963, Ch. IX.

perform in their roles—perhaps somewhat "against their will" but still in agreement with what they want, lest something worse happens to them. In this regard there is a parallel between roles as external determinants of intentions and rules and symbolic challenges as external determinants of actions. But as with rules it is also the case with roles that it is essential to our notion of a functioning society that role-performance should on the whole *not* be motivated by normative pressure, but should be "internalized", that is: the duties unquestioningly accepted as an ultimate determinant of what we intend.

It is perhaps right to say that duties implicit in various roles more than any other determinants mould men's intentions and therefore indirectly guide their actions. But the extent to which this happens is different within different societies and with different roles. Therefore questions of role-distribution within a society are inseparably connected with the problems of individual freedom.

So-called "free-time" is that part of a man's life when he can do what he *wants* and temporarily forget the demands on him of at least some of his assigned roles. When a man has no time for his wants, only for his duties, he is a slave to his roles. This he can be both as servant in the meanest position and as a master endowed with the greatest power.

X

In addition to wants and duties there is also a third type of factor which determines a man's intentions—and through the intentions his actions: his *abilities*.

Unlike wants and duties which "prompt" people to action, abilities determine actions negatively, restrictively. They delimit the "horizon" or "domain" or "range" of a man's freedom to act. This range will then wax and wane with variations in ability.

To have an intention to do something presupposes that the agent thinks, rightly or wrongly, that he can achieve the object of his intention. What he does not think he *may* accomplish, he will not attempt either. To say this is to make a *conceptual* observation on the relation between the volitional and epistemic attitudes involved in a practical argument. There is not, be it observed, a corresponding relation between "want" and "can". A man may want to do things he knows he cannot do. But if his want is not to remain merely an "idle wish", he will have to form an intention to acquire the ability. He may, for example, be resolved to learn to do it. This again presupposes, logically, that in his subjective estimate, he *can learn* to do the thing in question.[8]

Abilities are either "innate" or else determined by biological and physical

---

[8] On the relation between want, intention, and ability cf. above pp. 6ff and pp. 20ff.

factors, or they are acquired. Intelligence and memory, health and bodily strength are gifts of nature—and nature endows people unequally and also makes the abilities which depend upon these endowments vary within the lifespan of the same individual. But within rather broad limits people are *roughly* equally endowed in these regards, and the differences which exist between them can to some extent be equalled out as a result of care or training.

Acquisition of abilities happens through learning, instruction, and education. These are largely socially institutionalized processes. But new abilities are also acquired thanks to individual inquiry into the possibilities of doing things and thanks to creative efforts. Of abilities, thus acquired, those which have the character of *technological innovations* occupy an important and peculiar place, chiefly because of their consequences on the social level.

The fact that learning and education are parts of the social fabric can be responsible for great inequalities in the possibilities which men have of acquiring abilities. A man may not be able to afford or his social position may not allow him to avail himself of facilities for education which some other men enjoy. The range of things he is able to do may on this account remain very restricted. Then it is also likely that within this range his duties, "the pressing necessities of life", much more than his wants, will determine his intentional actions.

There are thus a great many abilities which a man "by nature" could acquire but which for deontic reasons, i.e., reasons built into the normative structure of the community of which he is a member, he cannot acquire.

Many abilities, moreover, require for their exercise *equipment* in the form of instruments or machinery. This is true of all abilities which are conditioned by technological innovations, but particularly of the ability to use technology for the production of commodities. This fact is the greatest source of inequalities in the freedom of men and also the greatest urge to make men equal by changing the institutionalized restrictions on what each one of them *can do*.

The prospects of social philosophizing which open up here are easily recognized—but their further exploration must remain outside the scope of this paper.

XI

What a man can do in a given situation is, however, only partly conditioned by his abilities. An equally important condition is formed by the *opportunities*. A child may have learnt how to open a window, but if the windows in his surroundings are already open, it *cannot*, in that situation, open a window. The ability is a generic feature of an agent; the opportunity, again, an individual feature of a concrete situation.

Every action by any man creates and destroys opportunities for actions—by the agent himself and by other agents. By shutting a door I create an opportunity for opening it; by leaving the room I may destroy the opportunity for another man to request my help in an important job.

The opportunities are thus in a constant flux as compared with the *relative* stability of abilities and wants and duties—not to speak of their background in the institutions of society. Intentions fall in a middle zone here. As the situations change, creating new opportunities for action, intentions articulate under the already existing wants and duties and within the frame of given abilities. This interplay between situational change, intentionality, ability, and a motivational and normative background I shall call the *logic of events*. It constitutes the cogwheels of the "machinery" which keeps history moving.

Sometimes the changed situation which makes new actions possible, or imperative, results from the working of natural forces alone. This is the case when, for example, an earthquake or a flood upsets human conditions. The intentions for acting formed under the impact of such changes are often the outlet for wants (and shunnings) shared by practically all men at all times and which might also be called a "will to survival". People seek refuge or migrate to new abodes—or they join hands to take various countermeasures such as building walls against floods or protecting the environment against industrial pollution. Such measures may in their turn require (in the sense of the second premiss of a practical argument) changes on the institutional level of society.

A very different type of logic of events is exemplified by changes in situations which primarily result from people acting in roles, for example when the actions are those of a government, or a corporation, or the army, etc. A country conquers a province from another to safeguard its borders. "Unless we do this, they might invade us" is now the reason-giving premiss of a practical syllogism. In the new situation, created by the conquest, the neighbouring country, i.e., its government, thinks it necessary to safeguard its independence by entering into an alliance with a third power. The two now jointly constitute a threat to the first and further actions become imperative for its rulers. And so forth. Each new action by one party "triggers off" the conclusion of a "latent" practical argument by another party—the "latency" of the argument consisting in the fact that the goal-structures, both the duties of the role-holders and the wants ("hopes and fears") of those who vest their expectations in the role-holders, are fixed, and the requirements of the situation appear univocal in the light of past experience or of traditional standards of assessing them.

Such chains of successively created sufficient reasons necessitating action are particularly impressive when events are heading for disaster or towards decay. The origins of imperalistic wars, the fall of empires, the decay of an economy often follows this pattern and thereby assumes an air of "historical inevitability".

Again a somewhat different type of "logic" is presented by the great creative innovations, particularly in the realm of technology, which open new possibilities of action and thereby become an outlet for latent wants rather than for pre-existing institutionally determined duties. The chain-reactions "let loose" by such changes often create a tension between the duties of role-holders and external objects of intention set by the rules on the one hand, and the direction given to the action-opportunities by the flux of situational change on the other hand. Internalization of the institutional forms becomes more difficult and more dubious, normative pressure increases and the "internal contradictions" of the community crystallize into grounds for changes in institutions.

XII

The description which I have tried to give of the motivational mechanisms and the working of chains of necessitation of action should help us answer the question whether there are "laws" in history.

In fairness to the question it should be said that if there existed law-like connections between concrete historical events, we should rather think of them as instantiations of general laws of sociology, and perhaps of economics, than as "laws of history" proper.

A number of so-called laws of economics easily come to the layman's mind: Say's or Gresham's laws, the law of supply and demand or of diminishing marginal utility, etc. In sociology there is much less unanimity about what deserves the name of a law—but candidates are not lacking, for example the several Marxian principles concerning the dependence of social structure upon productive forces and relations.

My suggestion now is that such laws are applications to specified types of activity and types of historical situation of the very general conceptual patterns which I have outlined in my paper. Even the most elementary laws of economics presuppose some institutionalized forms of exchanging commodities on a market and of rough standards of measuring the value of goods to a producer and a consumer. It is usually not too difficult to see under which assumptions concerning the institutional frame these laws are conceptual necessities about the way in which wants and abilities regulate behaviour. Within different frames different laws are valid. This means that different frames require different laws, if the logic of events is to be correctly described. The complexities of theoretical economic analysis largely consist in devising conceptual instruments appropriate to the description of economic behaviour within the institutional structure of a historically given situation. Thus, for example, in the strongly "manipulated" market of late capitalist societies the laws of "classical" market economy cannot be expected to hold good. For this reason it is sometimes said that the laws of economics and sociology are themselves subject to historical change—unlike the laws of nature which are valid *semper et ubique.*

Social "laws" are not generalizations from experience but conceptual schemata for the interpretation of concrete historical situations. Their discovery, or rather, invention, is a matter of the analysis of concepts and their application a matter of analysis of situations. On this account one can say that social study occupies an intermediate position between philosophy and history. It can move in the direction of the one or the other of the two poles, but it cannot live a self-contained life divorced from either of them.

History, when it is "scientific" and not mere chronicle or narration, is an inquiry into the logic of events in a fragment of the past with named actors and institutions. It is a study of history from a deterministic point of view in as much as it studies the interplay between historical change and the determinants of human action. As we have seen, these determinants have to a great, not to say overwhelming, extent their roots in the structure of the social fabric: in the distribution of roles and the institutionalization of behaviour-patterns. With changes in these societal determinants of actions, actions too will be different. But changes in the determinants are in their turn the results of action—except for the cases when they are man-independent changes in nature. Thus the actions of men are determined by their historical situation, but the historical situation is itself the result of the actions of men. There is no circularity of a logically vicious kind in this fact that mankind is both slave and master of its own destiny.

The determinants of natural change are causal laws—and them man cannot change. But he can use his knowledge of the laws to steer natural change by producing and suppressing opportunities for causes to work. Man's foresight, however, is limited and what further causal consequences his manipulations of nature will call forth may be humanly impossible to foresee. We are reminded of this by the eroded landscapes in lands of ancient cultures—but also by the ecological problems facing modern industrial society. That man has made himself master of nature to the extent he has is one of his greatest achievements as a species. To exercise the restraint and skill needed in order not to be dethroned is the most serious challenge facing him today. It is unlikely that it can be successfully met without profound changes also in that law-regulated realm in which man's mastery can never be challenged and where he is for ever sovereign, *viz.* his societies.

Explanation and Understanding of Action

I

To explain an individual human action is, one could say, to give a truthful answer to the question *why* the action was undertaken. "Why?" means "from what motive?" or "for what reason?". *Can* it also mean "from what cause?"? In a trivial sense, certainly. Motives and reasons are often called "causes" of actions. But in a non-trivial sense the question is problematic. The problem will be discussed later. Let it, however, be clear from the beginning that by "cause" I here mean what is also called a *nomic cause*. A nomic causal relation between two terms, C and E, should satisfy *at least* the following two conditions:

  i. C and E are *logically* independent of one another.
  ii. C and E are connected by a *universal law*. Whenever C occurs (in the frame or setting of some circumstances F), E follows.

II

It is worth saying a few words about the *motives* for action explanations. Why do we ask, why this or that was done?

The reason is seldom a "scientific" interest in action. Action explanation is not a species of "scientific explanation". Its motive is usually a wish to *evaluate* the action or the agent. Does what he did deserve praise or blame? We may not know until we have investigated the agent's motives. How does the action reflect on his character? What can we expect of this agent in the future? Is what he did perhaps something we should do ourselves once we know the reasons *he* had for doing it? Such questions reflect typical interests behind our ques' for action explanations.

There is, however, one "science"—if it can be called by that name—in which explanations of individual actions play a role. This is the study of history. Why did Caesar cross the Rubicon? Why did Queen Christina of Sweden abdicate her throne? These may be interesting questions. But as a species of historical explanation action explanation is not, I should say, of great prominence.

III

Reasons for actions have been extensively discussed in recent philosophic literature. But to the best of my knowledge, no systematic inquiry has been made into what might be called "the varieties of reasons". What *sorts of thing* count as reasons for actions?

Many actions are done *for the sake of an end*. The end is something the agent intends or wants to reach (produce, secure, enjoy). The action is thought to be either needed for or conducive to or in some other way "promotive" of the end. Such a volitive-cognitive combination of a "will" to an end and the thought of some means to its realization constitutes a *type of reason* for action.

For example: I hear voices in the corridor outside my room. I want to know what is going on. This constitutes a reason for me to open the door and look out. I believe that this will help satisfy my curiosity.

Reasons of this type I shall call *inner* or *internal*. They are *necessarily* reasons for action. By this I mean the following: No-one who is familiar with action discourse could, without committing an inconsistency, deny that aiming at something and thinking a certain action promotive of this aim is *a* reason for doing it. There may exist reasons *against* doing it—or one may know better means to the end.

Other actions—perhaps the majority—are done *in response to a* (symbolic) *challenge*. Two sub-types of challenge may be distinguished. One consists of challenges presented in what may be called *communicative action* patterns. Examples are orders, requests, questions. Traffic lights and (many) other signals also belong here. The other type consists of (prescriptive) rules or norms, and of norm-like things such as customs, fashions, or traditions within a community.

Example: Why did you stop your car? Because the traffic light turned red. Why do you stop in front of the red light? Because there is a rule prohibiting one to drive against this signal. Such answers give reasons for action.

Challenges I shall call *outer* or *external* reasons for action. Unlike internal reasons, challenges are *contingently*, and not necessarily, reasons. This means the following: Even though an agent recognizes the challenge and has learnt or otherwise knows how to respond to it, he need not *acknowledge* it as a reason *for him* to act upon. External reasons can thus be said to "exist" in two different senses. As *instituted* and presented to members of a community they exist, so to speak, "objectively". As *acknowledged* by individual agents as reasons for their acting they exist "subjectively". Their subjective existence cannot be inferred, in the individual case, from their objective existence.

IV

Agents are taught to participate in communicative action and to obey rules. When they are thus brought to acknowledge outer reasons as reasons for their (own) actions, the reasons will be said to be *internalized* with the agents in question. In order to understand how internalization comes about we must note the following connections between outer and inner reasons:

Outer reasons are often, though certainly not always, instituted to serve some ends. If the agents to whom the challenges are addressed share those ends, the agents have inner reasons for responding to the challenges. Example: Traffic rules are there to secure safety on the roads. Whoever wants to contribute to this end, has an internal reason for obeying the rules.

Such internal reasons may not exist or may not be effective for all agents, however. Therefore external reasons of a secondary type will have to be instituted which threaten the agents with some evil (coercive measures, punishment, reprobation, sanction) in case of non-conformity. Challenges and rules are thus being surrounded by what I have elsewhere[1] called an "aura of normative pressure". Agents who intend or want to avoid these evils have a secondary type of internal reason for conformity.

Internalization has taken place when the agent acknowledges an external reason as a reason for him to act on, independently of the "pull" of social ends or the "push" of normative pressure. Internalization admits of degrees and may be more or less well accomplished. In the individual case it may, for example, be difficult or even impossible to tell whether the agent obeyed an order *because* he had been ordered, or *because* he feared punishment for disobedience. His motives might have been "mixed". But it would be a distortion to think that his action *must* have had internal reasons and *could not* have taken place on purely external grounds.

V

Often reasons which explain actions are overtly neither of the kind I have called inner nor of the kind I have called outer. Such reasons I shall call "oblique".

Examples: Why did you take an overcoat when you went out walking? Because the sky looked threatening. Why did you bring your wife flowers? Because it is her birthday. These are explanations in terms of reasons. Normally we should understand them and regard them as exhaustive. But in order to understand why this is so we must establish a relationship between those reasons and reasons of an overtly internal or external nature.

The sky looked threatening and there might have been a rainstorm and I should have become wet. Getting wet is unpleasant, something I *shun*, i.e. want to avoid. My raincoat will protect me. So, I have an internal reason for taking it with me.

---

[1] See above, p. 39.

It is my wife's birthday—I want to do something which will please her. Bringing her flowers will make her happy. This constitutes an internal reason for my action. But also: It is customary to honour people on their birthdays. I am anxious to behave politely; I acknowledge the external reason constituted by the custom. Was it the inner or the outer reason that moved me to action? Perhaps my motivation was a "mixture" of both.

Compare: "I screamed because it hurt so badly" and "I shouted because I got angry with him". In the first case we should perhaps say that I could not help doing what I did. My screaming was more like a reflex than an action; the pain a cause rather than a reason. The second case *could* be like the first. He had been teasing me for a long time and at last I "exploded", could no longer control myself. Was this an action? But perhaps I thought "This cannot go on, I must stop him", and therefore I shouted at him angrily. Then what I did was clearly an action of mine and I had reasons for it.

VI

So far we have only spoken of reasons *for* an action. Reasons, however, may also be *against* an action. A reason against doing something can be defined as a reason for omitting the thing; reciprocally, a reason for doing is a reason against omitting.

Even though the two types of reason (*for* and *against*) are thus inter-definable, what we ordinarily think of as reasons against are considerations pertaining to some action which the agent *also* has or may have some reason for doing. Reasons against are typically "second thoughts". They are thoughts of something we either *shun* or *ought not* to do and which are consequences of or prerequisites for a contemplated action (*for* the doing of which something speaks).

Things we shun constitute *inner*, things we ought not to do *outer* reasons against doing something.

VII

When an agent had several reasons for an action of his, and no reason against it, his action will be said to have been *overdetermined*. When this is the case, one cannot tell for which reason the action was undertaken. A truthful answer to the question Why? will have to mention *all* the reasons actually present.

Of more interest is the case when there are reasons for but also against the action. In many, but not in all, such cases there is *deliberation* terminating in a *decision* to act.

Examples: I am about to go for a walk; shall I take an overcoat? It is heavy to carry—this is a reason against taking it. But it may be raining—this is a reason for taking it. I take it. Why? Because I would rather suffer the discomfort of carrying the coat than risk the discomfort of becoming wet. I *prefer* the first to the second.

Shall I visit my old mother this afternoon? She is expecting me; I have a duty towards her and I acknowledge this. Or shall I take part in the excursion which has been announced? The weather is fine and the company will please me. Here an outer reason for a certain thing is balanced against an inner reason for doing something else. This is the classic case of conflict between "duty" and "inclination".

Assume that duty conquers inclination. This may but need not mean that I want, or like better, to do my duty, i.e. that some inner reason "behind" the outer one carries the victory over another inner reason. But it would be correct to say, in any case, that I *prefer* to do my duty rather than follow my inclination.

Is a preference a reason (for action)? To call a preference a reason seems to me highly misleading. In the normal cases, a preference goes together with the existence of several reasons: some for, some against a certain action or some for one, others for an alternative action. These reasons are being "weighed", taken into consideration, and a "balance" formed. The preference *is* the resulting balance—*not* an additional reason to be thrown into the scale, so to speak. Therefore one should not call a preference for a certain course of action over another a reason for choosing the first.

How is such a balance formed? One can think of this as a decision-theoretic problem: we assign probabilities and values to the outcomes of alternative courses of action and calculate the "expected utilities". *Sometimes* something approximating to this takes place in real life. But the peculiar talent required for making choices which also in retrospect will seem to us the best or right ones is a "practical wisdom" without which decision-theoretic calculations, when at all possible, will be of no or little avail.

VIII

I began by saying that to explain an action is to answer truthfully the question why the action was performed (p. 53). When the motivation for an action is, in the sense explained above, *complex*, we cannot in a straightforward manner answer the question *why* the agent did it or say that he did it *because* he had such and such reasons for and such and such reasons against doing it. Another agent may have articulated a different preference on the basis of the very same set of reasons—and accordingly acted differently.

These limitations on action explanation are, I think, significant. It is a prejudice to insist upon answers to the question *why* or upon accounts in terms of *because* in the case of all *actions for reasons*. Many actions have a complex motivation which makes such accounts impossible. Still we *understand* the actions in the setting of their motivation. They are not "incomprehensible" or "unintelligible"—and *in that sense* not "inexplicable" either.

There is, however, another and entirely different case when the question why an action was done has no answer. This is the case of fortuitous or gratuitous action. I did something, but I did it *for no particular reason*. Yet, it was an action of mine—I am not willing to say in retrospect that I "could not help" having done it. I may even say that I then intended or wanted to do just this—though for no particular reason.

Cases of this sort occur. But they are relatively rare and we sometimes find them puzzling. If they occur repeatedly with an agent, we may look for "subconscious reasons" or try to find "medical causes" for his behaviour.

If we could not, *on the whole*, account in terms of reasons for what people do, it would be difficult for us to understand them *qua* agents. If this were the case with ourselves, we should cease to feel responsible for our actions, since we could not then on the whole account for them. We should perhaps think that we are at the mercy of uncontrollable outer or inner forces—maybe of a causal nature.

Free action and action for reasons are twin concepts. "Determination" of action through reasons is, one could say, a precondition of human freedom. Without this type of determination our very notions of agent and action would not exist, or be quite different from those we have.

IX

In spite of the above "limitations on action explanation" I therefore think it is right to say that there is an answer to *most* questions why, i.e. for which reasons, this or that action was undertaken. A good many of the actions we perform we *learn* to do by being trained to respond adequately to various challenges or conform to rules. When asked why we did this or that we often *justify* our action by relating it, as an adequate response, to a challenge or a rule. A justification of action has the form of an explanation (in terms of reasons) of the action. But it need not be a correct explanation. There is an important discrepancy to be noted between justification and explanation:

The reasons given in justification of an action can be there, exist as a matter of objective fact, and yet not be the reasons why the action was undertaken. For example: I pay a visit of condolence to Mrs *A* who lost her husband. Why? It is customary to do such a thing when one is a close acquaintance of the family. The custom justifies my action. But it need not be the reason why I paid the visit. Perhaps the reason was that I had *selfish* designs on the rich and beautiful widow.

If I acknowledge the custom as a reason for my visit but also had such designs, my justification of the visit was a *partial* explanation. A *full* explanation would then show that my action was overdetermined.

If, however, I had the selfish motive but do *not* acknowledge the custom as a reason, then the action had an acceptable justification which was *not* even partially a valid explanation. That I do not "acknowledge" the custom as a reason means the following: I have been taught that one is expected to observe this custom and recognize that many people do this but I should myself never conform to it unless I had *some independent reason* for doing so. If I conform and say that I do this because it is the custom, I am hiding the true motive of my action. I hide it from others—but maybe I even hide it from myself.

When *is* a justification an explanation? The answer obviously is: When the reason *R* given in justification of the action not only was there but moved the agent to action.[2] When it is true to say of the agent that he did it *because of R*.

But when *is* this true? To this question some philosophers would wish to answer that the statement is true when (the existence or occurrence of) *R* is, or is somehow "correlated" with, a *nomic* cause of the action. Those who give this answer are sometimes said to adhere (in one form or another) to a *causalist* theory of action. I shall try to show why I think this theory will not help us solve the problem.

X

It is useful to distinguish two aspects under which the relation between an action and its grounds may be viewed. I shall call them the aspect *ex ante actu* and the aspect *ex post actu*. The two aspects answer, roughly, to the distinction between *prediction* and *explanation* of action.

Prediction is *ex ante*: Given causes or reasons, we predict what will take place. For example: *A* intends to go to the theatre next Saturday. He knows that, unless he books in advance he will not get a seat. Therefore, we predict, he will take steps to book in advance. Or: *A* has been asked to report to the police within 48 hours. We predict that he will do so.

Explanation is *ex post*. The action is a *fait accompli*. We look back for causes or reasons. *A* turns up at the booking office. Why? Maybe he

---

[2] The terms "reason" and "motive" (for actions) are commonly used as rough synonyms. One could, however, try to separate their uses, and such separation might serve a philosophic purpose. One way of separating them would be as follows: *Reasons* are given in *justification* of an action—*motives explain* it. The motives, in other words, are those reasons which actually "move" the agent to actions. Other reasons which are objectively present but are not subjectively acknowledged are not motives. I am indebted to Professor Chaïm Perelman for conceptual observations in this area.

intends to attend Saturday's performance and thinks it necessary to book tickets in advance.

In writings on the philosophy of science it often used to be said that the predictive and the explanatory relations are *converses* of each other. What is prospectively a prediction is, if true, retrospectively an explanation, and *vice versa*. This view is an oversimplification even in the natural sciences. But it holds true, *by and large*, for prediction and explanation which subsume an individual case under a general law. Therefore it is true, on the whole, in the natural sciences. In my opinion, the situation in the human sciences is quite different. Many of the difficulties and obscurities in action theory arise from failure to appreciate the conceptual difference between the predictive and the explanatory point of view.

XI

If the *explanans* of an action is a (nomic) *cause*, then from knowledge of the presence of the cause one can predict the action "with certainty".

Predictability, however, does not presuppose causal laws. Reasons which are not causes may also provide good grounds for predictions. What is then predicted is, strictly speaking, not the *action*. In the case of internal reasons, the prediction is that the agent will not "change his mind" before proceeding to act, i.e. will not give up his intentions or alter his opinion of how to make them effective. If the reasons are external again, the prediction is that the agent will *acknowledge* such and such reasons, the presence of which is an objective fact, as reasons for him to act upon. Such a prediction does not rely on a *law* connecting the reasons with the action; but it may rely heavily on our *knowledge of the* (particular) *agent*.

The reliability of predictions of this kind may vary from agent to agent, and with the same agent in the course of his life history. When the motivational situation is simple, for example because all the known reasons point in the same direction, reliability may be very high. When again the motivational web consists of a great many reasons for and also against the action, prediction may be next to impossible. Another factor which affects the reliability of predictions is whether the motivational situation is "typical", i.e. in relevant features like a situation in which the agent has repeatedly been before, or whether it is a rare or even unique case, or a case in which it is difficult to tell whether the *known* reasons (for and against) the action are *all* the reasons which there in fact are.

The predictive relation which we are considering thus holds between a compound of *reasons* and (other) *facts* about the agent and the circumstances of the case on the one hand and the agent's proceeding to *action* on the other. I shall call these three factors R, F and A respectively. Our problem is: *Can* this relation acquire *nomic force*, i.e. can there exist a causal law connecting *R* and *A* as cause and effect in the frame or setting of the circumstances *F*?

For example: Someone at the dinner table asks me to pass him the salt.[3] The request is an outer reason for me to do something. Can this outer reason in combination with facts about me (my abilities, character, education, position at the table) nomically "force" me to proceed to a certain action?

One can discuss this question under two aspects. I shall refer to them as the "macroscopic" and the "microscopic" aspect respectively. The first concerns the existence of something which might, in some broad sense, be called a *psychological law* connecting *R* and *A* within the frame *F*. The second concerns the existence of a *physiological law* connecting events or states in my neural system, somehow "corresponding" to *R*, with bodily movements of mine, somehow "corresponding" to *A*? We shall consider in turn these two aspects of the problem.

XII

Let us assume that the description and identification of *R* causes no problem. We may think of some very simple case when there is only one reason present. How can we then specify the frame of accompanying circumstances *F* so as to make the purported psychological law testable? How can one make sure, for example, that the agent does not suffer from some "inhibition" which will prevent him from proceeding to the action *A* although this would be the adequate response in the presence of *R*? Can one be confident that no such "counteracting" factors are hidden in *F* except by making the action *A* itself a criterion of this? In other words: how can we ensure the *logical independence* of "cause" and "effect" here? It will suffice to pose the question—leaving open the answer.

Assume next that the specification of *F* is no problem, but that *R* is a compound of reasons for and against *A*. The agent has to form a "balance" of reasons before acting. Must not this balance, once formed, be a commitment either to do or to omit *A* such that if the agent, in the first case, does not proceed to action or, in the second case, proceeds to action, we must deny that he was committed? The difficulty, in other words, is again that of securing the logical independence of cause and effect.

Assume, finally, that the specification of neither *R* nor *F* is problematic. An example could be the appearance of a traffic light under entirely normal circumstances of driving or walking. The adequate response seems to follow without exception. If wanted, we can test the regularity experimentally. Could we not then say that the reason *R* under the circumstances *F* causally necessitates the action *A*? So that, viewing things

---

[3] Cf. above, p. 38.

prospectively, the agent cannot help initiating action or, viewing them in retrospect, he could not have acted otherwise? Is this possible?

I think we ought to be generous and admit that such cases are "just possible". But they are almost certainly *marginal*.

Suppose somebody suggested that they are marginal only in relation to our limited knowledge. In fact *all* cases are like this. If only we could specify *R* and *F* with ideal completeness it would necessarily be the case that those two components taken together causally necessitate (the initiation) of *A*.

The one who suggests this, however, has shifted the point of view from *ex ante* to *ex post actu*. Not the law itself but the *existence* of a law is now a tautologous after-construction. Whenever an agent proceeds to action we think that this could not have happened had it not been for some reasons which, under the circumstances, causally necessitate the action. But we do not claim to be able fully to specify which these reasons and these circumstances are and therefore do not claim to be able to test the causal law either. Those who are intellectually wedded to "a causalist point of view" may draw a certain amount of comfort from this "existentialist" construction. Those who are not thus prejudiced will think it idle.

XIII

A consistent statement of the "microscopic" point of view must, I think, be given in terms of external and internal stimulation of the neural system resulting with nomic necessity in certain bodily movements. The description of the stimuli and the movements should moreover, be "drained" of intentionality, i.e. the stimuli should not be described in the language of reasons, nor the movements in the language of actions. But there ought to exist a "correspondence" between the two levels of discourse, the "actionist" and the "physicalist" one. Some would prefer to speak of "alternative descriptions" of the same thing. The criteria of correspondence and of sameness constitute difficulties for this approach. We can, however, bypass these problems here.

We need not doubt that there exist nomic connections between stimulations of the neural system and bodily movements. Nor need we deny that such connections "work" when action for reasons takes place. That a causal law "works" or is "operative" shall mean that the cause is present within the frame of circumstances under which the law holds true. In what way would these causal connections now *explain* how the action is connected with the reasons?

If there are reasons for and against the action, a balance of reasons will have to be formed before the agent proceeds to action. If there are only reasons *for* the action, but the reasons are external, the agent will have to *acknowledge* the reasons (or some of them) as reasons for *him* to act upon. In neither case will the mere *existence* of the reasons move the agent. He will, in forming a balance, have to "take a stand" on them or, if they are external, "make (some of) them" his reasons in proceeding to action. Only when this has happened can we refer back to the reasons in an explanation of the action. But how does *this* happen? In what does the "making" the reasons reasons (for him) consist?

I submit for consideration that it is an urge to answer these questions that is the motive force behind the "microscopic" version of a causalist theory of action. To the reasons becoming operative there corresponds a "click" in the brain, the neural system, which is released by some stimuli corresponding to the reasons and which results in some movements corresponding to the action. Does such a "click" occur in the brain whenever an agent proceeds to action? We surely do *not know* whether it does—but perhaps we can imagine the possibility. I say "perhaps" because it is not entirely clear what we are supposed to "imagine". Granted that we can do this and that the possibility is an actuality, *must* it be this? That is: must it be the case that when an agent proceeds to action for such and such reasons there is a "correlated" physiological law simultaneously operating? Here the difficulty is with the "must". *In what sense* could this be a requirement? Merely postulating the correspondence seems an idle move—just as postulating a psychological law connecting the reasons with the action seems idle (cf. above p. 62). The answer must be that we could not otherwise *understand* how the reasons connect with the action.

Assume, for the sake of argument, that there is this parallelism between acting for reasons and the operating of physiological laws. Does this mean that an agent could not have acted for *those* reasons had it not been for the operating of *that* law? Or shall we say, on the contrary, that the law would not have operated had the agent not acted for those reasons? There is, I think, a presumption—deeply ingrained in and strongly nourished by the "scientism" of our culture—to say the first. But who can tell that this is not sheer prejudice and superstition?

My conclusion then is that the question of the "click in the brain" is *irrelevant* to action explanation. The truth of the statement that an agent did something for certain reasons is *independent* of the truth or falsity of the statement that to the existence of those reasons there "corresponds" events and states in the agent's body nomically connected with some bodily movements "corresponding" to the performance (or initiation) of the agent's action.

XIV

An agent did something, A, and maintains that he did this for the reason(s) R. If he is not lying, i.e. saying what he does not believe to be true, then in explaining or justifying his action he evinces his *self-understanding*. The reasons he gives constitute a "perspective" in which he sees his action.

Assume, however, that we doubt the agent's own account of the case. That is: we do not doubt that he did the action, nor that the reasons were "objectively" there. But we doubt whether he acted for *those* reasons.

How would one try to settle such doubts? Certainly *not* normally by examining his neural system. (In exceptional cases of a pathological nature a neurological examination may be relevant.) What one would do is to examine the agent's motivation in a *wider setting* either of his life history or of the present circumstances or both. We should press him with further questions, call in "witnesses", study records of his past.

Consider again the visit of condolence (above p. 58f). In the light of what we know about the visitor's character and conduct in the past, and also maybe in the light of things which took place *after* the visit, we may be convinced that he acted from selfish motives and not out of respect for the custom. The "coherence" of the picture we form ourselves of him "requires" this interpretation of his action.

When the agent is confronted with the way we understand him he may *confess* that he had been lying to us. But he may also be led to scrutinize himself and come to see that he had, in fact, been lying to himself, too. By way of his self-scrutiny and, maybe, under the influence of our opinion of him and of further facts about him to which we drew his attention he is *converted* to a new understanding of himself. Perhaps he says: "had I been sincere I should have admitted that I did this for selfish reasons—observance of the custom was only a pretext".

But what if he stubbornly refuses to see his action in the light we are convinced is the right one? Perhaps we say: "his lips refuse to confess—but in his heart he admits the truth". With what right can *we* say this? Hardly with any right at all, unless we foresee the possibility of a conversion. But what sort of "possibility" is this? Is it the possibility that the agent becomes "brain-washed" and a new self-understanding thus forced on him—or is it the possibility that he comes to see the Truth (which was always there to be seen)?

One must be cautious with the answer to these questions. One cannot separate the *truth* about the connection between the action and the reasons from the *understanding* of this connection. Therefore there is no unique way of deciding between the truth-claim of an agent's self-understanding and that of an observer's understanding from without.

There was a time when I believed that in the case of conflicting claims the agent's self-understanding must "in the last instance" be accorded priority.[4] The qualification "in the last instance" indicated that an agent's self-understanding may be defective and a "conversion" is needed to make him see the truth about himself. To think otherwise would, it seemed

---

[4] Cf. *The Varieties of Goodness*, Routledge & Kegan Paul, London, 1963, p. 190. See also above, p. 45.

to me then, be to assume an unjustifiable authority on the part of one man in matters relating to the "inner" life of another. The subject must be supreme judge in his own case, I used to say. But I am afraid that this position has to be abandoned. Self-understanding cannot be accorded ultimate authority. Understanding "from outside" *may* overrule its verdict.

XV

Behaviour sometimes is seemingly "causeless", "incomprehensible", "irrational"; we may even doubt whether it should be classified as "action" at all. But in a wider context it may assume a different appearance.

A person kicks another person in a crowd. He knows the person whom he kicked. He apologizes and says it was a "mistake". Perhaps it was. Next time they meet the first says something which hurts the feelings of the second. Unintentionally, he maintains. But we may begin to wonder. We learn that the second person once did something which made the first feel deeply wounded. A similar incident occurs for a third time. If the agent insists that it was all unintentional and by mistake, we may say: " 'Mistakes' simply are not all that often repeated. You kicked him because you wanted to pay him back, to revenge the wrong you thought he had inflicted on you". Even if the person were never to admit this, we may be convinced that we had understood his behaviour better than he does himself. Further consequences may confirm our belief. If we say that *we* have seen the Truth in the matter, this easily suggests a misleading picture of the case. But we may say that we have seen the truth *to the extent that there is a truth to be seen*.

XVI

It may be illuminating to draw attention to some distinguishing features between typical cases of action explanation, causal explanation, and deductive explanation.

In giving a deductive explanation we show that a proposition follows logically from a set of grounds or premisses in which its content is "implicit". In order to "extract" the conclusion from the premisses we ought to "analyse" or "explicate" their content.

In a causal explanation we *isolate* a fragment of nature from a wider context of "accompanying circumstances", and link a piece within this fragment or frame as "effect" with another piece as "cause". The ideal test of correctness of a causal explanation is *experimental*. *We* reproduce the cause within the given frame and watch whether "nature" will reproduce the effect. This requires that the frame too is reproducible and that what happens inside it is not affected by outside differences in the situations under which the reproduction takes place. A failure of the experiment is sometimes interpreted as a refutation of the causal law, sometimes as a "disturbance" caused by outside factors. If we can control the presence and absence of these factors we can reformulate the frame-conditions under which the law holds and continue to use it for causal explanations. If, however, we simply reject the law we must look round for a new explicative principle.

The characteristic pattern of an action explanation in terms of motives and reasons is different. Here we are never interested in *isolating* the context but sometimes in *widening* it so as to make the action to be explained match maximally well with the rest of the agent's life history. Usually we can stay content with a narrow context. All that is needed for our understanding of the case may be that the agent deemed his action necessary for something he coveted or thought adequate for meeting some requirement. It is on the whole only when the objects of his intentions or wants seem queer or "suspect" or his beliefs distorted or the requirements which his action is supposed to meet abnormal that we are anxious to widen the context so as to get a more coherent picture of the case. Some cases remain inexplicable. Usually they are laid aside as being of no consequence. Sometimes, however, they continue to puzzle us—for example if they are enigmatic but consequential actions of historically important personalities. Historians will perhaps again and again dig into the background, revising our previous understanding of the case and our assessment of its significance. The criteria for when we have succeeded in explaining or understanding an action may also change and vary. What satisfies our craving for an answer to the question *Why*? is not uniquely determined by the brute facts of the case, but depends also on the requirements which we put on an acceptable explanation.

The Foundation of Norms and Normative Statements

I

By a *normative statement* I understand a statement to the effect that something ought to or may or must not be done. Such a statement is often, but not necessarily, elliptic or incomplete unless it says, by whom this thing ought to (may, must not) be done, and whether it ought to (may, must not) be done generally or on some particular occasion, unconditionally or provided certain conditions are fulfilled.

I use the term "statement" here in that which I propose to call its "strict" sense. A statement in the strict sense is true or false.

By the *foundation* of a given normative statement I shall understand the content of a truthful answer to the question, *why* the thing under consideration ought to or may or must not be done. The foundation, in this sense, of a normative statement can also be called its *truth-ground*.

To answer the question of the foundation or truth-ground of a normative statement is to tell, what *would make* the statement true. The foundation of the statement is thus some "possible fact". If this possible fact is actual, the statement is true.

Very often, when a normative statement is made, a foundation for it is also supplied. "You ought to (may, must not) do this, because . . .", we then say. If a foundation is not supplied, it is often asked for. "Why ought I to (may I, must I not) do this?", we then ask.

People are far from always clear over the foundations of the normative statements, which they hear. And not infrequently are people unclear also about the foundation of normative statements, which they make themselves. This is true above all with regard to statements concerning so-called moral matters.

The philosophic *problem of the foundation* of normative statements is, in the first place, the question of the general form and nature of the truth-grounds of such statements. It will be seen that there are different forms or kinds or types of foundation for normative statements. Moreover, one and the same normative statement may have more than one foundation of the same or of different types. (Plurality of foundations.) The question will also become urgent, whether a normative statement could be true and yet lack a foundation, i.e. whether it could be true to say that something ought to or may or must not be done and yet not possible to tell *why* (on what grounds, for which reasons) this is so.

II

One important type of answer to the question "Why ought (may, must not) this or that to be done?" is the following: *There is a norm* to the effect that this thing ought to (may, must not) be done. The existence of the norm is here the foundation or truth-ground of the normative statement.

For example: I am told that I must not park my car this side of the street. Why? The answer could be that there is a by-law or regulation prohibiting this.

The word "norm" in English has many meanings. Here I use the word to mean something, which can also be called a prescription or a regulation or, sometimes, a law. Commands and orders are a species of what I here call norms. But a norm can be a permission; and a permissive norm is not ordinarily called "command" or "order".

Examples of norms, in the sense in which I here use the word, are the laws of the state, or by-laws and regulations issued by a magistrate. But also orders, which parents give to their children, or officers to soldiers in the army, are norms in this sense.

Norms are given by some agent to a certain other agent or agents. I shall call the first agent norm-*authority* and the second norm-*subject*(*s*). Calling the norm-authority "agent" should be compatible with the possibility that this authority is not a physical person, but e.g. a law-court or magistrate or legislative assembly.

The giving of norms requires the use of language. The norm-authority promulgates or makes known by means of signs to the norm-subjects, what he wants them to do or forbear. The signs which are used to announce the norm, I shall call *norm-formulation*. A norm-formulation can be a sentence in the imperative mood. Or it can be a sentence using the auxiliary verbs "ought to", "may" or "must not". We may call such sentences *deontic* sentences. Very often, however, the norm-formulation is an indicative sentence of the ("ordinary") declarative or descriptive type.

It is important not to confuse the norm itself with the norm-formulation, nor the existence of a norm with the uttering or other production of a norm-formulation. I shall not here discuss the logico-semantic nature of the relationship of the norm to its expression in words. I should only like to say, in passing, that I do not think it right to call the norm either the reference or the meaning or the sense of the norm-formulation.

Norms are neither true nor false. The notions of truth and falsehood do not apply to them. Norms fall outside the category of truth. In this respect they differ importantly from normative statements.

A *norm* is not true or false, but *that there exists a norm*, ordering or permitting such and such acts or forbearances, is true or false. The existence of a norm is a contingent, empirical fact. We shall not here inquire closer into the nature of this fact—of which we have already said that it cannot be identified with the existence of a norm-formulation.

III

A normative statement to the effect that a certain thing ought to (may, must not) be done may sometimes become founded on the existence of a norm, which is *expressly* to the effect that this thing ought to (may, must not) be done. This case is rather trivial. It is, however, not the only and perhaps also not the most common case.

Sometimes the truth-ground of a normative statement is *deduced* from (the existence of) one or several norms. For example: Let there be a norm to the effect that it is obligatory to do *p* and another to the effect that whoever does *p* ought also to do *q*. From these two norms we can deduce an obligation to do *q*, i.e. an (actual) truth-ground of the normative statement that *q* ought to be done. This is obviously a valid inference. Yet it is not an inference according to the "laws" of traditional logic. In order to account for the nature and validity of this inference an extension of the province of logic is required. I have elsewhere coined the name *deontic logic* for this new branch of logical theory. Deontic logic thus is important also to the question of the foundation of normative statements.

Norms are usually to the effect that acts of a certain category or kind ought to (may, must not) be done. A normative statement again is often about some individual act. The question may then arise, whether an individual act, about which a normative statement is made, falls or may become *subsumed* under some category of acts regulated by norm. We could call this a question of *interpretation* ("interpreting law").

The final answer to such questions of subsumption and of interpretation, it should be observed, is never set by "theoretical considerations" relating to the nature of individual acts. It is set by the reaction of the norm-authority to the disputed case. If the case is doubtful and the norm-authority has not yet reacted to it, the nearest we can come to an answer to our question may be a *conjecture* about this reaction and therewith also about the normative status (obligatory, permitted, forbidden) of the act. When a person or a corporation takes legal advice about some planned action of theirs, the advice often has the form of such a conjectural normative statement. A prospective agent may be anxious to know, what the ruling of a law-court would be, if a case were brought against him—say for unfair competition or for having injured somebody's privileges. In unclear cases it is for the law-court to decide, whether acts should be counted as obligatory, permitted or forbidden according to existing norms (laws).

What has just been said means that the existence of a norm is partly dependent upon the hypothetical reactions of norm-authorities to the conduct of norm-subjects. These reactions are not always easy to foresee in the individual case. It is probably these two facts in combination, which are responsible for the view—entertained by some legal philosophers— that the (legal) norms themselves were a kind of *prediction* (mainly about the reactions of law-courts). This is, I think, an utterly mistaken view of the nature of norms—legal and other. But the existential statements, on which normative statements are founded, sometimes have to be enunciated in the form of predictions about the future reactions of norm-authorities.

IV

From the problem of the foundation of normative statements one must distinguish the problem of the foundation of the norms themselves. Many things can be meant by the "foundation" of a norm. I shall here mention and briefly discuss *two* of the senses, in which one may speak of the foundation of a norm, when "norm" is understood as we do it here.

A foundation in the first sense is again an answer to the question "Why?". Someone may wish to know, *why* there is (exists) a norm to such and such effect.

This question "Why?" is not a question of truth-grounds. It is a teleological question, a question of ends. It concerns immediately, not the norm itself, but the act or activity of the norm-authority, when giving or issuing this norm or rule. Why, i.e. for what reason or with a view to what end, has the norm-authority ordered or permitted this action to the norm-subjects? Not of every truthful answer to this question would it sound plausible to say that it provides a "foundation" of the norm. But if the answer satisfies certain requirements, it is natural to say that it *justifies* the act of giving the norm and thereby provides a *foundation* of the norm itself.

I shall call the giving of a norm *normative action*. The problem of foundation and of justification may now be put as follows: Which conditions must the answer to the question "Why?" satisfy in order to justify normative action?

That something is done *for the sake of an end* can mean two things. Firstly, it can mean that this act is considered necessary for the attainment of the end. That the act is necessary means that unless it is done, the end will not be attained. In other words: the act *must be* done, if the end is to be attained. Action, which must be done for the sake of an end, I shall call a *practical necessity*.

Secondly, that something is done for the sake of an end can mean that the act is thought to favour or promote the attainment of the end, without being necessary for this. The act is then said to be a *good* or a *useful* thing to do with a view to the end.

What has been said also applies to action of the type, which I have called "normative". A norm-authority may consider it useful or even necessary with a view to some end of his to prescribe certain acts or forbearances to certain norm-subjects.

That something is necessary or useful for the attainment of an end is an "objectively" true or false proposition. Since this is so, an agent may also be mistaken in thinking that something is necessary or useful with a view to some end of his. The end may be, for example, that people should behave in a certain way and the mistake consists in thinking that one could make them behave in this way by commanding them. Gentler means of persuasion may be effective, where normative action is ineffective.

We can make these observations a ground for distinguishing between a "subjective" and an "objective" justification of normative action. The giving of a norm is subjectively justified, we shall say, when the norm-authority gives it, because he believes this to be useful or necessary with a view to some end of his. And it is objectively justified, when the belief which (subjectively) justifies it is true to fact.

When normative action has, in the sense just explained, an objective justification, I shall say that the norm, in which it results, has a *teleological foundation* in the norm-authority's ends.

We have so far viewed the norms in the perspective of the norm-*authority*'s ends. One can, however, also approach the problem of the justification of normative action and the foundation of norms from the point of view of the norm-*subjects'* ends.

As the giving of norms may be necessary or useful for the ends of the norm-authority, in a similar manner the having or receiving of norms may be useful or even necessary for ends of the norm-subjects. There is, needless to say, no "pre-established harmony" between these two sets of ends, from the point of view of which the necessity and usefulness of norms may become judged. What the norm-authorities want the norm-subjects to do or forbear may be badly in conflict with what the norm-subjects want to do themselves. It seems to me to be a useful mode of approaching some of the central problems of political philosophy, to formulate them as questions concerning this harmony of ends in normative relationships. This approach to the problems is not altogether new, but I think it can, within a modern theory of norms, be given a clearer expression than before.

One could give a new sense to the terms "subjective" and "objective" as attributes of a justification of normative action. Normative action might be called *subjectively* justified, when it has a justification ("subjective" *or* "objective" in the old sense of these terms) from the point of view of the ends of the norm-*authority*. Whether normative action, which is subjectively justified, is also *objectively* plausible, might then be made dependent upon considerations relating to the ends of the norm-*subjects*, or upon some other considerations.

V

From the teleological foundation of norms in ends one must distinguish that which I shall call the *normative* foundation of norms. A foundation in this second sense is not the content of an answer to the question, *why* there is such and such a norm. It is provided by an answer to the question whether the authority of the norm has a *competence* or *right* to issue the norm.

The normative, like the teleological, foundation of a norm is in the first place relevant to the *act* of giving the norm—and only *via* this act to the norm itself.

Like any other type of human action, normative action can be subject to norm or rule. There can be a norm to the effect that a certain agent may or may not issue regulations of such and such a kind. Norms regulating normative activity can conveniently be called *competence norms*. The subjects of such norms are themselves authorities of other norms.

That which I call the normative foundation of a norm can now be defined as follows: A norm has a normative foundation if, and only if, there exists a competence norm which permits the act of issuing this norm to the authority, who actually has issued it.

It is *one* of the uses of the terms "valid" and "invalid" in legal and other normative contexts to say of a norm, the giving of which is permitted by norm, that it is *valid* and of a norm, the giving of which is prohibited by norm, that it is *invalid*. In particular this use of "invalid" is common. That a norm is invalid very often means that the authority, who issued it, transgressed its competence as determined by the law.

There is also another use to be noted of "valid" and "invalid" as attributes of norms. Then the terms mean the same as "in force" and "not in force" respectively. To say that a norm is in force is another way of saying that it exists. To say that it is not in force is usually to say that it no longer exists—e.g., to say of a law that it has passed out of existence because of *desuetudo*.

As far as I can see, a great deal of confusion in legal philosophy has been due to failure to keep distinct these two, completely different, notions of the validity of norms.[1] Every norm, which has come into being within a given legal or other normative order, either is valid in the sense that it is in force or invalid in the sense that it has become repealed or otherwise passed out of existence. But it is not the case that every norm within a given legal or other normative order is either valid in the sense that it was issued by a competent authority or invalid in the sense that the authority, who issued it, transgressed its competence. For all I can see, it is even logically impossible that every norm within a given normative order should possess that which I have here called a normative foundation. There must, it seems, exist at least one supreme competence norm, which is void of this kind of foundation.

One can, however, also define "competence" or "right" to issue norms in a way, which is independent of the existence of norms concerning this competence. I shall not here discuss, how such a definition may be given.

---

[1] For a fuller treatment of the two notions of validity see *Norm and Action*, pp. 194ff.

Be it only said that an aspect of the question of the right to prescribe rules for the conduct of others is intimately connected with the question, which we discussed in Section IV, of the justification of normative action and therewith also with that which I called the *teleological foundation* of norms.

VI

I now move on to discussing another type of foundation, which normative statements may be given, i.e. another type of answer to the question, *why* something ought to or may or must not be done. It will be seen that this second type of foundation, although different from the first type of foundation of normative statements, is in a characteristic way related to the first type of foundation of *norms*, which we have been discussing.

Consider the following case. A builder orders beams from a carpenter for a house, which he is building. He says the beams ought to be so and so many inches thick. If he is asked, why the beams ought to have this thickness, his answer is perhaps that, unless they are thus thick, the roof will (or may) break down. This statement of the builder's could also be cast in the following form: In order to support the roof (safely) the beams ought to be thus and thus thick. Instead of "ought to be" we could here also say "must be" or "have to be".

I shall call the "unless"-statement, and its alternative form the "in-order-to"-statement, *anankastic* statements.

In an anankastic statement there is mention of two states of affairs or events, of which the one is said to be (or not to be) a necessary condition of the other. For example: the roof being safely supported and the beams being thus and thus thick. Now it may happen that the conditioned state or event is an end of human action, something we want to achieve. Then the conditioning state or event becomes something which, for the sake of attaining this end, we ought to produce or bring about. For example: we want the beams to support the roof safely, and therefore we ought to take care that they are of the needed dimensions.

Of the sentence "If you want the roof to be safely supported, you ought to make the beams thus and thus thick" I shall say that it expresses a *technical rule*. Technical rules must be distinguished both from anankastic statements, which are statements of (logical or natural) necessity, and from norms or rules of action, which are somebody's order (or permission) to somebody else.

Now consider the normative statement that the beams ought to be made—by whoever makes them—thus and thus thick. Let the question "Why?" be raised for this statement. And the answer given "Or else the roof will (may) collapse." That this could be a satisfactory answer will, I think, be readily admitted. Yet it is only provided two things are taken for granted that the answer is satisfactory. The one thing is the truth of the anankastic statement that unless the beams are of certain dimensions, the roof will (may) collapse. The other thing is the fact that preventing the roof from collapsing is an aim or end of the person, who orders the beams to be made. These two things in combination, the end and the necessary connection, I shall say, constitute a (teleological) *foundation* of the normative statement. Alternatively, we could say that (pursuing) the end and (believing in or being aware of) the necessary connection *justify* the (making of the) normative statement.

Given the end and the normative statement, we can tell what is supposed to be the necessary connection "linking" the two. The technical rule "if you want, etc." we can therefore regard as a way of justifying a normative statement aiming at the given end.

There is an easily recognized logical relationship between the foundation of a normative statement in ends and necessities on the one hand and that which we have previously called the teleological foundation of norms on the other hand. The relation, briefly speaking, is this: Whenever ends and necessary connections justify a normative statement to the effect that a certain thing ought to (may, must not) be done, then a command (permission, prohibition) to somebody to do this thing, given by somebody in pursuit of these ends, has a teleological foundation in the ends of the norm-authority. The converse of this, apparently, does not hold. Considerations of utility (goodness) may provide a teleological foundation of norms even in the absence of necessary connections linking means to ends (cf. above, Section IV).

We have thus become acquainted with two principal answers to the question, *why* a certain thing ought to or may or must not be done. The one is to say that there exists a *norm* ordering or permitting or prohibiting the doing of this thing. The other is to say that *ends and necessary connections* make (or do not make) the doing or forbearing of this thing a practical necessity.

On the basis of the above we could also say that the idea of "ought" has two main sources. The one source is in the will of a commanding agent or norm-authority. The other is a double source in ends of human action and necessary connections between things.

In themselves, the two sources are of a rather different nature. But they are related to one another through the notion of a foundation of a norm (as a manifestation of the will of a norm-giver). Norms are frequently, perhaps one could say: normally, given for the sake of some ends. For this reason it may happen that the "ought", which flows from a commanding will, becomes supported by the "ought" of a technical rule and will rest on this latter "ought" as on its foundation.

VII

The question may be raised: Do all normative statements have a foundation of either of the two types, which we have so far been discussing? In particular, one may wish to know, whether normative statements relating to so-called *moral* matters, may be given a foundation of these types.

The answer to the second question will partly depend upon what one understands by a *moral* normative statement (or by "moral matters"). Trivially, one can define a moral normative statement as a statement to the effect that doing or forbearing a certain thing is morally obligatory or morally permissible. This leaves open the non-trivial question, what makes action, *in a moral sense*, obligatory or permissible. I shall return to this question in Section X.

An *example* of a normative statement which, I think, nobody would hesitate to call "moral", is the statement that promises ought to be kept. It is, moreover, an example of that which I shall call a statement of *moral principle*.

Only some moral normative statements, i.e. statements to the effect that something or other is morally obligatory or permissible, state moral principles. Consider, for example, the statement that I ought to help my neighbour to paint his house. Let the question "Why?", i.e. the question of its foundation, be raised. And the answer given "Because I have promised."

This answer to our question would normally be regarded as completely satisfying. Only under special circumstances would we raise the further question "Why ought you to do that which you have promised to do?". To raise it would be to raise a question of moral philosophy.

The answer "Because I have promised" is, of course, not the *only* possible answer to the question, why I ought to help my neighbour to paint his house. There could, in some community, exist a law or regulation to the effect that one ought to help one's neighbours with this kind of job. Or the reason for the "ought" here could be some "technical" considerations, relating to ends and wants and to what will happen, *if* . . . For example, that unless I help my neighbour now, he will not help me on some other occasion, or my reputation will suffer, or . . . These answers need not be exclusive of one another nor of the answer "Because I have promised."

That fact that I have promised to do a certain thing is thus a possible foundation of the normative statement that I ought to do this thing. As a foundation of the statement it is, moreover, a truth-ground of it. (See above, Section I.)

It is, however, plain that what makes the fact that I have promised to do *p* to be a foundation of the normative statement that I ought to do *p*, is the moral principle that promises ought to be kept. It is because promises ought to be kept that I ought to do *p*, if I have promised to do *p*. The normative statement is founded on the *principle* of promise-keeping in combination with the *fact* that I have promised. We could also say that the moral statement has become *subsumed* under the moral principle.

Subsumption under a moral principle is thus a type of foundation of normative statements. Many moral normative statements have this type of foundation. It is, however, impossible that they should *all* become thus founded. At least some statements of moral principle must, for logical reasons, be void of this type of foundation.

Subsumption of moral normative statements under moral principles is an analogue to the foundation of normative statements on (the existence of) norms (see above, Sections II and III). Moral principles are analogous to norms. They are indeed quite commonly called "moral norms". There is no objection to this terminology. But it is important to realize that, *prima facie*, moral principles are very different from norms in the sense of prescriptions for action, given by some norm-authority to some norm-subject(s).

As a foundation of moral normative statements subsumption under moral principles may be said to possess only a "relative" value. For the question will instantly arise, how statements of moral principle then may become founded. Until we have answered this question, we do not even fully understand the nature of the foundation, which the moral principles themselves provide for the various moral normative statements that are subsumed under them.

VIII

There are many answers to the question, which we raised at the end of the preceding section. The answers correspond to well-known positions in moral philosophy.

One answer is to take the view that moral principles *are* that which we have here called "norms"—or something very much like this. One could term this the *legalistic* or law-conception of morality. The historically most important version of this conception is the view that moral principles are the commands (commandments, laws) of God to men.

This view of morality cannot be dismissed as being an "anachronism". Maybe we must reject it. But if no other attempted foundation of morality satisfies us, we are in a serious predicament. As Dostoevsky put it: "If God does not exist, then everything is permitted." If there is no satisfactory answer to the question, why one should do, as the moral principle says one should do then why should one be moral? This is no purely "theoretical" problem, but also a "practical" one.

To say that no moral normative statement is founded on the existence of a norm is tantamount to saying that the fact that somebody has commanded or permitted a certain conduct to somebody is never a reason, why this conduct is *morally* obligatory or permissible.[2]

If we accept this thesis, we must look for a foundation of moral normative statements in some other source beside the normative activity of a God or of men. But the thesis is in no way incompatible with the fact that norms and human normative activity are, to a very considerable extent, concerned with moral matters, i.e. with regulating conduct which is considered morally obligatory or permissible. This is true both of the laws of the state and of the rules of conduct, which parents and teachers try to make children obey.

Consider, for example, the principle of promise-keeping. Agreements and contracts are kinds of promises. The *legal* obligations, which people have under contract, are therefore obligations to keep a kind of promise. But we are inclined to think that the *moral* obligation to keep promises, even when *safeguarded* by law, is not *founded* on law. This means: We think that the proper answer to the question, why it is *morally* obligatory to keep promises, is *not* that there is some norm or norms to this effect.

One could, in a broad sense of the word "legal", call those normative statements, which have a foundation in norms, *legal* normative statements. Then one could, if one rejects the law-conception of morality, say that it is a characteristic logical difference between legal and moral normative statements that they hold opposite relationships to norms. Legal normative statements are *secondary* to norms in the sense that the existence or non-existence of norms determine their truth-value. Something is a legal obligation or right, *because* the norm (law) so requires. Moral normative statements are not secondary to norms, and nothing is morally obligatory or permissible, *because* it is prescribed. But many *norms* are secondary to moral principles in the sense that we issue and enforce the norms, because we want people to behave morally.

Rejecting a law-conception of moral principles thus does not mean that the logical ties between morality and norm (law) are completely severed. This must be taken into account, when discussing the possibility of a moral without a religious foundation.

---

[2] Note the difference in meaning between "permitted" and "permissible" in ordinary usage. "Permitted" suggests that somebody has given permission to somebody. "Permissible" does not suggest this. It does not sound natural to call something "morally permitted", but it is perfectly in order to call something "morally permissible". Perhaps this observation can be instanced as showing a certain unnaturalness of a law-conception of morality.

IX

Another possible answer to the question of the foundation of a statement of moral principle would be to say that such statements have no foundation —at least not in that sense of "foundation", which we are here discussing. On this view, it is not possible to tell, *why* that thing ought to or may or must not be done, which according to the moral principle is obligatory or permissible. This impossibility does, of course, not exclude that one could answer the question, how people *have come to think* that certain things are morally obligatory or permissible. But the answer to this question would not provide a foundation of moral principles—but a (causal) explanation of certain moral attitudes and opinions.

If statements of moral principle lack a foundation, does it then follow that they have no truth-value? In other words: If it is "in principle" impossible to tell *why* something or other ought to (may, must not) be done, is then the statement *that* it ought to (may, must not) be done neither true nor false? Statements in the "strict" sense of the term are true or false, we have said. Thus, if we accept an affirmative answer to the above questions, we should have to say that statements of moral principle are no statements in the "strict" sense. They do not express "propositions", are not accepted or rejected on the basis of acts of "cognition".

The view that statements of moral principle, because void of a foundation, are neither true nor false, would be a form of the position, which has become known as *non-cognitivism* in ethics. It is much in fashion among contemporary writers.

It should be observed, however, that the mere fact that the question, *why* it is thus and thus, cannot be answered for a given statement to the effect *that* it is thus and thus, is not sufficient to show that this statement has no truth-value. There are a great many statements which are true or false, but which have no truth-ground "outside their own content" so to speak.

Perception-statements, for example, may be regarded as being of this category. Consider the statement that I hear my own voice, when reading this paper to my audience. There may exist a physiological explanation, why it is that I hear my own voice. But the truth of the statement that I hear my voice, is not logically grounded on any further fact beside the fact that I hear it. There is no answer to the question, *why*, i.e. for which reason, it is true. The statement is true or false, depending, as we say, upon whether I hear or do not hear my voice.

In view of this, could it not be the case that moral principles too lack a foundation but yet possess a truth-value? To give an affirmative answer would be to think that the statement that something or other ought to (may, must not) be done could be true for no other reason but that this thing ought to (may, must not) be done.

The opinion that statements of moral principle are true or false, but not grounded on anything outside their own content, is known as the *deonto-logist* position in ethics. Adherents of it sometimes wish to make an analogy between moral normative statements and perception statements, and some-times between moral normative statements and mathematical statements. The truth of statements of moral principle, they say, can be "intuited" or is a matter of "self-evidence".[3]

When viewed in the perspective of the problem of foundation of norma-tive statements, the deontologist and the non-cognitivist positions thus come to be related. They share the opinion that for an important category of normative statements one cannot answer the question, why it is as the statements say that it is. In other regards the two positions differ sharply. Both are, in my opinion, unsatisfactory as attempts to give an account of the nature of moral principles.[4]

X

The chief alternative, in the history of ethics, to a law-conception of moral principles is a *teleological* view of them. The so-called utilitarianism is a variant of teleological ethics.

One can characterize the difference between the legalistic and the teleo-logical conception of morality as follows: The first regards the foundation of normative statements on the existence of norms as the pattern, according to which statements of moral principle have to be founded. The second again regards the foundation of normative statements in necessities and ends of action as being the proper pattern. On the first view, the moral "ought" is the "ought" of a command. On the second, it is the "ought" of a technical rule. Just as the command behind the "ought" must be a very special sort of command (e.g. by a God) in order to constitute a *moral* "ought", in a similar manner, the technical rule behind the "ought" must be of a very special sort in order to justify a statement of *moral* obligation.

---

[3] The position sometimes called an *ethics of conscience* may be regarded as combining elements of a law-conception and a deontologist conception of morality. My conscience "bids" me to do and forbear certain things. As such an inner voice it is like a norm-authority. But by consulting my conscience I also come to "see" or understand that such and such is my duty. As a supposed source of knowledge of duty, conscience may be said to resemble perception as a source of knowledge about the sensible world.

[4] For assessing the correctness of non-cognitivism as a position in ethics, it is important to distinguish clearly between norms and values, and between normative statements and value-judgments. Unfortunately, this is seldom done with sufficient clarity by adherents of the position. It seems to me that as a theory of the nature of valuations and value-judgments, non-cognitivism contains much that is both true and important. To call statements of moral principle, e.g., that promises ought to be kept, "value-judgments" would, however, be to blur important logical distinctions. To point this out is not to deny that moral principles may have logical connections with valuations.

We shall here consider the problems confronting a teleological view of moral principles in the light of an example. The example will be the principle that promises ought to be kept.[5] This principle has presented those philosophers in the past, who have been inclined towards a teleological view, with notorious difficulties. It is therefore a good test-case for the possibility of giving to statements of moral principle a foundation in ends and necessary connections.

That the institution or practice of promising is of value to those who participate in it, is not only an obvious fact. It is, moreover, true for reasons of logic. This is so, because the objects of particular promises, i.e. the things which the givers of promises promise to do, are things in which the receivers of promises take an interest. If I am indifferent to a thing, which is held forth to me as the object of a promise, I do not receive the promise. And if I loose interest in it, after having received the promise, I—as we say—"release" the promisor from the obligation to fulfil his promise. Only promises, the objects of which represent an interest (a "good" or "value") to the promisee, oblige. Hence every man who participates in the practice of giving and taking promises, necessarily has an immediate interest that those, who have promised *him* something, should keep their word. This is a common interest of all participants. It is not, however, a contingent interest of theirs, but a necessary interest or an interest inherent in the concept of promising.[6]

The *anankastic statement* underlying the principle of promise-keeping can be formulated as follows: People ought to keep their promises, lest others should forego the benefits of participating in the practice of promising and suffer the evil of being deceived. (This is not to say anything "over and above" the fact that, unless people keep their promises, others will lose a benefit and suffer some evil.)

From the anankastic statement must be distinguished the *techical rule* underlying the moral principle. The anankastic statement speaks of a necessary connection between a certain interest ("good", "value") and a certain practice or mode of conduct. The technical rule extracts an obligation to behave in a certain way from the pursuit of this *interest* as an end. It says that, if you want not to do evil to your neighbour, you ought to keep your word to him. The interest, of which the technical rule speaks as an end of my action, is, be it observed, not *my* interest (self-interest), but my neighbour's interest. It is for the sake of *my neighbour's good* that moral conduct is required of *me*.

By love of one's neighbour we can understand pursuit of one's neighbour's good "for its own sake" or, as it can also be called, as an "ultimate end" of action. It should be clear, in which sense love of our neighbour

---

[5] Cf. the essay "On Promises" in this volume.

[6] Cf. below, pp. 97ff.

can be said to demand or require moral conduct of us. Whether love can itself be required, imposed in the form of an obligation, we need not here discuss. What is certain, however, is that moral conduct, observance of moral principles, may become demanded of us otherwise than by our love of our neighbour. The way in which this may happen, is, moreover, essential to the logical picture we are trying to draw.

The common interest of all participants in the practice of promising that others should keep their word to them engenders the further common interest to *make* the givers of promises keep their word. This we try to achieve in a variety of ways: by teaching children the importance of being trustworthy, by urging people to keep their word, sometimes by calling for the arm of the law to enforce the obligation, and by the punitive measure of not trusting the faithless again, i.e. by depriving them of the benefits of further participation in the practice. The activity, in which men engage in order to make people keep their promises, is to a large extent of the type, which we have called normative activity. It includes both the commanding of children and the making of laws for the citizens of a state.

It is thanks to the fact that the interest at the source of the moral obligation engenders various kinds of normative activity that men *also* become self-interestedly concerned about obedience to moral rules. The self-interest, which men have in behaving morally, is the interest, which they themselves have to escape from the various evils which they threaten to visit on others, who behave immorally. In the case of promising, one of these evils, to quote Hume, is "the penalty of never being trusted again".

The interest which men have to escape the evils consequent upon immoral action is essential to the "mechanism of interests", whereby men become morally obligated. But pursuit of this interest is *not* the end of action, on which a statement of moral principle is founded. Not to be trusted again would not be a penalty for breach of word, unless continued participation in the practice of promising were a benefit. And participation would not be a benefit, unless the objects of promises were goods to the receivers. *This* is the interest, on the pursuit of which as an end the obligation to keep promises is founded.

My suggestion now is that a statement to the effect that something is *morally* obligatory or permissible is true if, and only if, it may be given a teleological foundation of the general form, which I have here illustrated using as an example the principle of promise-keeping. The interest at the source of a moral obligation is an interest, which each individual participant in a certain practice necessarily has that the other participants behave towards him in a certain way, defined by the practice. This is self-interest. Its pursuit does not oblige the interested party to the behaviour in question. But it may come to oblige his neighbours, his co-operants in the practice. The interest, from which the obligation on him arises, is not *his* but *theirs*. The obligation, which the moral principle imposes on him, is to observe the same mode of conduct which *he* self-interestedly demands of *others*.

This view of the nature of moral principles is not, in its spirit, new. It is a view which makes an idea of *justice* the core of morality.[7] It has an obvious affinity to the so-called Golden Rule. It is related too to Kant's maxim of universalization of action as a touch-stone of morality. (This is so notwithstanding the fact that Kant himself would have been strongly opposed to attempts to derive moral principles from considerations of interest.) But neither the Golden Rule in any of its usual formulations, nor Kant's maxim can be regarded as satisfactory expressions of the conditions, which a normative statement has to satisfy in order to qualify as stating a moral principle.

XI

My paper thus ends with a suggestion. This suggestion is a proposed definition of the concept of a moral principle in terms of a teleological foundation of morality. The suggestion could also be called a contribution to the moulding of the notion of a moral principle. Philosophical ethics, as I see it, is essentially such a moulding or shaping of the ethically relevant notions.[8]

Is there a test of truth for the results of this sort of inquiry? In some important sense, I think, there is no such a test of truth. But there are various tests of what may be called acceptability. The acceptability of the suggestion concerning the nature of moral principles which I have ventured to make, can be put to test in at least three ways. The first test is that normative statements, which we ordinarily regard as stating moral principles, can be given a foundation, which satisfies the suggested formal requirements. The second is that no normative statement, which has this sort of foundation, would commonly and naturally be regarded as *not* stating a moral principle. The third is connected with the fact that the suggestion provides a method for deciding, whether a proposed rule of action satisfies the requirement of being a moral principle. These are questions, on which moralists have notoriously disagreed and which may become thus decided. But on the further question, whether our suggested criteria are an acceptable basis for such decisions, moralists may nevertheless continue to disagree. The existence of such disagreement need not be deplored. It seems to me to constitute the life-nerve of philosophical ethics.

---

[7] A fuller statement of this view is given in *The Varieties of Goodness*, Ch. X.

[8] Cf. *The Varieties of Goodness*, Ch. I, Sect. 3.

On Promises

I

What is a promise? I.e., what sort of things are promises?, under which category do promises fall?

A promise is not an *utterance* or a *sentence* or anything which could be reasonably called a "linguistic" category. Nor is a promise an *act(ion)*, nor a *relation* between a promise-giver and a promise-receiver. It would also be false to say that a promise is a kind of *obligation*. But "utterance", "sentence", "act(ion)", "relation", and "obligation" are all of them needed for a satisfactory account of promises.

Promises belong to the same category as *agreements* and *contracts*. There seems to be no name for this category in ordinary language—and we need not here coin a name for it.

A promise is not an action, but promising or the giving of a promise obviously is a human action. Of this sort of human action the following features are characteristic:

(a) The action cannot be performed *solo*. It requires two parties, a promise-giver (promisor) and a promise-receiver (promisee). They are human beings.

I shall here disregard the case, when a promise is given collectively or jointly by several agents and also the case, when a promise has more than one receiver. It seems that these cases are essentially similar to the simpler case, which we are here discussing.

If acts of promising cannot be performed *solo* in the sense explained, then one cannot "strictly speaking" give a promise to oneself. Yet we sometimes do things which we describe as giving promises to ourselves. It seems to me, however, that promises to oneselves are promises in an *analogical* sense only. My reasons for this opinion will not be given here. They have to do with the notion of having an obligation to somebody.

Vows and *oaths*, be it observed in passing, are related to promises. They differ from promises, it seems, among other things in the nature of their receivers, who need not be human beings.

(b) The "performing" of the act of promising, its physical aspect so to speak, normally consists in that the promisor addresses the promisee—either orally or in writing—using a characteristic *form of words*.[1] We

---

[1] I adopt Hume's phrase "form of words". It seems to me better suited for the purpose of a logical clarification of promises than the term "promise-sentence". Prichard talks of "a

could call this verbal performance an utterance (in a broad sense of the word).

In English, the standard form of words used for promising is "I promise" followed by an expression for the thing promised, e.g. by the phrase "to come and see you tomorrow morning". The standard form admits of variations. "I give my word" is another form. I shall later mention a possible alternative form, which differs both from "I promise" and "I give my word" in that it is not of the form of an indicative sentence.

It is worth mention that the verbal performance of the promisor in giving a promise often consists merely in an affirmative answer to a question on the part of the promisee "Do (will) you promise to − − − ?" It seems to me that philosophers, who have written on promises, have tended to ignore the role of the promisee in the act of promising, or to view promising one-sidedly from the standpoint of the promisor. If someone addresses me with the words "I promise you to do p" and if I have not asked him to do p or otherwise manifested some interest in p being done, I should probably feel bewildered or embarrassed. "What does he mean?" "Is he perhaps joking?" are questions which arise. If I cannot understand, why he should be promising me to do this thing, I should probably refuse to enter into a relation of promisee to promisor with him. (The receiving as well as the giving of promises is a mode of voluntary action.) His verbal performance would then fail to constitute an act of promising.

The thing promised I shall call the *object* of the promise. The object of a promise is one or several future actions (and/or forbearances) on the part of the promise-giver. Promises necessarily refer to the future. One cannot promise to have done something. Nor that something *is* thus and thus, e.g. that twice two is four. But one can make *assurances* about such things. (Assurances sometimes have the appearance of "promises referring to the past".)

(c) In the act of promising the promise-giver acquires an obligation to the promise-receiver. This obligation is to do the promised thing (the object of the promise).

That x has an obligation to y to do (or forbear) certain things can be called a "normative relationship" between x and y. The successful performance of an act of promising thus establishes a normative relationship between two agents.

It should be observed that the obligations, to which acts of promising give rise, are of the peculiar kind which I here call *obligations to persons*. Not every obligation, under which a man may be, is an obligation to some

---

certain noise in connection with the phrase for some action". See his essay "The Obligation to Keep a Promise" in H.A. Prichard, *Moral Obligation*, Oxford at the Clarendon Press, 1949.

other man (or men). When *x* has an obligation to *y*, then *y* is said to have a *right* as against *x*, *viz*. the right to claim or demand that *x* fulfil his obligation (e.g. keep his promise). Such rights sometimes have a legal significance. This notion of a right, it seems to me, is logically rather different from that notion of a right which consists in a *permission* to the rightholder to do a certain thing in combination with a *prohibition* to others to prevent the right-holder from doing this thing, should he choose to avail himself of his right.

II

When, under which circumstances, do we say that a promise has been given, i.e. an act of promising successfully performed?

The urge to establish (decide, find out), whether a promise has been given or not, usually comes from the claim on the part of an alleged promise-receiver that an alleged promise-giver should keep his word. The urge to establish the existence of a promise, one could also say, usually comes from a claim that a certain agent is under an obligation to another agent. The existence of the promise is the justification of this claim.

The mere fact that certain words were uttered or written down on some occasion can never be *sufficient* for concluding that a promise has been given. The words, first of all, must have been *used* and not *mentioned* (e.g. by some philosopher in a discussion of the nature of promises). The words, moreover, must have been used by somebody to *address* somebody else.

It is sometimes said that the appropriate form of words must be used "in earnest" in order to constitute a promise. But this is not quite true. If an agent demands that another agent should do something on the ground that he promised, then this other agent cannot refuse to carry the burden of the obligation *merely* on the ground that he had been joking. Not the fact that he was joking makes a man's use of the words "I promise to − − −" not constitute an act of promising. But often, when it is clear that a man, who says "I promise to − − −", is not promising, we conclude that he is (perhaps) joking. If a person addresses me with the words "I promise to make you Emperor of China", he would (normally) not be promising me anything. Why should he nevertheless have said this? The answer may be that he was joking.

It does not seem possible to tell exactly, *how* words must be used in order to constitute a promise. Not even the use of words *with the intention of giving a promise* is sufficient to secure that a promise has been given. For the addressee of the words may fail to respond in the adequate manner. He is perhaps not even *capable* of entering into a relationship of promisee to promisor with another agent (cf. below).

Even though the use of words is not, by itself, sufficient to accomplish an act of promising, it seems that the use of words or signs is *necessary* to this end. Promising "essentially" involves the use of language. The giving and receiving of promises is therefore possible only among beings, who can communicate with each other by means of symbols.

I shall here mention and briefly discuss three more things, which may be regarded as necessary conditions (beside the use of a "form of words") for saying truly that an act of promising has been (successfully) accomplished or that a relation of promisor to promisee exists between two agents. It is not maintained that the four necessary conditions jointly constitute a sufficient condition. Nor is it maintained that it is possible to state necessary and sufficient conditions for deciding, when the four necessary conditions are, in the given case, fulfilled.

The proposing of necessary conditions is a contribution to the *moulding* or *shaping* (some would say "defining") of the concept of a promise. Rejecting some of the proposed conditions or replacing them by others would lead to different concepts of a promise. It cannot be claimed that the concept as shaped by us here is the "true" one, or the one which is "really" meant when we speak of promises in ordinary parlance. The concept of a promise is obscure. This is why it challenges philosophic reflection. And this is why the philosopher is to some extent free to shape the concept so that its logical features and relations to other concepts become clear. Nothing more will here be said about the justification of our procedure.

(*a*) A necessary condition of the origination or coming into being of a promise is that the parties concerned, i.e. the promisor and the promisee, should *know what they are doing* when giving and taking promises. They must, as we could also put it, be familiar with the institution or practice of promising. That a child has learnt to talk and also to say "I promise – – –" does not *ipso facto* mean that it can give and/or take promises. It is a logical peculiarity of the act of promising that it is possible to master the physical performance, which is an aspect of it and which consists in the production of some words or signs, without being able to accomplish the act. Ability to accomplish the act presupposes a certain "conceptual maturity" on the part of both agents, who engage in promising. It may be impossible to give necessary and sufficient conditions for deciding whether this presupposition is fulfilled in the individual case. Its character of necessary condition for saying that an act of promising has been accomplished is, however, not affected by this.

(*b*) From the fact that acts of promising give rise to *obligations* we may deduce the following necessary condition of saying that such an act has been performed: The promisor must be able to perform an action *of the kind* (category), to which the promised action belongs. (The question, whether he can perform the individual action, which would fulfil his promise, is not relevant to the question, whether he has given a promise or not.) If it is clear that the promisor cannot do the kind of action he says he promises to do (e.g., swim across the Atlantic), we dismiss his words as nonsense and do not regard them as constituting a promise. If again it is doubtful, whether he can do it or not, we sometimes say that he is under an obligation to *try* to do it. We then interpret what he did as the giving of a promise to try to do a certain thing. Explicit promises to try to do things are not uncommon. The objects of such promises are acts of trying to do.

Consider the case, when the giver of a promise knows that he cannot do the thing he "promises" to do, but the receiver of the promise believes that the promisor can do this. The promisor can then rightly be accused of having cheated the promisee. The cheat, however, does not consist in the promisor's breaking his word, but in his making the promisee believe that something has been promised. This seems to me to be a natural way of describing the situation. Yet we must not be pedantic about the use of language here. The cheated party would perhaps want to insist on saying that he had been given a promise, but that the promise was not kept. He would then be using "promise" in such a way that the promisor's use of a form of words, which is characteristic of promising, in combination with the promisee's belief that he has been promised something, entails that a promise has been given. His use of "promise" would correspond to a slightly different concept of promising from the one, which we are here moulding.

(*c*) Finally, from the fact that acts of promising give rise to obligations of the peculiar kind, which I have called *obligations to persons*, one may extract the following necessary condition of saying truly that an act of promising has been performed: The object of the promise must represent an *interest* to the promisee, must be *for him a good*, something he *wants* or *welcomes*. (I shall regard these phrases as alternative ways of saying the same thing.) It seems to me to be a logical feature of the concept of an obligation to a person that one can have such an obligation only on condition that its fulfilment is in the interest of the person, to whom one has this obligation. I shall not here discuss the criteria for judging that something is somebody's interest. The question is complicated. Parents, e.g., have obligations to their children which may involve the doing of things, which the children shun or hate in their ignorance of their "true good". But parents cannot have obligations *to their children* to do things which are either harmful or totally irrelevant to the welfare of the children.

In order to see the importance of interests to promising, it may be useful to consider the circumstances under which promises normally originate. The "initiative" is usually with the promise-*receiver*—and *not* with the promise-giver. For example: One man wants another man to do something. The second says he will do it, but the first is not quite sure. "Will you promise?", he asks. If the second man then gives his word, the first will, as a rule, feel more confident that he will get his wanted thing. Very often promising is linked with an *exchange of services* (goods). Then the connection with interests is in the nature of the case. One man asks another to help him with a certain task. The second agrees, but only on condition that the first promises a service in return on another occasion.

It sometimes happens that an act, which is in itself of no interest to the promisee, acquires an interest to him as a consequence of being mentioned in the form of words "I promise to – – –". For example: Someone asks me for an appointment and promises to come to see me tomorrow morning. It is of no interest to me, let us assume, to grant him the appointment; nor am I anxious that it should be tomorrow morning and not at any other time. But having taken his word, I arrange my day accordingly. Perhaps I make an appointment to see another person later in the day. If the first person does not turn up at the appointed time, his failing to do so may cause considerable annoyance and maybe even damage. I can insist that he should come in the morning, as promised, and I can accuse him of breach of promise, if he does not turn up then.

If something, in which a man takes no interest at all, is held forth to him by another person as the object of a promise, the first man will either acquire an interest in the thing and enter into the relation of promisee to promisor with the second man, or he will refuse to enter into this relation. In the second case, what the prospective promisor said and did failed to constitute an act of promising.

If a person addressed me with the words "I promise to make you Emperor of China", he would (normally) not be promising me anything (cf. above). One reason, why he *cannot promise* to make me Emperor of China is that, as we both know, he *cannot make* me Emperor of China. But even if he could make me Emperor of China, his words would fail to constitute a promise with me, i.e. with the writer of this essay on promises. For I am not in the least attracted by the prospect and my attitude to it would not change as a consequence of its being held forth to me as the object of a promise. I should *refuse* to enter into the relation of promisee to promisor with my interlocutor.

Sometimes it happens that the promisee loses or gives up his interest in the object of the promise before the promise is fulfilled. Then the promisor is *released*, as we say, from the obligation to keep his word. The relation of promisor to promisee ceases, dissolves. The promise, so to speak, passes out of existence before its fulfilment.

*   *   *

The form of words "I promise to – – –" is sometimes used for addressing a person, knowing that the action mentioned in the form of words *is* a thing which the addressee shuns. This sort of "promise" we call a *threat*. A threat, I would suggest, never creates an obligation *to the person, who is being threatened*, to make the threat effective. For this reason a threat, even when it is "dressed up" in the form of a promise, is not a (genuine) promise.

Normally, it does not make much difference, whether a person says to another "I shall punish you, if − − −" or "I promise to punish you, if − − −". But it makes a *great* difference, whether a person says to another "I shall do as you ask me" or "I promise to do as you ask me". In the first case, it is only a declaration of intention that carries weight—irrespective of which form of words has been used in announcing the threat. A threat of punishment *cannot* assume the obliging character of a promise (to the threatened person).

III

Some words should be said about certain features, which are *not* essential to promises or to deciding, whether a certain verbal performance constitutes an act of promising. The reason for mentioning them is that they may *appear* essential.

It is, first of all, not essential to the existence of a promise that it should be fulfilled or kept, i.e. that the promise-giver should actually do what he has promised to do. He may try but fail, or he may neglect the promised act altogether. *Broken* promises are a species of *unfulfilled* promises. Both are promises.

It is, moreover, not essential to the question of the existence of a promise that the promise-giver, at the time of promising, should *intend* to do what he promises to do. A promise is not a declaration of intention. Nor is it, of course, a *prediction* of what the promisor is going to do. Promising without intention to keep the promise can aptly be called giving a *false* promise. But it is not making a false statement (to the effect that a promise is being given). False promises, like broken and unfulfilled promises, are promises too.

The question may be raised, whether it is not essential to the (existence of the) *institution or practice of promising* that false and broken promises should be *exceptions*, i.e. that promises should on the whole be given with an intention of keeping them and also on the whole be kept. I shall not discuss this question here. Nor shall I discuss the problem, whether an attempt to promise, which uses some such form of words as "I promise you to do *p*, but I do not intend to do *p*", would be self-refuting, i.e. fail to constitute a promise, or otherwise "paradoxical".

IV

To the act of promising, we have said, the use of a characteristic form of words is essential. We shall now examine in some detail this form of words and its function.

The form "I promise to − − −" is that of an indicative sentence in the first person of the present tense. With it may be compared sentences of otherwise the same form but in different person and/or tense. For example: "He promises to − − −", "I promised to − − −", "He will promise to − − −".

The normal use of all members of this class of (forms of) indicative statements, with the exception of sentences in the first person of the present tense, is for *stating that* somebody is promising or has promised or will promise to do something. The normal use of the sentence in question is thus to make statements, which are either true or false as the case may be.

The sentences of the class under consideration—again with the exception of those in the first person of the present tense—are *not* normally used for *giving promises*. Sometimes, however, they are used for that purpose too— or for some closely related purpose. Thus, for example, "I promised to − − −" might be used to reinforce or renew a promise already given; and use of the words "I shall promise to − − −" might be understood to constitute a promise to promise.

The form "I promise to − − −" stands out from all the rest of the class of (forms of) indicative statements under discussion in that its normal use *is* for *giving promises*. Considering the peculiarity of its function, its outward similarity to the other members of the class may be regarded as "philosophically misleading". This means: its form may lead the thoughts of someone, who reflects on the nature of promises, in a wrong direction. It may therefore be helpful to consider the possibility of replacing the characteristic form of words, actually used in promising, by some other form.

The conventional form of words used for promising could be, for example, "On my honour, I shall do − − −". Is this an indicative sentence? I do not know what grammarians would say. I think there are some reasons for *not* calling it an "indicative sentence". It is, for one thing, not clear what its different tenses would be. Sentences of this type could not without the introduction of special linguistic conventions be used for stating that a promise has been or is or will be given. If "On my honour, I shall do − − −" were the standard form of words used for promising (and "I promise to − − −" were not), then philosophers would perhaps never have been strongly tempted to think that the use of words for making promises was a use of words for making statements.

To sum up: It is a *contingent* fact about the use of language that the form of words used for promising is that of an indicative sentence. But it is *necessary* that the form of words used for stating that promises have been or are or will be given either is that of an indicative sentence or can be translated without alteration of meaning into indicative sentences.

V

Can the form of words "I promise to − − −" be used for *stating that* I promise to − − −? Or, to put the question in a more precise form: Can the very same token of this form of words be used both for giving a promise and for stating that I give a promise?

One must distinguish between the possibility that the words "I promise to − − −" are used for making a statement, and the possibility that they express a true proposition. That they can do the second need not be doubted, I think. The words "I promise to − − −" express a true proposition if, and only if, it is the case that I promise to − − −. From the fact, however, that the words actually happen to express a true proposition it does not follow that they have been used for making a (true) statement. Words, as they stand, may express a (true or false) proposition, even though nobody is there to "contemplate" or "entertain" it. But words, it may be argued, are not used for making a statement, unless their user *intends* this use of them.

Accepting this, the answer to the question, whether the very same words can be used both for promising and for stating that a promise is being given, would depend upon whether one can have and carry into effect "at once" the two intentions of giving a promise and stating that one is giving a promise. (The problem, whether one can do this, is not a psychological problem, but a conceptual or logical one.) Now granting that one *can* have the two intentions in one act, it is fairly obvious that *normally* one does not have both intentions. Only on rare occasions, therefore, would I, in uttering the words "I promise to − − −", both accomplish an act of promising and state that I am accomplishing this act.

It would, of course, be utter confusion to say that a sentence (either type or token) of the form "I promise to − − −" can be both a promise and a true statement and a true proposition. It, the sentence, can be neither of the three. But a token of a sentence of this form can be *used for giving a promise*. And it can *express a true proposition*. Whether it can also be *used for making a true statement* is, as we have seen, somewhat problematic.

VI

Consider the third person sentence "*x* has promised *y* to do *p*". Its normal use would be for making a (true or false) statement about something, which has occurred between two persons. By an *analysis* of (the meaning of) this sentence one could understand a formulation of its truth-conditions (when used for making a statement). This analysis would throw light upon the question, *what x* has done, when he promised *y* to do *p*, or—as we could also put it—what it *means* (to say) that *x* has promised *y* to do *p*.

This would be a possible analysis of the above third person sentence: "By addressing *y* with a certain form of words (such as 'I promise you to do *p*'), *x* has put himself under an obligation to *y* to do *p*". This would be an "analysis" also in the sense that it mentions two main "components" or "parts" of a promise, *viz.* the use of a certain *form of words* and the *obligation* which the user of the words henceforth (and on account of having used them) has to another person to do a certain thing.

"With these words I put myself under an obligation to you to do *p*" is another *form of words*, which could be used for giving a promise. (It probably sometimes *is* used for this purpose.) This form of words is *equivalent* to the form of words "I promise you to do *p*" in the sense that the two forms may be used for doing exactly the same thing, *viz.* giving a certain promise. And one could call the longer form of words an *analysed* version of the shorter form of words, on the ground that the first sentence contains explicit mention of things which, though essential to promising, are not overtly mentioned in the second.

The notions of an obligation in general and of an obligation to a person stand themselves in need of "analysis" or of some form of philosophic clarification. This, however, is not in conflict with the fact that the notions are needed for an analysis or clarification of the notion of a promise.

Can one not teach a child what promising is without teaching it what obligations (to others) are? One can teach a child to give and receive promises, without mention of the word "obligation" or some equivalent word, e.g. "duty". But teaching a child what promising is *is* making it familiar with a kind of obligation.

Philosophically, the concept of an obligation may be said to be highly controversial and obscure. And the same may be said of the concept of a promise. The fact, however, that the nature of obligation and promise puzzles philosophers, in no way impairs the commerce of men (including philosophers) in giving promises and in entering into various normative relationships with each other.

VII

In the rest of the present essay I shall discuss some problems relating to *the obligation to keep promises*. Considering the obvious philosophic importance and interest of this notion, it is surprising that it has received relatively little attention. Hume dug deep into the problems connected with it.[2] The

---

[2] In *A Treatise of Human Nature*, Bk. III, Pt. ii, Sect. 5, entitled "Of the Obligation of Promises".

most interesting recent treatment, of which I am aware, is by the late Professor Prichard.[3]

The problem in this region, which chiefly occupied Prichard, could be formulated as follows: How can an act of promising or the production of "a certain noise in connection with the phrase for some action", to use Prichard's words, create (give rise to, bring into existence) an obligation? Prichard's way out was to suggest that the obligation must exist antecedently to the individual act of promising. In order to account of this antecedently existing obligation, he invented the fiction of an antecedent *promise* (agreement) never to cause a noise of a certain kind in connection with the phrase for some action without also going on to do the action.[4] This "second-order" promise, unlike ordinary promises, does not require the use of language.[5] Therefore, strictly speaking, it *is* not a promise at all.[6] Prichard's essay ends with the question, what this thing is, which must be presupposed in promising in order to make intelligible the obligation to keep a promise.

In order to resolve Prichard's difficulty, it is helpful to make a distinction which Prichard failed to make. It is the distinction between the (general) obligation to keep promises and the (particular) obligation to do *p* on account of having promised. The second can also be called the obligation to keep a particular promise.

It is clear that acts of promising have not created (cannot create) the obligation to keep promises. But individual acts of promising can quite correctly be said to create obligations to keep particular promises, i.e. obligations to do certain things *qua* promised. There is, as far as I can see, no difficulty or problem about this "creation" of obligations. Before we had promised to do *p*, it was irrelevant to our fulfilling of the obligation to keep promises, whether we did or neglected *p*. Having promised to do *p*, this is no longer irrelevant. The act of promising changed the relevance of our future doing or neglecting of *p* to the general obligation to keep promises. In this change consists the "creation" of the new obligation.

Instead of saying that an act of promising "creates" an obligation to do the promised thing, we can also say that an agent in giving a promise "puts himself under" an obligation to do the promised thing. The obligation, under which he is thus putting himself, is not the *general* obligation to keep promises. This is not an obligation, under which a man can put himself or from which he can withdraw or become released. He is, in a sense, always under it. The obligation, under which he can put himself

---

[3] The essay called "The Obligation to Keep a Promise", published posthumously in *Moral Obligation* (1949).

[4] *Op. cit.*, p. 172.

[5] *Op. cit.*, p. 179.

[6] *Ibid.*

through an act of promising, is the *particular* obligation to do a certain thing *p* on account of having promised it. But since the particular obligation did not exist antecedently to the giving of the promise, it seems to me better to say that one "acquires" it than to say that one "puts oneself under" it.

The answer to Prichard's question is thus *not* that the obligation to keep a promise presupposes a *promise* to keep promises. The answer is that the obligation to keep a promise presupposes—the obligation to keep promises. The answer may raise the further question whence this second obligation arises, what is its "foundation". As a solution to the (genuine) difficulty, which was puzzling Prichard, the answer nevertheless seems to me correct and satisfying.

The (general) obligation to keep promises, be it observed, is not an obligation of the kind which I have here called an *obligation to a person*. But the obligation to keep a particular promise, e.g. to do *p* on account of having promised, is an obligation to a person. Thus the obligation which is created (acquired) in promising is an obligation to a person, although the obligation to keep promises is not.

VIII

What is the "content" of the obligation to keep promises? What demand does it make on human action? The answer which immediately comes to our mind is this: The obligation to keep promises is the obligation never to promise to do a certain thing without also going on to do this thing.

I think that this answer is correct. Yet accepting it is connected with a certain logical difficulty. This can be stated as follows:

If the range of actions, which are the objects of promises, is unrestricted, then there is nothing inherent in the institution of promising to prevent a forbidden action from being the object of a (genuine) promise. A forbidden action is one which must not be done, i.e. which it is obligatory to forbear. A promised action is one which it is obligatory to do—not *simpliciter*, but *qua* promised. Now if somebody has promised to do a forbidden action, then it looks as though one and the same action had become both obligatory and forbidden, i.e. obligatory to do and obligatory to forbear. This, as such, can hardly be called a contradiction of logic. But it is plausible to regard it as a logical feature of the concept of an obligation that one and the same action cannot be both obligatory to do and obligatory to forbear (for one and the same agent on one and the same occasion). Promising the forbidden therefore appears to lead to something, which might be called a *contradiction of deontic logic* (the logic of obligation-concepts).

At this point someone may wish to say: Since promising the forbidden obviously is possible, how *could* it lead to a contradiction? But saying thus would be to take a much too simpleminded view of what promising is. Of course, the fact that *p* is something, which must not be done, does not in the least affect the logical possibility of addressing a person with the words "I promise you to do *p*". The serious question is, whether use of those words would constitute a promise, i.e. create an obligation for me to do *p*, if *p* is something which I must not do.

How shall that which looks like a contradiction here be resolved? A suggestion would be that the range of possible objects of (genuine) promises must, in the name of logic, be restricted to acts which are permitted. But in fact no such restriction is needed. This may be shown by elementary considerations of a logical nature.

What it means that the action *p* is obligatory, not *simpliciter* but *qua* promised, we can understand in the following way: It is obligatory *simpliciter* either not to give a promise to do *p* or to do *p*. Or, which means the same: It is forbidden *simpliciter* to promise to do *p* and leave *p* undone. From the prohibition *simpliciter* to promise to do *p* and leave *p* undone one cannot extract a prohibition *simpliciter* to leave *p* undone, i.e. an obligation *simpliciter* to do *p*. Therefore, that one and the same action is forbidden *simpliciter* and is obligatory *qua* promised, is, in fact, no contradiction at all.

The following logical point about promising the forbidden is worth noticing:

Consider an action which is forbidden (*simpliciter*). With regard to it we have two obligations. The first is not to do it. The second is either not to promise to do it *or* to do it. Under the first obligation we are not allowed to promise to do the action *and* do it (since we are not allowed to do it at all). Under the second obligation we are not allowed to promise to do the action *and not* do it (since this would be breaking our word). Thus under all circumstances, i.e. independently of whether we do or do not do the action, we are not allowed to promise to do this action. *The act of promising to do the forbidden is, for reasons of (deontic) logic, itself a forbidden action.*[7]

Although promising the forbidden does not lead to a *contradiction*, it can quite correctly be said to lead to a *conflict of obligation*. A man ought to do *x*, because he has promised it. But he also ought to forbear *x*, because *x* happens to be a forbidden action. What shall he do in such a situation? This is an ethical problem, often of considerable interest. It cannot be solved by means of considerations of a formal logical nature. It can be solved only on the basis of considerations of an *axiological* nature.

---

[7] This principle is a consequence of what might be called the Jephthah Theorem of deontic logic—alluding to the story of Jephthah in the Book of Judges. For further comments on the theorem and on the notions of conflict of obligation and predicament, cf. my *Essay in Deontic Logic and the General Theory of Action*, North-Holland Publishing Co., Amsterdam, 1968, pp. 78ff.

By these I mean considerations relating to the question, whether it is *worse* (a greater bad or evil) to break the promise to do *p* than to do the forbidden thing *p*. It may be doubted, whether a general answer to the question can be given.

IX

Is it true that we ought to keep our promises? Ought we really to keep our promises? Whence, if from any source at all, does the obligation to keep promises get its "binding force", its "validity"? I shall say that these and similar questions refer, in a confused and unprecise way, to the problem of the *foundation* of the obligation to keep promises.[8]

This problem, as far as I can see, presents two rather different aspects. I shall here allude to them with the two questions "*Ought* promises to be kept?" and "*Must* I do *p*, if I have promised to do it?" respectively. The first question refers to the (general) obligation to keep promises, the second (directly or primarily) to the obligation to do a particular thing on account of having promised to do it.

Ordinary usage does not maintain a *sharp* distinction between the sense of "ought to" and "must". A distinction can, however, be made and is important to observe.

I shall say that something *must be done*, when doing this is (causally) necessary for the attainment of some end. I shall call such necessity of action a *practical necessity*. The question, whether I must do *p*, if I have promised to do it, is thus a question whether promise-keeping here is a practical necessity (with a view to some end).

A useful mode of attacking the question, whether keeping his word is a practical necessity for the giver of a particular promise, is to consider what the consequences would be of a breach of promise. If the consequences are something, which the promisor shuns, would not want to befall him, then it is necessary for him to keep his word in order to escape this evil. (Whether keeping his word is also sufficient for the attainment of this end, is, of course, another question.)

It is clear that a breach of promise *may*, in the individual case, not affect the welfare of the giver of the promise at all. It is also clear, however, that it may affect his welfare considerably—and in various ways. The party, whom he has wronged, may try to revenge himself. Or he will perhaps resort to the aid of legal justice to force the promisor to keep his word or to punish him for not having kept it. Even if the giver of the promise has to fear neither of these evils, he may yet by not keeping his word risk "the penalty of never being trusted again"—to quote Hume's words.

---

[8] On the obligation to keep promises, see also the essay on the foundation of norms in this volume, above, pp. 80ff.

The penalty of never being trusted again could also be called excommunication from further participation in the practice (institution) of promising. Excommunication is a *penalty*, i.e. an evil for the individual concerned, only provided participation is a *benefit*. To most men participation is a benefit, permanent forfeiture of which will make their lives most unhappy (cf. Section X). The facts that forfeiture is not always permanent and that it is not always consequent upon a single breach of promise, tend to make people forgetful of the severity of being refused the benefits of participation in the practice of promising.

Considerations, when they arise, as to whether a particular promise must be kept, are usually conducted in terms of the *risks* (probabilities) of various unwanted consequences of a breach of promise. An agent may be prospectively willing to take risks, which he retrospectively regrets having taken. He may come to think that he should have kept his word, considering what happened as a consequence of his breaking his promise. He had been judging falsely of a practical necessity.

To try to argue that *every* promisor is *always* under a practical necessity to keep his word does not seem realistic. To think that *practically all* agents are for *the most part* well advised to keep their promises is good common sense.

X

Consider the following situation. A person maintains that he ought to do a certain thing. We ask him: "Why is it that you ought to do this?". He answers: "I have promised to do it."

There is a way of understanding "ought to" here, which is such that the above answer (if truthful) to the above question would be *completely* satisfying. On this understanding of "ought to", if the questioner went on and asked "Why is it that you ought to do that which you have promised to do?", we could say that he has not grasped what promising *is*. Promises *ipso facto*, by their very nature, ought to be kept.

If, however, the questioner went on and asked "Ought you really to keep your promise?", he *could* also be asking something, which is fully compatible with understanding the nature ("meaning") of promising. He could be asking, for example, whether the other man *must*, whether it is necessary for him to keep his word. He would then be viewing the question of promise-keeping in a new perspective. He would be asking, whether that which is, of course, an obligation is *also*, perchance, a practical necessity.

When the question "Ought promises to be kept?" is so understood that "I promised" is a completely satisfactory answer to the question "Why ought you to do this?", we view the obligation to keep promises as *inherent* in the nature of promising. It is a feature of the concept. The obligation, we could also say, exists as a necessary part of the institution or practice of promising.

Consider now a particular promise, of which it is true that the giver of the promise is not under a practical necessity of doing what he has promised, that he *need not* do this. We can then still say truly that he is under an obligation to do what he promised, that he *ought* to do this. The question, however, may be raised: Is saying this anything "over and above" stating the bare fact that the agent has promised, given his word to do a certain thing? If not, we may feel that the obligation to keep a promise, when lacking a foundation in the practical necessity of action, is only an "empty word" and has no "binding force".

The feeling of uneasiness, which may be felt here, is relieved, I think, by further considerations pertaining to the *interests*, which are associated with the obligation to keep promises, generally and in the particular case. Of one such interest we have just been talking. This is the interest which a man may have to escape some bad thing, consequent upon a breach of promise, and which sometimes assumes the force of a practical necessity of keeping one's word.

The evil which a man may have to suffer as a consequence of not having kept his word, is inflicted upon him by the actions and reactions of other men. It is in the nature of things that a man should be interested in avoiding that which is, for him, an evil. But why should men be willing and even anxious to visit promise-breakers with evil?

It will here be necessary to remind of the fact that the obligation to keep a particular promise is an obligation of the peculiar kind, which I have called an *obligation to a person*. The fulfilling of an obligation of this kind, we have said, represents an *interest* (a good) to the person, to whom the obligated agent has this obligation. If the obligation is not fulfilled, the "wronged" party suffers disappointment. The bad of suffering such disappointment is sometimes minimal. But sometimes it amounts to grave damage.

It is because the objects of promises are of value to the promise-receivers that sharing in the practice of promising is a good thing and exclusion from the practice a bad thing to people. The good of participating in the practice of promising and the bad or evil of being punished for breaking one's word by becoming excommunicated from the practice are thus *correlative values*.

It is because sharing in the practice of promising is a good thing that people are interested in *making others keep* their word. This they try to accomplish in various ways: by teaching children the importance of being trustworthy, by urging people to keep their word, sometimes also by calling for the arm of the law to enforce the obligation, and by the punitive measure of not trusting the faithless again. These and similar measures to make people keep their promises "institute" promise-keeping as an *obligation*, as something which we think *ought to be done*.

The interest which men have in making others keep their word I shall call the *foundation* of the obligation to keep promises. I have tried to show, how this interest and the interest, which makes dutiful action a practical necessity, are linked with one another thanks to the correlative value of the good of participation in and the bad of excommunication from the practice of promising.

On the Logic of Norms and Actions

1. Deontic Logic as Modal Logic—Analogies and Disanalogies

I

In what may be called the prehistory of modern deontic logic one can distinguish two main traditions. The one goes back (at least) to Leibniz, the other (at least) to Bentham.[1]

Bentham entertained a grand idea of a Logic of Imperation or of the Will. It was going to be a new branch of logic, "untouched by Aristotle". Bentham did not develop it systematically. This was left to the Austrian Ernst Mally in his work *Grundgesetze des Sollens, Elemente der Logik des Willens* (1926). Mally seems not to have been aware of Bentham's pioneer work which remained practically unnoticed until the late mid-twentieth century. As an aftermath to Mally's work one may regard discussions in the 1930s and early 1940s on the logical nature of imperatives—including some constructive efforts at developing a Logic of Imperatives and of Optatives.

The discipline which now goes under the established name Deontic Logic did not evolve in the tradition of Bentham and Mally. It was born as an off-shoot of Modal Logic. None of its founding fathers, however, seems to have been aware that their leading idea had been anticipated, quite explicitly, by Leibniz who in the *Elementa juris naturalis* (1672) wrote: "Omnes ergo Modalium complicationes, transpositiones, oppositiones ab Aristotele et Interpretatibus demonstrate, ad haec nostra Iuris Modalia non inutiliter transferri possunt". With these words the birth of deontic logic can truly be said to have been announced.

II

By the *Iuris Modalia* Leibniz meant the deontic categories of the obligatory (*debitum*), the permitted (*licitum*), the prohibited (*illicitum*), and the facultative (*indifferentum*). And by saying that to the deontic modalities may be transferred all the "complications, transpositions, and oppositions" of Aristotelian modal logic, Leibniz was in the first place thinking

---

[1] Actually, the history of the formal logical study of norms and normative concepts can be traced back (at least) to the fourteenth century. See the interesting essay by Simo Knuuttila "Deontic Logic in the Fourteenth Century", in *New Studies in Deontic Logic*, ed. by Risto Hilpinen; D. Reidel Publishing Co., Dordrecht, Holland, 1981.

of the relations of interdefinability which obtain between the traditional (alethic) modalities.

I shall refer to these observations by Leibniz as *analogies of interdefinability* between alethic and deontic modalities. The analogies can be exhibited in the following table:

it is possible, M	it is permitted, P
it is impossible, $I = \sim M$	it is forbidden, $F = \sim P$
it is necessary, $N = I \sim$	it is obligatory, $O = F \sim$
$\quad = \sim M \sim$	$\quad = \sim P \sim$

We shall omit from special consideration here the category of the facultative, i.e. the neither-obligatory-nor-forbidden, answering to the alethic category of the contingent. Then interdefinability, as shown by the table, means that one can, taking *one* of the concepts as basic or primitive, through a process of "double negation" define or engender the other concepts of the triad. Which of the three one regards as *Grundbegriff* is indifferent.

As far as the interrelatedness of the basic deontic categories is concerned, Bentham seems to have been of the same opinion as Leibniz. But Bentham did not note the analogies with the modal concepts. The first author to study in detail both the analogies and the interdefinability relations seems to have been the Austrian Alois Höfler in a paper written in the 1880s but not published until 1917.[2]

III

The analogies of interdefinability do not, by themselves, suffice for the construction of an (interesting system of) deontic logic. To this end some logical laws or principles governing the deontic notions must be found or suggested.

The additional observation which gave a decisive impetus to my efforts in the area, concerned the distributive properties of the alethic and deontic modal operators. For the notion of possibility we have the distribution law $M(p \vee q) \leftrightarrow Mp \vee Mq$. It seemed to me then that an analogous principle holds for the notion of permission (permittedness). Accepting this *and* the analogies of interdefinability gives us the following *analogies of distributivity*:

$M(p \vee q) \leftrightarrow Mp \vee Mq$	$P(p \vee q) \leftrightarrow Pp \vee Pq$
$I(p \vee q) \leftrightarrow Ip \,\&\, Iq$	$F(p \vee q) \leftrightarrow Fp \,\&\, Fq$
$N(p \,\&\, q) \leftrightarrow Np \,\&\, Nq$	$O(p \,\&\, q) \leftrightarrow Op \,\&\, Oq$

---

[2] "Abhängigkeitsbeziehungen zwischen Abhängigkeitsbeziehungen", *Sitzungsberichte der kaiserlichen Akademie der Wissenschaften, Philosophisch-historische Klasse*, **181**, 1917.

The first to pay attention to the distributive properties of the deontic concepts was, as far as I know, Mally. In Mally's *Deontik* the law (answering to) $O(p \& q) \leftrightarrow Op \& Oq$ holds. The analogy with modal logic, however, passes unnoted.

IV

By the *Minimal System* of deontic logic, I shall understand a calculus which can be characterized syntactically as follows:

Every tautology of propositional logic (PL) is a valid formula of the system when the propositional variables are replaced by deontic formulas. The sole (additional) axiom of the system is the formula $P(p \lor q) \leftrightarrow Pp \lor Pq$. The definitions $F =_{df} \sim P$ and $O =_{df} \sim P \sim$ are accepted. In addition to the usual inference rules of substitution and detachment we have a transformation principle to the effect that provably equivalent PL-formulas are intersubstitutable *salva veritate* in deontic formulas. This last principle may be regarded as a version of what is sometimes also called Leibniz's Law.

Bentham regarded it as a law of his Logic of the Will that if something is obligatory (Bentham says "commanded") then it is not also prohibited. In our symbolism above: $OP \rightarrow \sim Fp$. In the minimal system this is equivalent with the formula $\sim (Op \& O \sim p)$ which is equivalent with $Op \rightarrow Pp$ which again is equivalent with $Pp \lor P \sim p$. By virtue of the distribution axiom, finally, this last is equivalent with Pt where "t" stands for an arbitrary tautology of PL.

Bentham's Law is also valid in Mally's *Deontik*. Mally, moreover, recognized the role Leibniz's Law plays in the proofs of deontic theorems. His system, one could say, has all the ingredients of a "sound" deontic logic, but also contains additional ingredients which, unfortunately, from a formal point of view vitiate the whole undertaking. The "unsound" features of Mally's system have to do with his way of treating *conditional* obligations.

The system of deontic logic which I presented in my 1951 paper[3] was the Minimal System embellished with one additional axiom. This was the formula $Pp \lor P \sim p$. I coined for it the name Principle of Permission. Accepting the relations of interdefinability this, as we have just seen, is but another form of what above I called Bentham's Law.

For the Minimal System embellished with Bentham's Law I shall, *faute de mieux*, propose the name the *Classical System* of deontic logic.

Any normal modal logic accepts as valid the formulas $Mp \lor M \sim p$ and $\sim (Np \& N \sim p)$ and their "contracted" form Mt. Thus Bentham's Law too has an analogue in modal logic.

---

[3] "Deontic Logic", *Mind*, **60**, 1951.

From the Classical System we reach what I shall, following Bengt Hansson,[4] call the *Standard System* by making the following two modifications: The deontic operators are understood as operating on and resulting in propositions. Leibniz's Law is replaced by a stronger inferential principle which says that, if *f* is a valid formula of the deontic system, then *Of* is so too.

Both modifications strengthen the analogy with modal logic. The analogue of the inferential principle allowing the inference from *f* to *Of* is in modal logic known as the Rule of Necessitation.

The Standard System may be said to stretch the analogy between modal and deontic logic to its utmost limit. The only significant deviation lies in the fact that whereas traditional modal logic accepts as valid the formulas $p \rightarrow Mp$ and $Np \rightarrow p$, a "sound" deontic logic must reject their analogues $p \rightarrow Pp$ and $Op \rightarrow p$. It has to rest content with the weaker forms of those analogical formulas which are represented by the Principle of Permission and by Bentham's Law respectively.

When building the Classical System I took the view that the deontic operators operated on names of (categories or types of) action, and not on propositions. In the Classical System, therefore, "mixed" formulas, such as e.g. $p \rightarrow Oq$, or "higher order" formulas such as e.g. *OPp*, were not regarded as well-formed. To logicians these restrictions may seem impediments to the development of deontic logic. Their removal within the Standard System has gained more or less universal acceptance. There may nevertheless have existed some good and serious reasons against taking the step from the Classical to the Standard System—and even against the step from the Minimal to the Classical System.

V

Suggestive and, from a formal point of view, fertile as the analogies between the alethic and the deontic modalities may be, they are also open to doubts. The more I have reflected on the nature of norms and normative concepts, the stronger have these doubts grown with me. I shall next mention some points on which one may focus such doubts.

(a) Disanalogies of interdefinability

It seems much more plausible to regard the operators (concepts) *O* and *F* as being interdefinable than to regard *P* and *O*, or *P* and *F*, as being so. One can ask: is permission to do something simply the absence of prohibition to do this same thing? That permission should entail the absence of a "corresponding" prohibition seems clear. But does the reverse entailment

---

hold? Is not permission something "over and above" mere absence of prohibition?

This question is in fact a classic problem of legal philosophy and theory. Do permissions (rights) have an independent status in relation to prohibitions (obligations) or not? I think it is correct to say that opinions continue to be *very much* divided on this issue.

To say that prohibition to do is tantamount to obligation to forbear (omit) one and the same thing, and to say that obligation to do is tantamount to prohibition to forbear, seems uncontroversial. What is not clear and uncontroversial, however, is whether the relation between doing and forbearing (omission of action) is simply the relation between something and its *negation*. This is a grave problem for a "logic of action".

(b) Disanalogies of distributivity

Doubts concerning the analogies of interdefinability may, but need not, affect the analogies of distributivity. One might, for example, reject the formulas $\sim Fp \rightarrow Pp$ and $\sim O \sim p \rightarrow Pp$ and yet regard disjunctive permissions as being disjunctively distributable and conjunctive obligations as conjunctively distributable. In building a calculus or system of deontic logic one would then have to lay down independently in axioms the distributive properties of permissions and obligations respectively.

One can, however, for other reasons doubt the analogies of distributivity. Since its beginnings, deontic logic has been beset by some "anomalies" or "paradoxes". The best known and most discussed one is Ross's Paradox. Two others are the Paradox of Derived Obligation and the Paradox of the Good Samaritan. The last two ones may be regarded as variant formulations of the first. And all three have their roots in the formulas $O(p \& q) \rightarrow Op$ or, alternatively, $Pp \rightarrow P(p \lor q)$ of "traditional" deontic logic—whether in the "minimal", the "classical", or the "standard" version. Therefore, in a deontic logic which rejects the implication from left to right in the equivalence $O(p \& q) \leftrightarrow Op \& Oq$ while retaining the implication from right to left, the "paradoxes" would not appear.[5]

Analogous "paradoxes" are known from modal logic. The Paradox of Derived Obligation, for example, is an analogue in deontic logic to what is known as the Paradox of Strict Implication in modal logic. But the conflict between "intuition" and "formalism" of which the paradoxes are symptomatic seems to be much more serious in deontic than in modal logic. In this fact I would see an indication that the analogy between the two logics is not as perfect as many people have thought.

On a normal understanding of the word "or" in normative language, disjunctive permissions are *conjunctively*, and not *disjunctively*, distribut-

---

[5] See A. Stranzinger, "Ein paradoxenfreies deontisches System", *Forschungen aus Staat und Recht, Band 43: Strukturierungen und Entscheidungen im Rechtsdenken*, 1978.

able. If someone is told that he may work *or* relax this would normally be understood to mean that he is permitted to work but also permitted to relax: it is up to him to *choose* between the two alternatives. Disjunctive permissions of this character I have called Free Choice Permissions.[6] Opinions on their logical status differ considerably. Some logicians think that they only apparently conflict with the distribution law $P(p \lor q) \leftrightarrow Pp \lor Pq$. Another attitude is to reject, at this point, the analogy with modal logic and build a deontic logic which incorporates a distribution principle $P(p \lor q) \leftrightarrow Pp \& Pq$.[7] Such a deontic logic, however, will have to differ in many other features as well from the traditional systems.

(c) Disanalogies in the rules of inference

In a "normal" modal logic the contradiction is pronounced impossible and the tautology necessary. A "normal" modal logic, moreover, accepts the Rule of Necessitation (above p. 103) and all tautologies of PL. From the Rule of Necessitation and the distribution principles of the modal operators one easily derives Leibniz's Law (above p. 102). Since $p \lor \sim p$ is a theorem, $N(p \lor \sim p)$ is a theorem, too. By virtue of Leibniz's Law and the interdefinability of the modal operators, Nt and $\sim M \sim t$ are theorems. However, taking $N(p \lor \sim p)$ or $\sim M(p \& \sim p)$ as *axioms*, one can, with the aid of Leibniz's Law, derive the Rule of Necessitation.

What I have called the "standard" system of deontic logic accepts the deontic analogue of the Rule of Necessitation. That which is, in deontic logic, provably true is also obligatory. This always seemed to me highly counterintuitive, sheer nonsense. Most logicians, however, seem willing to swallow the absurdity—presumably for reasons of formal elegance and expediency. I cannot regard this as an acceptable ground. The "classical" system, therefore, did not accept the necessitation rule and, since it accepted Leibniz's Law, it did not regard Ot, the deontic analogue of Nt, as logically true. This still seems to me a sound attitude.[8]

(d) In standard modal logic

Here, the operators operate on propositions. The expressions are read "It is possible (impossible, necessary) *that* . . . ". The place of the blank is taken by a descriptive *sentence*. The deontic phrase "it is permitted (forbidden, obligatory)" is sometimes, in ordinary parlance, continued "that . . . ". Equally often, however, or maybe more often, it is continued "to . . . ".

In "it is permitted to . . . " the place of the blank is taken by a *verb* (or

---

[6] *An Essay in Deontic Logic and the General Theory of Action*, p. 22 and *passim*.

[7] This is done in my paper "Normenlogik" in *Normenlogik*, ed. by H. Lenk, Verlag Dokumentation, Pullach bei München, 1974.

[8] However, as the reader will see from the next essay "Norms, Truth, and Logic" I have since come to take a different view of the acceptability of the "obligatoriness of tautologies". (1983).

verb-phrase) for (a category or type of) *action* or *activity*. For example: "to smoke" or "to walk on the grass".

As mentioned above (p. 103), in my first effort to build a deontic logic I regarded the variables in the deontic formulas as standing for *names* of actions. This suggests yet a third reading of the deontic operators. By names of action one could understand nouns such as "smoking" or "trespassing". On this conception, *Pp* might be a schematic representation for "smoking permitted", and *Fp* for "trespassing prohibited". It is feasible to think, however, that such phrases can be translated into the idiom using verbs for actions. "Smoking (is) permitted" and "it (one) is permitted to smoke" seem to say very much the same thing.

The readings of the deontic operators with "that" and with "to" respectively may be said to answer to two different types of deontic logic. The one is a logic of that which ought to, may or must not *be*, and the second a logic of that which ought to, may or must not *be done*. To use a terminology which has become established in German, it is a difference between a deontic logic of the *Sein-Sollen* (*-Dürfen*) and the *Tun-Sollen* (*-Dürfen*) type.[9] The Classical System was intended to be a logic of the *Tun-Sollen-*; the Standard System is by its very nature a logic of the *Sein-Sollen*-type. It follows from what has been said above that only a deontic logic of the second type *can* preserve a perfect analogy with modal logic.

It is problematic whether deontic sentences prefixing the operators to verbs of action can be "translated" into sentences prefixing the operators to sentences. Consider, for example, the sentences "it is permitted to smoke" and "it is permitted that everyone smokes". It is doubtful whether they mean the same. Another rendering of the first sentence might be "everyone is permitted to smoke"—replacing the impersonal "it" by the universal quantifier "everyone". This sentence then says that permission is given to everyone. But the sentence "it is permitted that everyone smokes" seems to say that a certain state of affairs is allowed, *viz.* the one when everyone is (maybe at the same time) smoking. This is something different from permission given to everyone.

There is of course no objection to thinking that the variables *p*, *q*, etc. of the Standard System represent sentences describing actions ("action sentences"). But this by itself, as seen from the above considerations, does not mean that the *Sein-Sollen* nature of the Standard System could capture and do justice to the *Tun-Sollen* logic which the Classical System intended to formalize. As a formal system, the Classical System is much poorer than the Standard System. But from the point of view of intended content the former aims at embracing something which seems out of reach of the latter.

In the third part of the present paper I shall try to sketch a new type of

---

[9] On this distinction more will be said in the next essay. See below, pp. 196–209.

deontic logic which I hope will do justice to the intentions implicit in my first venture into the subject. But first we must say something more about action.

2. On Action Sentences and the Logic of Action

I

As the basic type of action sentence one may regard one which says that an agent *a* on an occasion *o* does a certain thing *p*. The content of such a sentence can often be viewed, alternatively, under two aspects. I shall call them the aspect of *achievement* and the aspect of *process*. The two aspects are related, loosely, to the ideas of *making* and *doing* respectively. They are also related to the distinction between *act(ion)* and *activity*.

a on *o* opens a door, say. By his activity he achieves the opening of the door and it is, at least for a short time, open. What he thus achieves is the *result* of his action in opening the door. He makes the result come about, happen. (Whether we think of the result as the *event* of the door's opening or as the *state* of its being open is, for present purposes, immaterial.)

The connection between an action and its result is *intrinsic*. Had the door not opened, the agent would not have opened the door; this is "logically true".

The opening of the door makes a creak and the noise wakes a sleeping child, say. These effects of the result of the action are also called *consequences* of the action. The connection between an action and its consequences is *extrinsic*.

The phrase "the opening of the door" is ambiguous. The process denoted can be *the door's opening*, the fact that the door opens. This can be the achieved result of an action. But it may also come about independently of action, as when the wind blows the door open. The process, however, can also be *the agent's opening the door*. This consists, for example, in his seizing the handle, pressing it down, and pushing. These are *bodily movements* and *muscular activity* displayed by the agent on the occasion of his acting. I shall call them, for short, *bodily activity*. By "the action process" I shall mean the bodily activity involved in the performance of the action.

Every action which can be viewed under the aspect of achievement also presents an aspect of process. But some actions seem to consist solely in bodily activity, for example running or walking. They need not "result" in anything, produce any state in the world which remains, at least for a short time, once the activity has ceased.

It may be argued, however, that also such "pure activities" can be viewed under an aspect of achievement. The activity of running, for example, manifests itself in the transportation of a human body through a stretch of space. That a body was thus transported is an achievement which may be said to have resulted from the activity. Moving a limb, e.g. raising one's arm, results in a change of position of the limb in question. In the activity of moving a limb "back and forth" this position is restored but the (repeated) transportation of the limb through a stretch of space has been achieved. These observations seem to support a view according to which "pure activity" also presents an aspect of achievement and result. But whether this is a correct view or not I shall not try to decide here.

I shall use the symbol $[p]$ (a, o) as a schematic representation of the sentence that a certain agent on a certain occasion does a certain thing. The symbol "p" will have a different significance, depending upon whether we view what is being said in the sentence under the aspect of achievement or under that of process. When the sentence is viewed under the aspect of achievement, "p" is a schematic representation of a *sentence* describing either some state of affairs or some event, for example that the door is open or that it is opening. When again the sentence is viewed under the aspect of process, "p" is a schematic representation of a *verb* or verb-phrase denoting some type of action or activity, for example door-opening.

Adopting the achievement point of view, the schema $[p]$ (a, o) may be read "a on o makes (it so) that p". Adopting the process point of view, the reading could be "a on o is p'ing".

It should be noted that the sentence represented by "p" in our schema does not express a true or false proposition, but describes something which I propose to call a *generic* state or event. A generic state (event) is one which may or may not obtain (occur) on a given occasion o. That the state, e.g. that this door is open, obtains on the occasion o is a true or false proposition.

II

The meaning of $\sim [p]$ (a, o) is obvious, both on the achievement and the process view of action sentences. If, for example, $[p]$ (a, o) says that a on o opens the door, then $\sim [p]$ (a, o) says that a on o does *not* do this. On the achievement view this means that the agent does not make the door open—and on the process view that he does not engage in the bodily activity of door-opening.

Negation, however, need not be of the whole schema. It can also be of the part "p" in it. If "p" stands for "the door is open" (or for "the door is opening"), then "$\sim p$" stands for "the door is not open(ing)", i.e. it says that the door is (stays) closed. This is entirely obvious. If, however, "p" stands for "opening the door", how shall we then understand "$\sim p$" or the phrase "not-opening the door"? This is not immediately clear since the phrase can hardly be said to have a settled place within ordinary usage.

We need not, however, reject it as meaningless. It can be understood as another, somewhat "primitive", way of saying that the agent in question abstains from or *omits* opening the door. As far as he is concerned, he leaves the door closed, lets it remain closed.

One could say that, on the achievement conception, the symbolic form $[\sim p]$ (a, o) signifies the un-doing of a certain existing state of affairs or its suppression on an occasion when otherwise it would come to be, and that, on the process conception, $[\sim p]$ (a, o) signifies omission to engage in a certain activity.

As seen, it is possible to give a sense to the negation-sign when it stands in front of a verb or verb-phrase. It is obvious that "and" and "or" may be used for joining verbs (for example, "read and write", "read or write"). Junctors applied to sentences expressing true or false propositions, junctors applied to sentences describing generic states or events, and junctors applied to verbs or verb-phrases should be distinguished from one another. It cannot be taken for granted that they all behave in the same way logically. But we shall nevertheless use here *the same symbols* for the three kinds of junctor.

III

The notion of *omission* of action is notoriously tricky. Omission is a non-action—and yet it is, at the same time, a "mode of action or of conduct". It is something for which an agent can be held responsible. Omissions are *imputed* to agents. A logic of action, clearly, has to take this into account and treat omission as something different from mere *not* doing something.

It may be suggested that omission could be defined in terms of not doing and the notions of *ability* ("can do") and *opportunity*. On this view, *a* omitted to do a certain thing on *o* if he could have done this thing but did not do it. The expression of this view in a symbolic language requires some kind of "modal operator". If $M[p]$ (a, o) means that *a* can do *p* on *o*, then $M[p]$ (a, o) & $\sim [p]$ (a, o) says that *a* on *o* omits doing it.

The notion of omission thus defined may be called "omission in the widest sense". In ordinary language, the word "omission" would hardly be used for a good many omissions in this widest sense. On most occasions there are innumerable things which I could do then but which I do not do simply because it does not occur to me to do them. (They do not fall within what may be called my "horizon of intentionality" on *o*.)[10] Normally we should not say that I omitted to do these things then. But if I had a *reason* for doing or was *expected* to do some of the things, for example because it

---

[10] On this notion see *Freedom and Determination*, p. 25 and *passim*. Cf. also the related idea of a "preference horizon" in the essay "The Logic of Preference Reconsidered" in the second volume of my *Philosophical Papers*.

was my duty or because I had promised to, then we may say that I omitted what I did not do. Such omission is often called *neglect*. If again, upon deliberation, I decide not to do some action, we call the omission *forbearance*, sometimes also *refrainment* or *abstention*.

IV

For sentences of the schematic type $[p]$ (a, o) one can build a calculus, "Logic of Action". Such calculus is "based" on ordinary propositional logic (PL) in the sense that all tautologies of PL are theorems of the calculus when action sentences are substituted for the variables (in the formulas of PL). The inference rules are those of PL, i.e. Substitution and Detachment, *and no others.*[11]

When action sentences are being viewed under the aspect of process the following four principles intuitively seem valid:

A1.　$[\sim p]\,(a, o) \rightarrow \sim [p]\,(a, o)$
A2.　$[\sim \sim p]\,(a, o) \leftrightarrow [p]\,(a, o)$
A3.　$[p\,\&\,q]\,(a, o) \leftrightarrow [p]\,(a, o)\,\&\,[q]\,(a, o)$
A4.　$[\sim (p\,\&\,q)]\,(a, o) \leftrightarrow [p\,\&\sim q]\,(a, o) \vee [\sim p\,\&\,q]\,(a, o)$
　　　　　　　　　　　　　　　　　$\vee\,[\sim p\,\&\sim q]\,(a, o)$

The question may be raised whether one could not replace the fourth axiom by a weaker distribution principle to the effect that $[\sim (p\,\&\,q)]\,(a, o) \leftrightarrow [\sim p]\,(a, o) \vee [\sim q]\,(a, o)$. But consider what it means that an agent *omits* engaging in two different activities on one and the same occasion. The answer most in agreement with intuition seems to be that this is to omit engaging in both or omit engaging in one of them *while engaging in the other*. For example: What is it to omit (abstain from) reading-and-writing? The best answer seems to be that one reads but neglects to write or writes but neglects to read or neglects the one as well as the other. Why not simply say that it is to omit at least one of the two activities? One could say this—but it may strike one as "unnatural". For it would mean that if an agent on some occasion omitted to read, which, say, he was expected to be doing, then one could say *a fortiori* that he omitted to read-and-write although perhaps he was not expected to be writing or he cannot write or could not have written on that occasion. We need not try to decide which one of the two views on the nature of a "conjunctive omission" is the right one. If one takes the more restrictive view which also strikes me as the "natural" one, then one would have to accept for action sentences when viewed under the aspect of process the principle A4 above.

---

[11] There is a somewhat fuller description of this type of action logic in my papers "Deontic Logic Revisited", *Rechtstheorie*, **4**, 1973 and "Handlungslogik" in the anthology *Normenlogik*, ed. by H. Lenk, Verlag Dokumentation, Pullach bei München, 1974.

We may define the notion of a "disjunctive activity" as follows:

$$[p \vee q] \, (a, o) = {}_{df} \, [\sim (\sim p \, \& \sim q)] \, (a, o)$$

An agent is engaged in the disjunctive activity of, say, reading or writing, if, and only if, he omits the conjunctive omission of both.[12] By virtue of A4 and A2 this is equivalent to saying that the agent engages in both or engages in the one while omitting to engage in the other.

The calculus of action sentences with the axioms A1–A4 is decidable and semantically complete.[13] Every formula of the calculus may be shown to be provably equivalent with a formula which is a truth-functional compound of "constituents" of the simple types [ ] (a, o) or [$\sim$] (a, o) where the place of the blank is held by a single variable p, q, etc. Truth-values may be distributed over the constituents in a truth-table subject to the sole restriction that constituents [ ] (a, o) and [$\sim$] (a, o) of the *same* variable cannot both be given the value "true". This is a simple consequence of A1 or of the truth that one and the same agent cannot on one and the same occasion both commit and omit the same thing. If, observing this restriction, a formula gets the value "true" for all distributions of truth-values over its constituents, it will be said to be an action(-sentence) *tautology*. All such tautologies are provable in the calculus and provable formulas of the calculus are action(-sentence) tautologies.

We may introduce quantification into our action logic. This can happen in steps. We can quantify the sentences with regard to agents and let the sentences refer to the same (arbitrary) occasion o; or we can quantify them with regard to the occasion and let the sentences refer to one and the same (arbitrary) agent a; or we can combine these two modes of quantification. Finally, the calculus may also become quantified in the "proposition-like" variables p, q, etc.

For action sentences when viewed under the aspect of achievement one can also build a logic. This will have to have a somewhat more complex structure than the above "logic of action as process". In its fully developed form the variables p, q, etc. would stand not only for sentences describing results of action but also for sentences describing states which are, or are not, transformed through the action. Only then can one, for example, express in the formal system the important distinction between *productive* and *preventive* action.[14]

---

[12] I am indebted to Professor Carlos Alchourrón for a correction of a previous attempt of mine to define the notion of a disjunctive activity.

[13] Cf. the papers mentioned in fn. 11 above.

[14] A logical study of action under the achievement aspect is found in *An Essay in Deontic Logic and the General Theory of Action*, Ch. II. At that stage, however, I did not see clearly the relevance to a logic of action of the distinction between the two aspects of achievement and of process, respectively. For a new attempt, see the next essay in this volume.

V

One can distinguish between act-*categories* or *generic* actions, such as door-opening, murder, or smoking and act-*individuals* or *individual* actions, such as for example the murder of Caesar by Brutus.

Opinions differ on the question whether the deontic attributes *primarily* apply to generic or to individual actions. If one takes the view that they apply primarily to act-individuals, then the question will arise: Do they apply as operators to action-sentences or are they genuine attributes or properties of some individual things ("logical individuals")? Those deontic logicians who have opted for the second alternative in answering the first question have almost invariably opted for the first alternative in answering the second.

The question whether one can make good sense of the conception of actions as logical individuals is not uncontroversial.

Consider the schematic form of a sentence describing an individual action "*a* on *o* does *p*". (The action could be, for example, that of opening a door.) One cannot individuate this as "the action performed by *a* on *o*". It is logically possible to do more than one action on one and the same occasion.[15] From the name of an individual action it must also be plain *what* it was that *a* did on *o*, i.e. we must mention a generic characteristic of the action. The phrase "the opening of the door by *a* on *o*" names an individual action or, in pure schematic form, "the doing of *p* by *a* on *o*".

Individual actions have various properties (attributes, features). The individual action of *a*'s opening a door on *o* has the "property" of (being a case of) door-opening. This is trivial. But when an action is being individuated or identified as an act of a certain category or kind the question will sometimes arise whether it may not also be classified as an action of a certain other category or kind. This question is often a preliminary to evaluating the action or to qualifying it deontically. For example: A child has been ordered to stay at home for the afternoon studying, perhaps as a punishment for a minor offence. It stays at home reading a book. Is this studying? If the child in reading was doing its homework for the school, its activity would probably count as studying. If the reading was of a novel, the child's activity would probably not count as studying. A person spat. Was what he did perhaps an act of insulting somebody? Was the killing of *b* by *a* a case of murder? When such questions are considered

---

[15] The notion of "occasion" is vague. In this there is nothing objectionable. One could make the notion sharper by stipulating that the occasion must be restricted to the time-span of one single action. This would exclude that an agent on some occasion *first* does a certain thing and *then* another. But this restriction would not remove the possibility that at the same time as the agent did a certain thing he also did a certain other thing.

and decided, properties are in a nontrivial sense being attributed to individual actions.

The property which, as we said above, "trivially" belongs to an individual action I shall also call its *essential* property or characteristic. It is the property which we use for *identifying* ("picking out") the act-individual under consideration. Some of the properties which an action may have in addition to its essential characteristic belong to it by virtue of *the way in which* the action was performed.[16] Suppose that the agent opens a door by pressing a button and pulling. Then his action, *viz.* his action of opening the door, is also a case of button-pressing and of pulling. It has these two additional characteristics.

Further additional properties may belong to an action by virtue of its consequences. Let us assume that the agent by opening a door lets cool air into the room. His action is thus also one of cooling the room. It has the property of being a "room-cooling action".

A non-essential property of an action is not necessarily either a causal prerequisite or consequence of its performance. Suppose *a* on *o* is waving his arms. In doing so he might be giving a signal. His action is thus also a case of signalling. It is this because there is a convention giving a "meaning" to the arm-waving.

The two events of a button sinking down and a room getting cool are different events from the event of a door opening. But the event of a pair of arms moving in a certain way is not a different event from the appearance of a certain signal.

Unintended consequences of an action may also constitute properties of the action. The agent who lets cool air into the room by opening the door may, as a consequence, catch a cold. His action is then a cold-giving action.

Which property of a given individual action is singled out as essentially belonging to it, is to a large extent a matter of choice. The choice may depend on our *interest* in the action, on what is *important* about it. The person who opens a window may "primarily" be ventilating a room. The essential property of his action is then that it is a case of room-ventilation. But because of the way the action was done, it was also an action of opening a window—and because of its consequences perhaps also an action of making a person sneeze.

The (causal) consequences of an action will normally materialize some time after the action was performed. At the time of performance it may

---

[16] The "way" in which an action is performed here means an(other) action which is instrumental for the achieving of the result of the first action. This sense of "way" must be distinguished from adverbial modifiers such as (doing something) quickly or silently or well, etc. One could distinguish the two senses as "way" and "mode" (of acting), respectively.

therefore not be clear (known) which (all) the consequences will be. *a* runs over *b* with his car in the street. *b* is badly injured and dies soon after. Medical expertise attributes the death of *b* to the injury. It may be a matter of decision for a court whether *a*'s action of running over *b* should be deemed the *cause* of *b*'s death. But if it is thus regarded, *a* can correctly be said to have killed *b*; *a*'s action of running over *b* was a case of killing a man.

If the running over is regarded as the essential property of *a*'s action under consideration, then this action can be said to acquire a property, *viz.* that of being a killing, which initially it did not possess. If again the killing is regarded as the essential property, then this action may be said initially to have consisted in (causing) a car accident.

Is *a*'s running over *b* and *a*'s killing *b* one and the same action? The result of the action of running over *b* is the event that *b* gets under a car, and the result of the action of killing *b* is that *b* dies. Getting under a car and dying are two different events (even if they take place at the same time). But *a*'s action of running over *b* and his action of killing *b* are one and the same action. Some philosophers would say that they are one and the same action "falling under different descriptions".

At the generic level, i.e. as act categories, running over and killing, door-opening and room-ventilation, etc. are, of course, *different* (types of) *actions*.

Could we not say, therefore, that e.g. the person who ran over a man in the street thereby causing his (later) death performed *two* actions? We can do this if thereby we mean that his (one) individual action on a certain occasion exemplifies two (or more) generic actions. But it is important to distinguish this from the case when a man actually performs two individual actions on one and the same occasion, for example, opens a window and closes a door. Even if those two actions take place simultaneously and not successively they would be two different *individual* actions.

Once it is accepted that actions may be regarded as logical individuals there seem to exist no obstacles of a conceptual nature to regarding also deontic attributes as properties of individual actions. One such property would be permittedness. Actions of a certain category are, let us assume, permitted. Then the performance of an action of this category by a certain agent on a certain occasion may (but need not) have been a permitted individual action (cf. below p. 122).

Not all properties of individual actions, it seems, mark generic actions. Let it be granted that deontic status, e.g., permittedness can be a genuine property of an individual action. This seems plausible. But it does not seem plausible to say that there is a generic action "doing the permitted". One cannot *identify* an individual action as being a case of doing the permitted. It must be identified as a case of doing such and such, *the doing of which is permitted*. Since permittedness cannot be used for identifying individual actions, it cannot be an essential property of an action either. Essential properties can only be those which name act-categories.[17]

As noted above (p. 113), an individual action may be identified, now by one, now by another essential property. It may, for example, be identified as a case of flipping a switch or as a case of illuminating a room or as a case of alerting a prowler who was about to enter the room—to allude to a famous example from the literature in the philosophy of action.[18] Depending upon which property is used for identifying the action, the set of its properties is differently divided into a subset of prerequisites and consequences. If we identify the action as one of illuminating a room, then its being prowler-alerting is a "consequential" property of the action. If again we identify it, as the prowler himself may do, as a prowler-alerting action, then both its being a room-illuminating and a switch-flipping action are accidental properties which belong to the action as its causal prerequisites.

If "two" actions have all their properties in common but different essential properties, are they then "the same" action, or not? It seems to me that we are free to mould our criteria of identity so as to answer the question either by Yes or by No. But I should prefer to answer Yes, and I have a surmise that those who prefer to say No are misled by the fact that the *individual* action under consideration exemplifies several (different) *generic* actions.

VI

Omissions too can be individuated and treated as logical individuals. The individuation of an omission is the identification (labelling) of the conduct of an agent on a certain occasion as an omission to do a certain thing. How is such an identification done? We may verify that a on o did *not* do p. The occasion was one when one could have done p; the occasion in other words provided an opportunity for doing the action. We know, e.g. from previous experience, that a can perform actions of the kind in question, that he has the required ability. If these are established facts, then it is also established that he omitted to do p—in the widest (weakest) sense of "omission" (above p. 109). We can now speak of "the omitting by a on o to do p" as of a logical individual. If "omission" is not understood in the weakest sense but in some stronger sense, such as not doing what one is expected or has a duty to do (above pp. 109f), then these additional criteria too will have to be taken into consideration in determining whether the

---

[17] What is here said of deontic predicates is true also of "moral" predicates of individual actions such as, e.g., an action being "good" or "evil", "courageous", "temperate", or "self-sacrificing". Cf. *The Varieties of Goodness*, pp. 139ff.

[18] This much discussed example was introduced by Donald Davidson in his influential paper "Actions, Reasons and Causes" in *The Journal of Philosophy*, **60**, 1963.

agent should be said to have omitted this or that action on such and such occasion.

An omission of an action is usually "constituted" by the performance of some other action. For example, an agent is engaged in reading and thereby omits turning off the tap from which water is pouring into the bath-tub. As a consequence there is a flood in the bathroom, let us assume. We do not say that by reading he flooded the bathroom. But by omitting to turn off the tap he did so.

The agent's omission to turn off the tap does not "consist" in the *tap* being on (and the water pouring into the bath-tub). It "consists" in *his* reading in combination with the fact that he *could* have turned off the tap on that occasion—maybe even had a reason or was expected to do so ("instead of reading" as we should say).

There is a sense in which omissions can be called causes. What this means is that something, e.g. the tap remaining on, that happens because something else is omitted, e.g. the tap being turned off, causes a third thing, e.g. a flood, to take place.

An omission may have a less definite dating than a "corresponding" action. But in principle actions and omissions are on a par in this regard. The window was closed and *a* opened it at 11:15 a.m. On another occasion, the window remained closed the whole morning and *a* did not open it although he was there and could have opened the window, maybe even was expected to do so. The occasion for his omission to open the window was that (whole) morning.

It does not follow that the agent's opening, say, a door at 11:15 is identical with his omission that whole morning to open the window in the room. But his opening the door at 11:15 also constituted an omission to open the window at 11:15. And this "bit" of his failure to open the window in the course of the entire morning is, as an action individual, identical with his opening the door then.

Omissions can have further properties in addition to being omissions to do so and so. Someone stands by and sees another person drown. The first could have saved the second but omitted to do so. By his omission he became responsible for the death of a person. Depending upon the circumstances, a court may even pronounce his omission a case of murder.

The question may be raised whether an omission must always be "constituted" on the basis of some *other action* which the agent performs. Perhaps it is usually the case that one omits to do something because one is engaged in doing something else. But I do not think that it must be so. An agent need not do anything at all on a given occasion, he may stay completely passive. Then his passivity is omission to do every one of the things which he is able to do and for the doing of which the occasion of his passivity affords an opportunity.

VII

The Logic of Action which was described in outline in Section III is a logic of *action-sentences* of the schematic prototype form "*a* on *o* does *p*". The actions described in such sentences, we have seen, may be regarded as logical individuals, the prototype name form of which is "the doing of *p* by *a* on *o*". Under this conception of actions we get yet another type of Logic of Action. Its objects of study are sentences attributing properties to individual acts. The prototype form of such sentences is "the doing of *p* by *a* on *o* is *A*" where "is *A*" is a schematic representation of such phrases as, for example, "is (a case of) murder" or "is ventilating a room". One can, if one wishes, call such sentences action-sentences too. But then it should be remembered that, unlike the above prototype form of such sentences, they do not say that something or other is being done, but that something or other which was done has a certain characteristic or property.

Similarly, we shall have to count with sentences attributing properties to individual omissions. "The omission of *p* by *a* on *o* is *A*" might say that *a*'s omission to save a person from drowning was, on that occasion, a case of murder.

I shall use *x*, *y*, etc. as variables for individual actions or omissions and *A*, *B*, etc. as schematic representations for names of properties. Names of properties will also be called *predicates*.

The logic of the sentences now under consideration could be regarded as simply a fragment of "classical" (monadic) predicate logic and quantification theory. Then it is of no independent interest as a "logic of action".

There is, however, good reason for studying sentences attributing properties to individual actions within a more "refined" calculus than the traditional predicate calculus. I have elsewhere described this more refined calculus and coined for it the name Logic of Predication.[19] Its characteristic feature is that it allows us to make a distinction between denying that an individual has a certain property and affirming that it lacks a property. The distinction, in other words, is between two kinds of negation, an external negation which is of sentences (propositions) and an internal negation which is of properties. To use Aristotle's example,[20] between something not being white and something being not-white.

---

[19] "Remarks on the Logic of Predication", *Ajatus*, **35**, 1973.

[20] Cf. *Analytica Priora* 52a1–2 and 52a25–. Cf. also my paper "On the Logic of Negation", *Societas Scientiarum Fennica, Commentationes Physico-Mathematicae*, **XXII** (4), 1959, in which originally I introduced and discussed the distinction between the two types of negation, weak and strong, external and internal—which here I distinguish with the aid of the symbols ~ [ ] and [~].

What then is the difference between (simply) not having a property and lacking a property? Roughly speaking: the things which lack a given property fall within the "range" of that property: they *could* have the property in question although in fact they have not got it; things outside the range neither have nor lack the property in question.

This is a rough characterization only and its application to specific properties is, often at least, a matter of decision. It is for us to give a meaning to the distinction in question. This, however, can often be done in a way which seems both enlightening and natural. Thus, for example, that an action is not permitted can be taken to mean that it is forbidden, or it can mean that it simply has no deontic status at all. What is forbidden "lacks" permittedness; an action void of deontic status neither has nor lacks permittedness.

If there are several ways of doing an action and the action is performed in one of the ways to the exclusion of the other, then it lacks the characteristic of being an action of the second kind. For example: Let it be that one can open a door either by pressing a button or by turning a key. Then an individual act of opening this door may (accidentally) have the property of being an act of button-pressing and lack the property, which it could have possessed, of being an act of key-turning.

When an action lacks a property which an action performed by that agent on that occasion could have had, it is, normally, "constitutive" (above, p. 116) of an omission. If a child is reading a novel instead of the text he is supposed to be studying (and which he could have read then), his action of reading also constitutes an *omission* of his to study and can therefore be said to lack the property of being a case of studying.

VIII

The same device as before, square brackets [   ], will enable us to mark the distinction between not having a property and lacking it. Thus $\sim [A]x$ says that x is *not* A, and $[\sim A]x$ says that x is not-A. The axioms of a Logic of Predication are, with minor notational difference, the same as those of our above Logic of Action. One can debate whether a weaker version (cf. above, p. 110) of A4 is valid for predications. Ordinary usage of the negation words is hardly settled, so the answer to the question is a matter of decision. On the whole it seems to me more natural to opt for the strong version. This would mean that a thing is said to lack the conjunction of two properties if, and only if, it belongs in the range of both but has at most one of the two. The axioms are then:

A1. $[\sim A]x \rightarrow \sim [A]x$

A2. $[\sim \sim A]x \leftrightarrow [A]x$

A3. $[A \& B]x \leftrightarrow [A]x \& [B]x$

A4. $[\sim (A \& B)]x \leftrightarrow [A \& \sim B]x \vee [\sim A \& B]x \vee [\sim A \& \sim B]x$

We can now also define the notion of a "disjunctive property": $[A \vee B]x$ $=_{df} [\sim (\sim A \,\&\, \sim B)]x$. By virtue of A4 and A2 it follows that, for example, something has the property "red or round" if it has the one but lacks the other or has both the "simple" properties. But if "red" denotes the colour and "prime" a characteristic of some numbers, then nothing has the property "red or prime". There simply is no such disjunctive property because the range of things which are possibly red and of those which are possibly prime (numbers) have no common member.

The rules of inference are the usual ones of Substitution and Detachment. For quantified sentences one would have two additional axioms:

A5. $(Ex)([A]x \vee [B]x) \leftrightarrow (Ex)[A]x \vee (Ex)[B]x$

A6. $\sim (Ex)([A]x \,\&\, \sim [A]x)$

and an additional inference rule (Leibniz's Law) to the effect that formulas which are provably equivalent on the basis of A1−A4 are interchangeable *salva veritate* in quantified formulas.

3. DEONTIC LOGIC—A NEW APPROACH

I

Let it be agreed that deontic status can, in the genuine sense, be predicated of *individual* actions. I shall use "*F*" for the property of being forbidden, "*O*" for that of obligatoriness, and "*P*" for permittedness.[21] "$[F]x$" may be read "x is forbidden". "$\sim [F]x$" says that x is not forbidden, and "$[\sim F]x$" that x is not-forbidden, that it lacks the property of being forbidden. In what way the second is a stronger statement than the first will be discussed presently.

Undeniably, deontic status is often also attributed to generic actions or categories of action. I shall use the letters "$\mathcal{F}$" to stand for "forbidden", "$\mathcal{O}$" for "obligatory", and "$\mathcal{P}$" for "permitted" when this kind of attribution of deontic status is in question. Under this use, the deontic words are not predicates, but operators. About the difference more will have to be said later.

Let "$[A]x$" say, for example, that x, an individual action, is a case of murder. "$\mathcal{F} A$" then says that murder is forbidden or that it is forbidden to (commit) murder. The *kind of action* called "murder" is forbidden.

The expressions formed by deontic operators followed by a predicate or a molecular compound of predicates denoting generic actions may be used

---

[21] This use of the three letters, *O, F,* and *P,* is different from the use made of them in the first part of the present study and thereby also different from their established use in writings on deontic logic.

to express *norms* (of action). Norms are given to agents acting on certain occasions. Norms can be either for named individual agents, or for agents of a certain category, or for agents unrestrictedly. Analogously, they can be either for specified individual occasions, or for occasions satisfying certain conditions, or for occasions unrestrictedly (which provide opportunities for doing the actions in question).

II

The attribution of deontic status to individual actions will be called *deontic predication*.

What does it mean that an individual action x is a forbidden action? As was indicated above (pp. 114f), one cannot pronounce an individual action forbidden unless one has first identified it as an action of a certain category or kind. Assume that A is the essential property used for identifying the action. If there is a norm $\mathcal{F} A$ prohibiting actions of this kind, then x is (was) a forbidden action. Let us think, however, that there is no such norm. It does not follow that the action then is not forbidden. For x may possess some other property beside A, say B, such that actions of *that* category are forbidden. Then, obviously, x was a forbidden action (to the agent who on some occasion did it).

We can now define what it is for an individual action x to be a forbidden action, as follows: $[F]x = {}_{df}(EX)([X]x \& \mathcal{F} X)$. In short: an action is forbidden if, and only if, it falls under some forbidden category of action. Or, in other words: an agent's action on some occasion is forbidden if, and only if, in performing this action he does something forbidden.

The commission of an individual action is obligatory if, and only if, the action is of a kind such that it is forbidden to omit actions of this kind. Conversely, the omission of an individual action is obligatory if, and only if, the omission is of a kind such that it is forbidden to commit actions of this kind.[22]

This interrelatedness between obligation and prohibition in the terms of commission and omission of actions calls for some further comments.

Consider the following example. The agent a enters a garden on an occasion o. The action is thus the entering of the garden by a on o. This action, let us assume, can be performed in three different ways. One can enter the garden either through one of two gates, g_1 and g_2, or by jumping the fence surrounding it (which is low). It is, however, forbidden to jump the fence. (There are flowers at the foot of the fence.) The agent entered the garden through g_1. His action of entering the garden was thus also a case of passing through g_1. If $x =$ the entering of the garden by a on o, and

---

[22] I am indebted to Carlos Alchourrón and Eugenio Bulygin for useful observations relating to these matters.

A is the "property" of being a passing through g_1, then the action x is A. The action *could* have been a passing through g_2 (B) or a jumping the fence (C). But it *lacked* (p. 118) these two properties. In our symbolism: $[\sim B]x$ and $[\sim C]x$. By virtue of lacking the property C, the action x also constitutes (p. 116) an omission on the part of a to jump the fence on o. If the fact that the action x lacked the property C is considered sufficient ground for saying that a omitted to jump the fence on o, then this *omission* on a's part was obligatory. His action, what he *did*, was not, as such, obligatory. But in entering the garden a behaved *in accordance with duty* since he passed through the gate and observed the prohibition to enter by jumping the fence.

Obligatory omissions of action, i.e. the observance of prohibitions, could also be called "*negative*" obligations.

Assume next that our agent had been commanded to enter the garden and to do so through gate g_1. He was, in other words, not only forbidden to jump the fence but also to pass through g_2. Then his individual action x was an obligatory action by virtue of the fact that it had the property A, *viz.* that of being a case of passing through g_1. Had it lacked this property, it would have been a forbidden action.

Obligatory commissions of action might also be called "*positive*" obligations. Positive obligations often have the character of fulfilling *commands* (orders, imperatives).

As seen the *predicates* "forbidden" and "obligatory" can both be defined in terms of the operator "forbidden". The *operator* "obligatory" again can be defined in terms of the operator "forbidden", thus:

$$\mathcal{O}X =_{df} \mathcal{F} \sim X.$$

The two operators are interdefinable. This is in agreement with the "traditional" view of the matter.

Neither "in logic" nor "in real life" is there anything to prevent one and the same individual action (or omission) from being both obligatory and forbidden. If Jephthah had sacrificed his daughter, his action would have been obligatory because it was the fulfilment of a promise to the Lord, and forbidden because it was homicide. $[F]x \,\&\, [O]x$ is not a contradiction. It says that the individual action x is of a kind which is forbidden but also of a kind which is obligatory. It is forbidden by virtue of one of its characteristics and obligatory by virtue of another.

The *predicates* "forbidden" and "obligatory", be it observed, are *not* interdefinable. This is a simple consequence of the fact that individuals cannot be "negated". "$[F] \sim x$" and "$[O] \sim x$" are meaningless signs.

III

To deny that an individual action is forbidden is to affirm that it does not fall under any kind of action which is forbidden or, in other words, that *all* its features signify not-forbidden properties (of individual actions). In symbols:

$$\sim [F]x \leftrightarrow \sim (EX)([X]x \,\&\, \mathcal{F}X) \leftrightarrow (X)([X]x \rightarrow \sim \mathcal{F}X).$$

Shall we say that an action which is not forbidden is thereby permitted? This is an aspect of the much debated question whether permission is anything "over and above" the absence of prohibition. I think we are well advised to distinguish between things being permitted in the weak sense of simply not being forbidden and things being permitted in some stronger sense. Exactly in what this stronger sense "consists" may be difficult to tell. That which is in the strong sense permitted is, somehow, expressly permitted, subject to norm—and not just void of deontic status altogether.

The *predicate* "strongly permitted" we can define as follows: $[P]x =_{df} (X)([X]x \rightarrow \sim \mathcal{F}X) \,\&\, (EX)([X]x \,\&\, \mathcal{P}X)$. The (in the strong sense) permitted individual action does not fall under any forbidden kind of action but falls under at least one (in the strong sense) permitted one. This definition, of course, does not say anything about the meaning of the (strong) permission-*operator*.

As easily seen from the above, we have $[P]x \rightarrow \sim [F]x$.

IV

Nothing has so far been said to give meaning to the *lack* of the properties *F*, *O*, and *P*. An action *x* of which it is true that $[F]x$ falls under some norm prohibiting a certain kind of action. An action *x* for which it is true that $\sim [F]x$ *need not* fall under any norm at all. But it *may* fall under a permissive or obligating norm. And similarly for the expressions $[O]x$ and $[P]x$ and their negations.

The following suggestions therefore appear natural: That an action *lacks* the property of being forbidden means that it is *not* forbidden but *is* either obligatory or (in the strong sense) permitted. That an action *lacks* the property of being obligatory means that it is *not* obligatory but *is* either permitted or forbidden. That an action *lacks* the property of being permitted, finally, means that it is *not* permitted but *is* either forbidden or obligatory. Thus we have the following three identities:

$$[\sim F]x =_{df} \sim [F]x \,\&\, ([O]x \vee [P]x)$$
$$[\sim O]x =_{df} \sim [O]x \,\&\, ([P]x \vee [F]x)$$
$$[\sim P]x =_{df} \sim [P]x \,\&\, ([F]x \vee [O]x)$$

The identities imply equivalences which may then be distributed into conjunctions of (two) implications. Since, in the Logic of Predication, lack of a property in a thing entails that the thing in question has not got this property, we also have the following relations: $[\sim F]x \rightarrow [O]x \vee [P]x$

and $[\sim O]x \rightarrow [P]x \vee [F]x$ and $[\sim P]x \rightarrow [F]x \vee [O]x$. Moreover, since we already proved $[P]x \rightarrow \sim [F]x$ we can now from the first of the above three identities derive the stronger formula $[P]x \rightarrow [\sim F]x$.

V

I have thus taken the view which seems to be reasonable, that when deontic status is predicated of an individual action, this predication is grounded in the deontic status of some category or kind of action under which this individual action falls. As a consequence, we have to regard the deontic predicates as *secondary* to the deontic operators.

By *normative sentences* I shall understand expressions of the forms $\mathcal{O} -$, $\mathcal{F} -$ and $\mathcal{P} -$ and their molecular compounds, the place of "$-$" being taken by an atomic or molecular predicate (of actions).

Normative sentences will be called *norm-formulations*. A characteristic use of them is for giving (issuing, laying down) norms or rules for human agents. When this use is in question, the normative sentences may be said to *express norms* (cf. above, p. 120).

Normative sentences, however, can also be used for making statements to the effect that there are (have been given or issued) such and such norms or rules. When used in this way, normative sentences express what I propose to call *norm-propositions*.

This ambiguity of usage is a very characteristic and important feature of atomic norm-formulations. Also molecular normative sentences can be used either for expressing norms or for expressing norm-propositions. But their use in the second way seems much more common.

Let there be a prohibition with a disjunctive content (action), $\mathcal{F}(A \vee B)$. Individual actions with the generic characteristic "$A \vee B$" are actions which either have both the characteristics or have the one but lack the other. $[A \vee B]x \leftrightarrow [A \& B]x \vee [A \& \sim B]x \vee [\sim A \& B]x$ is a logical truth in the Logic of Predication. This fact will also be expressed by saying that the predicates $A \vee B$ and $A \& B \vee A \& \sim B \vee \sim A \& B$ are logically equivalent (predicates). We shall lay down the following

> *Principle of Deontic Equivalence*: Logically equivalent predicates are intersubstitutable (*salva veritate*) in norm-sentences (expressing norm-propositions).

By virtue of this principle we may regard $\mathcal{F}(A \vee B) \leftrightarrow \mathcal{F}(A \& B \vee A \& \sim B \vee \sim A \& B)$ as a "truth of deontic logic". Now consider the following: Any individual action by the performing of which an agent may observe or violate this prohibition is an action which can have or lack the characteristic A *and* can have or lack the characteristic B. For this reason it appears natural to say that a prohibition of actions with a disjunctive characteristic is logically equivalent with a conjunction of prohibitions of actions of any one of the various kinds (the individual members of) which fall under the disjunctive kind. Thus we may regard as a logical truth about norms the formula

(1) $\mathcal{F}(A \vee B) \leftrightarrow \mathcal{F}(A \& B) \& \mathcal{F}(A \& \sim B) \& \mathcal{F}(\sim A \& B).$

Let there be a norm to the effect that actions of the category A are forbidden. Then an action x with the property A is a forbidden (individual) action: $\mathcal{F} A \& [A]x \rightarrow [F]x$. This can also be written: $\mathcal{F} A \rightarrow ([A]x \rightarrow [F]x)$. Since this holds for any arbitrary individual action, we also have $\mathcal{F} A \rightarrow (x)([A]x \rightarrow [F]x)$.

The first implication in the formulas, be it observed, does not hold in the reverse direction. It might be the case that all actions of the category A actually are forbidden actions, though not on the ground that they have the property A, but because every one of them happens to belong to *some* (not necessarily the same) forbidden kind of action. We are thus not suggesting, which would be quite wrong, that norms are logically equivalent with general statements about the deontic character of individual actions of certain kinds. (Deontic attributes of individual actions, be it remembered, were defined with the aid of deontic operators.)

From the fact that actions of a certain type are forbidden it thus follows that all individual actions of this type are forbidden; but from the fact that actions of a certain type are permitted it does not follow that all individual actions which are of this type are permitted individual actions. In doing something which is, "as such", permitted an agent may also be doing something which is forbidden. He may, for example, do what he does *in a manner* which is forbidden. Or his action may *lead to* something forbidden.

If a disjunctive action, for example reading or writing, is (generically) permitted, then any individual action which has both the permitted features and no forbidden feature is permitted; and so is also any individual action which has one of the permitted features, is lacking the other, and has no forbidden feature. This seems as good a ground as could possibly be required for holding that

(2) $\mathcal{P}(A \vee B) \leftrightarrow \mathcal{P}(A \& B) \& \mathcal{P}(A \& \sim B) \& \mathcal{P}(\sim A \& B)$

is a norm-logical truth.

We already noted that, if an individual action is permitted, then, by definition, it cannot be a forbidden action. (Above p. 122.) On this basis we may hold that a norm permitting actions of the type A excludes a norm prohibiting actions of that same type:

(3) $\mathcal{P} A \rightarrow \sim \mathcal{F} A.$

What shall we think about the principle $\sim (\mathcal{F} A \& \mathcal{F} \sim A)$ and its equivalent form $\sim (\mathcal{O} A \& \mathcal{O} \sim A)$?

First we must warn against a misunderstanding. $\mathcal{F} A \& \mathcal{F} \sim A$ would not have as a consequence that an agent could not perform anything but forbidden actions, so that whatever the poor man does he sins against the law (norms). Because not all individual actions need be such that they either have or lack the feature *A*. They may not fall within the range of actions of this kind at all. (An agent who does *not* do a certain thing omits doing it, we have said (p. 109), only if, on the occasion in question, he *could* have done it.) Why does nevertheless $\mathcal{F} A \ \& \ \mathcal{F} \sim A$ strike us as absurd? Obviously because, for reasons of logic, an agent who is in position to do an action of the type *A* will, whether he does it or not, commit an offence. Is this a *logical* impossibility? Rather than calling it a logical impossibility we should, I think, say that a normative order which happens to contain those two prohibitions is "irrational"—and that therefore the legislator should, "in the name of rationality", lift at least one of the two prohibitions or make them conditional upon different types of situation when they apply.

A "rational" normative order should therefore satisfy the principle

(4) $\sim (\mathcal{F} A \ \& \ \mathcal{F} \sim A)$.

VI

The formula $\mathcal{P} (A \ \& \ B) \ \rightarrow \ \mathcal{P} A$ cannot be accepted as generally valid in a sound logic of norms. From the permittedness, in the strong sense, of the kind *A & B* of actions, one cannot conclude to the permittedness, in the strong sense, of the kind *A* of actions. But, as we shall see presently (below p. 127), the permittedness of the kind *A & B* is "rationally incompatible" with the forbiddenness of the kind *A* (and the kind *B*). Hence one may from the permittedness, in the *strong* sense, of the kind *A & B* of actions conclude to the permittedness, in the *weak* sense, of the kind *A*.

What then of the distribution formula $\mathcal{O} (A \ \& \ B) \ \leftrightarrow \ \mathcal{O} A \ \& \ \mathcal{O} B$?

Consider first the implication from left to right. This clearly—although contrary to what might be expected from knowledge of "traditional" deontic logic—cannot be a truth of logic. From the fact that an agent is under an obligation to perform actions which exhibit two characteristics, it does not follow that he is under an obligation to perform actions which have (only) one of the characteristics. From the fact that he has been ordered to enter a garden through a certain gate, it does not follow that he ought to enter the garden regardless of how he does it. We need not think that he is forbidden to jump the fence. But if he finds the gate locked and cannot open it, then he cannot conclude "logically" that, because of the order given, he must now jump the fence—a feat which, let us assume, he could perform.

Consider next the implication from right to left. The agent has two obligations. It is not certain that he can satisfy both by performing just one individual action. But it may be that, on some occasions, it is possible to satisfy both obligations by doing just one thing *and in no other way*. Then clearly he is obligated to do this conjunctive action. If, however, he can, on that same occasion, do something which satisfies the one and something else which satisfies the other of his two obligations, then there is no need for him to do the *one* action which satisfies both.

Example: An agent has been asked to see to it that the window and the door in a certain room are shut. If he finds the window open, he ought to shut it—and similarly with the door. If he finds both open, he has to shut both. Perhaps he can do this by operating a mechanism, say by pressing a button. If that is the *only* way this can be done, he ought of course to press the button. But if one can also shut the window and the door separately he is not obligated to do this by pressing the button.

Thus there is not a relation of entailment either way between the conjunction $\mathcal{O}\,A\,\&\,\mathcal{O}\,B$ of two norms and the conjunctive obligation $\mathcal{O}\,(A\,\&\,B)$.

VII

Let it be that $\mathcal{F}\,A$. In the Logic of Predication we prove $(x)([A\,\&\,B]x \to [A]x)$. This means that if an agent performs an action with the two characteristics A and B he will necessarily disobey the norm $\mathcal{F}\,A$. Must we not therefore say that if there is a prohibition to the effect that $\mathcal{F}\,A$ then there is also (implicitly at least) a prohibition to the effect that $\mathcal{F}(A\,\&\,B)$? So that $\mathcal{F}\,A \to \mathcal{F}(A\,\&\,B)$ would be a "law of deontic logic"?

I do not think that there is any clearcut answer Yes or No to this question. From the fact that there are individual actions of the kind A it does not follow that there are any of the kind $A\,\&\,B$. Maybe it is quite impossible, either for reasons of logic or for reasons of human ability, to perform actions with these two characteristics, although it is possible and maybe even easy to perform actions with either one of the characteristics. It seems silly then to say that actions of the (empty) kind $A\,\&\,B$ *are* forbidden, on the grounds that actions of the kind A are forbidden. Maybe the lawgiver would even permit actions of the kind $A\,\&\,B$, if they could be done. (Perhaps possessing the characteristic B would "make good" for the bad which actions with the characteristic A do and which motivated the prohibition $\mathcal{F}\,A$.)

Assume now that actions of the kind $A\,\&\,B$ actually are permitted. We thus have a norm $\mathcal{P}\,(A\,\&\,B)$. Must the lawgiver then repeal the norm $\mathcal{F}\,A$ if there was one before? If there are the two norms $\mathcal{P}(A\,\&\,B)$ and $\mathcal{F}\,A$, then no agent could avail himself of the permission without breaking the prohibition. This is logically true. And this fact would make it, if not "illogical" at least "irrational" to let permission $\mathcal{P}\,(A\,\&\,B)$ and prohibition $\mathcal{F}\,A$ co-exist within the same code of norms. A rational code should therefore satisfy the principle

(5) $\mathcal{P} A \& (x)([A]x \rightarrow [B]x) \rightarrow \sim \mathcal{F} B.$

Since $(x)([A]x \rightarrow [A]x)$ is logically true, it follows from (5) that $\mathcal{P} A \rightarrow \sim \mathcal{F} A$ or that what is (generically) permitted cannot be (generically) forbidden.

Thus the principle (3) which was already accepted as a "truth of deontic logic" is seen to be a consequence of a more general deontic principle to the effect, loosely speaking, that "what follows from the permitted cannot be forbidden".

In a similar manner it may be shown that the principle (4), one of the traditional corner stones of a deontic logic, is but a special case of a more general principle which, in the name of "rationality" if not in that of "logic", seems acceptable, *viz.*

(6) $\mathcal{F} \sim A \& (x)([A]x \rightarrow [B]x) \rightarrow \sim \mathcal{F} B.$

This principle says that if all (individual) actions with an obligatory characteristic also have another characteristic, then this other characteristic cannot be (generically) prohibited. Let it be observed, however, that this other characteristic need not itself be (generically) obligatory; it might even be the case that all actions which are B without also being A are forbidden actions.

If in (6) we for "B" substitute "A" we obtain $\mathcal{F} \sim A \& (x)([A]x \rightarrow [A]x) \rightarrow \sim \mathcal{F} A$ which reduces to $\mathcal{F} \sim A \rightarrow \sim \mathcal{F} A$ which is the same as $\sim (\mathcal{F} A \& \mathcal{F} \sim A)$ or $\sim (\mathcal{O} A \& \mathcal{O} \sim A).$

VIII

The facts upon which I have here based my arguments for accepting and for not accepting certain statements about the relations between norms are *logical truths*. They are derived from the definitions of the deontic predicates with the aid of principles of the Logic of Predication. The accepted statements themselves we might call truths of (a) Deontic Logic. But I feel a certain hesitation calling them "logical truths" at all. The reason for this is that it seems to be a matter of extra-logical decision when we shall say that "there are" or "are not" such and such norms. Shall we, for example, say that "there is" a $\mathcal{F}$-norm with a disjunctive norm-content, if there are (have been given, issued) norms concerning all the various ways in which this disjunctive norm-content may be realized through action? Perhaps the norm with the disjunctive norm-content was never formulated or even thought of. Yet it was there "implicitly" one could say. Had the norm been given in the disjunctive formulation, it would have imposed exactly the same demands and granted exactly the same freedom to agents as the norms about the disjuncts would have done jointly.

The distribution principles (1) and (2) are conceptually on a somewhat different footing from the principles (3) and (4) and the more general principles (5) and (6) from which (3) and (4) may be derived. (1) and (2) are in a sense "linguistic", concern the way "and" and "or" are used when speaking of prohibitions and permissions. The principles which say that the permitted cannot also be forbidden or that prohibitions (obligations) with contradictory contents cannot co-exist are more of the nature of requirements of rational legislation than of strictly logical thinking.

Thanks to the distribution principles any molecular compound of norm-formulations can be split up into atomic constituents consisting of the letters " $\mathcal{F}$ " and " $\mathcal{P}$ " followed by atomic predicates or conjunctions of predicates and their negations. Over these constituents we can distribute truth-values subject to the two restrictions imposed by the principles (5) and (6). For example: If there are two constituents $\mathcal{F} A$ and $\mathcal{P} (A \& B)$ and the first is given the value "true", then the second must be given the value "false". If, under all permissible distributions of the truth-values, the molecular formula assumes the value "true", it might be called a "deontic tautology".

IX

The deontic operators which we have been studying so far are prefixed to names of action-categories. The "deontic logic" which emerged from this study, could be called a logic of what one ought to, may or must not *do*. The things which tell what ought to, may, or must not be done, we called *norms*.

Deontic operators, however, can also be prefixed to action-sentences— or to sentences generally. For example: it ought to be the case that *a* on *o* does *p*.

In order to avoid confusion I shall introduce the symbol N_d for obligation ("deontic necessity") and M_d for permission ("deontic possibility").[23] No special symbol for prohibition will be needed now. For sentences I shall employ symbols $s, t, u, \ldots$ from the end of the alphabet.

One can build a deontic logic for sentences of the form "$N_d s$", "$M_d s$" and their molecular compounds. Such sentences say that a certain thing, e.g. that so and so does that and that on such and such an occasion, ought to or may or must not *be*.

This deontic logic may rightly be regarded as an off-shoot of modal logic. Just as there are several modal logics, one may also construct several systems of such a deontic logic. But I see no particular reason why it should be constructed in a manner which deviates considerably from the well-known modal logics—except in that it rejects the formula $s \to M_d s$. I

---

[23] These symbols N_d and M_d correspond to the symbols O and P respectively of traditional deontic logic.

shall not here inquire into the interest of preserving within such a deontic logic the distinction between strong and weak permission and of having a permission operator which distributes conjunctively over disjunctions. Perhaps there is no good motivation for these pecularities at all.

The more interesting variations of this type of deontic logic arise, I think, when instead of the variables s, t, etc. we employ action-sentences $[p]$ (a, o), etc. and their compounds. Then the basis on which the deontic logic stands is not propositional logic alone but also a Logic of Action of the type sketched in Part II of this paper.

Of particular interest will now be problems connected with quantification.

There can be no obstacles of a logical nature to applying deontic operators also to quantified action sentences. For example: $N_d(a)(o)$ $[p]$ (a, o) says that such a state of affairs is obligatory that everybody on all occasions does p.

The logical situation changes radically when we consider quantification *into* deontically qualified contexts. Consider, for example, the expression $(a)(o)N_d$ $[p]$ (a, o). Here "$[p]$ (a, o)" is *not* a sentence which expresses a true or false proposition but a *generic* sentence (open sentence, propositional function).

What could $(a)(o)N_d$ $[p]$ (a, o) possibly mean? It might be an attempt to say that a norm which makes obligatory actions of a certain *kind* is addressed to all agents on all occasions. Then we are not concerned with the obligatory character of a certain *state of affairs* but with a norm obliging *agents*. Instead of N_d $[p]$ (a, o) we have a norm θA which is being given to every agent and is for all occasions. How this universal character of the norm shall be properly expressed in a symbolism is not easy to tell. Perhaps we should introduce a *normative relation*, R, which holds between an agent, an occasion, and a norm, $R(a, o, \theta A)$. This relational sentence could then be quantified, e.g. so as to become $(a)(o)R(a, o, \theta A)$.

In which relation do the expressions $(a)(o)R(a, o, \theta A)$ and $N_d(a)(o)$ $[p]$ (a, o) stand to one another? We shall assume that the action which is the doing of p by a on o is an action of the category A. The answer to the question, I suggest, is as follows: The two types of deontic expression are not, "by themselves", related to one another in any way whatsoever. If it is a deontic necessity that all agents always do a certain thing it does not follow that there is any norm addressed to all agents ordaining them always to do this thing. But a lawgiver who is anxious to see to it that, if possible, all agents on all occasions behave in this way may issue a norm to the said effect. He may, however, issue such a norm also *without* deeming it necessary for any particular end of his that all agents always behave as he has ordained.[24]

---

[24] The vistas which here open are discussed more fully in the concluding part of the next essay. (1983)

Norms, Truth, and Logic

1. DEONTIC LOGIC AS A LOGIC OF NORM-SATISFACTION

I

A philosophic difficulty connected with the idea of a "logic of norms" has been the following:

A "logic", presumably, is concerned with such relations as entailment (logical consequence) or compatibility and incompatibility between the entities which it studies. The most natural way of explaining what is meant by those relations makes use of the notion of truth and of various truth-functional notions. For example: that something follows logically from something else seems to "mean" (something like) that if the second is *true* the first must be true, too.

It is, however, a common, even if not universally shared, opinion among philosophers that norms have no truth-value, are neither true nor false. Therefore it is at least doubtful whether norms can have a "logic"— whether for example one norm can be said to follow logically from another norm.

Ernst Mally,[1] who was the first to try to develop in a systematic fashion a logic of norms, seems not to have been troubled by such doubts. The first to articulate them were some philosophers and philosophical logicians of the logical positivist trend in the 1930s.[2] Normative discourse was by those thinkers labelled "atheoretical" and sometimes even said to be "meaningless". Norms were assimilated to imperatives and value-judgements to exclamations, i.e. to entities which quite obviously cannot be said to have truth-value.

Like Mally, I too was not troubled by the problem of truth when in 1951 I designed my first system of deontic logic.[3] This is perhaps surprising, considering that I then was, and still am, firmly of the opinion that (genuine) norms lack truth-value. At first, I did not "combine" this opinion of mine with my work in logic. But soon I noticed that I had been overlooking a problem. My first reaction to it was to think that logic "has a wider reach than truth". "Deontic logic," I wrote in the Preface to my book *Logical Studies* (1957), "gets part of its philosophic significance

---

[1] *Grundgesetze des Sollens, Elemente der Logik des Willens*, Leuschner & Lubensky, Graz, 1926.

[2] Notably Dubislav, Jørgensen, and Alf Ross. Cf. W. Dubislav, "Zur Unbegründbarkeit der Forderungssätze", *Theoria*, 3, 1937; J. Jørgensen, "Imperatives and Logic", *Erkenntnis*, 7, 1937–38; and Alf Ross, "Imperatives and Logic", *Theoria*, 7, 1941.

[3] In the paper "Deontic Logic", *Mind*, 60, 1951.

from the fact that norms and valuations, though removed from the realm of truth, yet are subject to logical law."

I know that some people have hailed this extension of the province of logic beyond the confines of truth as a satisfactory answer to the problem. It seems also to agree with the view implicitly taken by the vast majority of writers on deontic logic since the time of the subject's (re-)birth in the early 1950s. Few only have bothered to question its superficiality.

II

In *Norm and Action* (1963) I made a tripartite distinction which I think is useful between norms, norm-formulations, and norm-propositions. Norm-formulations have a characteristic "ambiguity": one and the same form of words may be used both *prescriptively* to enunciate a norm or a rule of conduct and *descriptively* for stating that there is (exists) such and such a norm or rule. Accordingly, I distinguished between a prescriptive and a descriptive interpretation also of the formalized counterparts of norm-formulations constructed by means of the deontic operators O and P and constants and variables belonging to a Logic of Action, of Change, and of Propositions. My view was then that Deontic Logic is a logic of descriptively interpreted formalized norm-formulations. This made the application of truth-connectives and of such meta-logical notions as entailment, consistency, and contradiction uncontroversial. But something remained problematic about the whole undertaking. As said in the book (p. 134): "Deontic Logic is a logic of descriptively interpreted expressions. But the laws (principles, rules) which are peculiar to this logic, concern logical properties of the *norms* themselves, which are then reflected in logical properties of norm-propositions. Thus, in a sense, the 'basis' of Deontic Logic is a logical theory of prescriptively interpreted O- and P-expressions."

The deontic logic developed in *Norm and Action* was thus a sort of conflation or mixture of a "logic of norms" and a "logic of norm-propositions". The basis of the logical principles *at the descriptive level* governing the norm-propositions were definitions *at the prescriptive level* of norms of the notions of self-consistency (of a norm), consistency (of sets of norms), and entailment (between norms). I was aware of the fact that these notions were not "purely logical" but related to ideas about *rationality* ("rational willing").[4] This, I think, was a basically sound insight. I did not then draw from it what now seems to me the appropriate conclusions.

For the sake of arriving at clarity in these matters it is necessary to make a *sharper* separation than was done in *Norm and Action* between the descriptive and the prescriptive interpretation of the deontic formulas. On the descriptive interpretation they express propositions to the effect that

---

[4] Cf. *Norm and Action*, pp. 151f.

such and such norms exist. These propositions are true or false and obey the laws of "ordinary" logic. If, in addition, they obey special principles of a logically necessary character this must be due to conceptual peculiarities connected with the notion of the *existence* of a norm. We need not doubt that there are such peculiarities. In *Norm and Action* I said something about them[5]—but I shall not here repeat or defend my past position.

On the prescriptive interpretation deontic formulas have a "prescriptive meaning" and do not express true or false propositions. It makes no sense to speak of relations of contradiction or entailment between the formulas when thus interpreted. The positivistic sceptics who, like Alf Ross, doubted the possibility of a deontic logic were in an important sense right in maintaining that *norms have no logic* or that normative discourse is "alogical". But norm-giving activity, and also the norms themselves, can be judged under various aspects and standards of *rationality*. Some such aspects, moreover, can be associated with considerations of a strictly logical character—and in the logical patterns which emerge from such considerations we can recognize the structures which deontic logicians (in the now traditional sense of the term) have studied and tried to systematize. How this happens I hope to be able to show in the sequel.

III

I shall in the following construct more than one formal system of deontic logic. The calculus or system constructed in this first part of the present paper answers, relatively closely, to what may be called the *standard* systems of deontic logic.[6] The calculus has the following vocabulary:

(*a*) Variables *p*, *q*, etc. They represent sentences describing states of affairs or processes which may or may not obtain (go on) at a given time or on a given occasion. Such sentences are *open*, i.e. the propositions which they express are not "in themselves" true or false, but acquire a truth-value when associated with an individuating, spatial and/or temporal determination. Such propositions will also be called *generic*.

(*b*) Sentential connectives ~, &, ∨, →, ↔ for forming molecular compounds of sentences.

(*c*) The deontic operators, *O* and *P*, symbolizing the deontic status of obligatoriness and permittedness respectively.

(*d*) Brackets ( ).

---

[5] *Ibid.*, especially Ch. VII, pp. 107–28.

[6] The term "standard system" seems to have been coined by Bengt Hansson (see above, p. 103). I here use it in a somewhat more restricted sense than the one proposed by Hansson in that "mixed formulas" are not regarded as norm-formulations.

The well-formed formulas of the calculus are schematic norm-formulations. They are defined as follows:

(*i*) A variable, or molecular compound of variables, preceded by a deontic operator, is an atomic norm-formulation of the first order.

(*ii*) A molecular compound of norm-formulations is a norm-formulation.

(*iii*) A deontic operator followed by a norm-formulation or by a molecular compound of variables and norm-formulations is a(n atomic) norm-formulation of higher order.

Rules for the use of brackets need not be stated here; they should be obvious from the contexts of formulas appearing below.

Examples. $O \sim p$ is an atomic norm-formulation. The formula should be read "it ought to be the case that it is not the case that p" or, shorter, "it ought to be that not p". $Pp \lor P \sim p$ is a molecular norm-formulation (of the first order). POp is an atomic norm-formulation of the second order. $POp \lor Oq$ is a norm-formulation. $p \to Oq$ is *not* by our definition a norm-formulation—but $O(p \to Oq)$ *is* a norm-formulation.

Expressions occurring within the scope of a deontic operator will also be referred to as (expressions for) *norm-contents*.

IV

A problem which calls for special attention has to do with the application of sentential connectives to norm-formulations.[7]

Consider first negation. How shall we understand, for example, $\sim Op$? "It is not the case that it ought to be the case that p." This form of words could be used for stating that there *is* not (does not exist) a norm to the effect that it ought to be the case that p. But then the sentence expresses a norm-proposition. It is descriptive, not prescriptive. Has the sentence no prescriptive use then? I think it cannot be rightly denied that it has one. But what does the sentence *mean* when used prescriptively? As far as I can see, the only plausible meaning which can then be associated with it is that of the sentence "it is permitted that it is not the case that p". But for that we also have the symbolic expression $P \sim p$.

Similarly, the form of words "it is not permitted that it is the case that p" or, which says the same, "it is not the case that it may be the case that p" can be understood either descriptively or prescriptively. Descriptively understood, the words mean that there is no permission to the effect that it may be the case that p. No such permission has been given, issued, or, if once given, has later been withdrawn or cancelled ("derogated"). Prescriptively understood, the words state a prohibition, mean that it must not be

---

[7] This problem was mentioned, and discussed rather extensively, in *Norm and Action*, pp. 130ff.

the case that p, i.e. ought to be the case that not-p. For this last we also have the symbolic expression $O \sim p$.

I shall, following the terminology adopted in *Norm and Action*, say that Op and $P \sim p$ and, similarly, Pp and $O \sim p$, when used prescriptively, express the *negation-norms* of one another.

That "and" has a genuine prescriptive use for joining norm-formulations seems beyond doubt. "It ought to be the case that p and may be the case that q" could be a genuine prescription.

The notion of disjunction, i.e. the particle "or", is more problematic. The same problem attaches to the word "not" when prefixed to a string of norm-formulations joined by "and".

"It ought to be the case that p or it may be the case that q" can, of course, be used for stating that either there is (exists) a certain obligation or a certain permission. But could the same form of words be used for giving a prescription? The question is confusing. If someone is told that it ought to be the case that p or may be the case that q he would not be told anything definite about the normative (deontic) status of those two states of affairs. But if he himself is in a position to *make* things obligatory or permitted, then being told this might be an *injunction* (command, norm) to him either to make a certain thing obligatory or a certain other thing permitted. This would surely be a genuinely prescriptive use of the form of words in question. A superior norm-authority might use them in addressing a subordinate norm-authority.

Similar observations apply to the form of words "It is not the case that it ought to be the case that p and may be the case that q" or, in symbols, $\sim (Op \,\&\, Pq)$. Accepting the usual transformations of expressions formed by means of sentential connectives, this last formula could also be written $\sim Op \lor \sim Pq$. And accepting what was just said about negation and norms, this again could be transformed into $P \sim p \lor O \sim q$. "It may be the case that not p or ought to be the case that not q". A prescription thus worded would, I think, most naturally be understood as an injunction to someone either to permit something or to make obligatory something else.

It thus seems that disjunctions of norm-formulations and negations of conjunctions of norm-formulations can be prescriptively understood. On what seems to me to be the most natural way of thus understanding them, the molecular constructs in question do not prescribe the deontic status of the states of affairs themselves involved in the atomic components, but prescribe which deontic status some states of affairs ought to or may be given.

Consider an arbitrary formula F of our calculus. By the *normative negation*(-formula) of F I shall understand the formula which is obtained from $\sim F$ by pushing the negation-sign $\sim$ as far "inside" as allowed by the rules of propositional logic (PL) and making the shift from $\sim O$ to $P \sim$ and from $\sim P$ to $O \sim$.

Examples. The normative negation(-formula) of $Pp \vee O \sim q$ is $O \sim p$ & Pq, that of POp is $OP \sim p$, and that of $O(p \rightarrow Oq)$ is $P(p$ & $P \sim q)$.

V

Norms of higher order have been something of a neglected problem-child of traditional deontic logic. In a system of deontic logic in which the "contents" of norms are thought of as actions, norm-formulations of higher order are not even well-formed. This is the case, for example with my first or 1951 system.

In a system of deontic logic in which the contents are thought of as states of affairs, expressions of higher order may be regarded as well-formed. But their interpretation is open to question.

Consider for example the expression POp or "it may be (the case) that it ought to be (the case) that p". If we stick to the view, taken here, that the content of a norm is a state of affairs then not only the variable "p" in the expression but also the compound "Op" must represent a state of affairs. The state of affairs represented by "Op" is that a certain thing (state of affairs) is obligatory. "Op" is thus the schematic form of an expression to the effect that a certain norm exists. In other words, "Op" must be interpreted descriptively. As norm-formulation it expresses a norm-proposition and not a norm.

The higher-order expression POp, however, may be interpreted either descriptively or prescriptively. Descriptively interpreted it states that there is permission to the effect that it may be the case that it is the case that it is obligatory that p. In other words it says that the state of affairs which obtains when there is a norm which makes it obligatory that p is itself a permitted state. Prescriptively interpreted the expression permits, i.e. gives permission to create, this state. It might, for example, be permission which a higher authority gives to a subordinate one to make certain things obligatory under norm.

As seen, norm-formulations of higher order can be given a prescriptive interpretation. But any norm-formulation which occurs itself within the scope of a deontic operator has to be interpreted descriptively.[8] This necessity of combining a prescriptive with a descriptive interpretation of expressions occurring in one and the same formula may strike one as surprising. But once the necessity is clearly seen it ought not to strike us as problematic.

In view of the fact that a norm-formulation which is part of the descrip-

---

[8] This observation has also been made independently by C. Alchourrón and E. Bulygin in an essay "von Wright on Deontic Logic and the Philosophy of Law", in a volume *The Philosophy of Georg Henrik von Wright* for the series Library of Living Philosophers.

tion of the content of a higher-order norm has to be interpreted descriptively one can raise the question why, in the formation of negation-norms of a given (higher-order) norm, the shifts from $\sim O$ to $P \sim$ and from $\sim P$ to $O \sim$ should be allowed (cf. above, p. 134). Why should we say, for example, that the negation-norm of POp is $OP \sim p$ rather than saying that it is $O \sim Pp$? I shall try to answer this question later when discussing what I propose to call the Transmission-of-Will Principle for norm-giving activity (see below, pp. 147 and 163).

VI

The status of permissions is traditionally a much debated question in the philosophy of norms, and particularly in legal philosophy. Is permission an independent category, or can permission be defined in terms of obligation? That obligation and prohibition are interdefinable has seldom, if ever, been doubted. The question of the independence of permission is usually raised in the following form: Is permission anything "over and above" the absence of prohibition?

It should be noted in passing that if permission can be defined in terms of prohibition (obligation), then also the reverse is true. The above question could therefore also be put: Is prohibition anything "over and above" absence of permission? It is worth reflecting why the question is seldom, if ever, put in that way. Prohibitions and obligations are somehow ontologically more "basic" or "real", it would seem, than permissions. This presumably is connected with the fact that neglecting obligations and breaking prohibitions is normally connected with "sanctions" of one form or another such as legal punishment or moral reprobation.

In legal philosophy, the question of the status of permissions is related to the problem of "gaps" in the law. If things which are not prohibited are *ipso facto* permitted, then any action or state has a legal status: it either is prohibited (and its "opposite" obligatory) or else it is permitted. The legal order is of necessity in this sense *closed*. It has no "gaps". A forceful proponent of this opinion was Hans Kelsen. Other legal philosophers, perhaps even the majority, do not find this position satisfying. They would argue that beside things which are permitted and prohibited there are also a good many things which are not regulated by norm at all and therefore lack deontic or legal status. They are not prohibited, but they are not (thereby) permitted either.

I think that this dispute can be settled once and for all by strictly observing the distinction between descriptive and prescriptive discourse.

"Absence" is a descriptive term. "Absence of prohibition" means that there *is* no prohibiting norm, that no norm to the effect that a certain thing is prohibited *exists*. To maintain that absence of prohibition is tantamount to a permission is to make a statement at the level of *norm-propositions*; and I do not think that this statement could be proved true by logical argument. The question of "gaps" in the law is not a question of logic. It is rather a question of accepting or not accepting certain "meta-norms".

One could, for example, argue that it is part of the idea of a *Rechtsstaat* or "reign of law" in a society that only deeds which are prohibited by an already existing law may be punished as criminal offences. *Nulla poena sine lege*, or *nullum crimen sine lege*, as the sayings go. In a society where this meta-norm is actually observed anyone can do what is not forbidden without having to fear sanction. Then one could also say that in this society everything which is not legally forbidden is legally permissible. But this argument concerns an "ideal" legal order and is not an argument in logic.

There are, moreover, systems of normative relationship in which the principle that anything which is not forbidden is permitted may appear unreasonable. The relations between parents and their children (before a certain age) might serve as example. There are things which have never been prohibited to the child—but for the doing of which the child may yet be reprimanded or punished. It must not do these things without first, as we say, having *asked permission*. The parents will then consider which "deontic status" these actions should have.

At the prescriptive level things are different. If in saying "this is not prohibited" I *give a prescription* and do not just speak about what has and what has not been subjected to norm, then surely what I do is that I permit this thing to be done or to exist. And vice-versa, if I say "this is not permitted" and "mean" this as a *prescription*, then surely I thereby prohibit a certain thing.

Thus in prescriptive language "not permitted" means "forbidden", and "not forbidden" means "permitted". Similarly, "not obligatory that" means "permitted that not" and "not permitted that not" means "obligatory that". In the prescriptive language of norms we can therefore safely assume "P" = "$\sim O \sim$" or "O" = "$\sim P \sim$" and, if we wish, dispense altogether with one of the two operators. This is also what is usually done in known systems of deontic logic. But not always for the right reasons. And in a logic of norm-propositions, i.e. of descriptively interpreted norm-formulations, we have no right to assume the above identities and to dispense with one of the operators. Here both operators are needed.

VII

Most norms come into existence and pass out of existence in the course of time. They may come into existence through an act of issuing or promulgation by some "norm-authority", and pass out of existence through an act of cancellation or derogation. This is normally the case with legal norms;

but it need not always be the case. Some legal norms pass out of existence by what is called *desuetudo*, and some come into existence from customs which in due course acquire the force of legal obligations or rights.

The existential status of moral norms is more complicated.[9] Moral codes and various moral taboos have a connection with custom and with religious beliefs and teaching. But rules such as that promises ought to be kept, or that it is immoral to tell a lie, seem rather different. I do not know what to think about their status in time. Their existence cannot truly be said to depend on historical contingencies such as the enacting of a law or even the gradual formation of a custom. They are rather meant to be valid *semper et ubique*, like the laws of nature. On the other hand, the rule that promises ought to be kept presupposes the existence of the *institution* of promising. This institution need not be universal. It may exist in some societies but not in others. Something similar holds true of moral rules condemning theft. The institutions themselves of contract and property are, however, also legal institutions. Custom, law, and morality are thus inseparably interwoven.

Norms with a history I shall call *positive* norms. The clearest example of positive norms is statutory law. I shall not here inquire whether there are norms of an essentially unhistorical nature and whether the logical study of such norms would have peculiarities which distinguishes it from a "normal" deontic logic.

VIII

A norm to the effect that it ought to be the case that *p* is *satisfied*, I shall say, if, and only if, at *all* times in the history of this norm, it is the case that *p*. And it is dissatisfied if, and only if, at *some* time in its history it is *not* the case that *p*. For norms enjoining or prohibiting *actions* the situation is a little more complex. The norm to the effect that *X* ought to be done is satisfied, I shall say, if, and only if, *X* is done on *all* occasions when there is an opportunity for doing it—and dissatisfied if, and only if, *X* is not done on *some* occasion when there is an opportunity (cf. below, p. 197).

Whenever *X* is done by a norm-subject, the subject obeys the norm; whenever *X* is not done by a subject when there is an opportunity for him to do *X*, the norm is broken or disobeyed. Satisfaction, as here defined, thus means exceptionless obedience to the norm.

If a lawgiver prohibits something or makes it obligatory, he will have to count with the possibility that the norm will not always be observed. But

---

[9] Cf. above, pp. 75f.

he may be said normally to want or desire, to "will", that what he has enjoined should without exception be the case. He wants the norms to be satisfied. If for some reason or other it would be *impossible* that the obligatory states always (in the history of the norm) obtain, we might say that his wish (will) is not "rational", since it *cannot* be fulfilled. The irrationality would be particularly glaring, if an obligatory state could never obtain and a prohibited state consequently always had to obtain. This would be the case, for example, if the lawgiver had enjoined a contradiction, p & $\sim p$, to be the case.

If a lawgiver had made obligatory both of two mutually contradictory states, then one of the obligations may be satisfied but only at the expense of the other necessarily remaining dissatisfied. If one of the two states obtains at some time, and the other at some other time, neither obligation is satisfied. Since it is impossible that both be satisfied, it was surely irrational, foolish, on the part of the lawgiver, to enact both norms. Doing this may also diminish his prestige in the eyes of his subjects.

But could he not issue contradictory orders merely with a view to placing the subject or subjects in an "unsolvable predicament"?[10] So that he can punish them whatever they do. Surely this is possible. Must it be "irrational"? Not if the purpose is to perplex or punish people. It is irrational only relative to the *normal* purpose which the institution of giving orders serves; *viz.* to achieve the states of affairs consequent upon fulfilment of the orders. Perhaps one should in the imagined case call the order "perverse" rather than "irrational".

Permissions are in a somewhat different position. Normally, a permitted state of affairs is not also obligatory, but its contradictory is permitted too. A lawgiver may perhaps hope or wish that his subjects never avail themselves of a permission he has granted, i.e. hope that a permitted state of affairs should never obtain. (Perhaps he was forced to grant the permission under duress.) But if it were quite impossible for this state to obtain, its permittedness would only be a "joke". It would be a "mock-permission". It is therefore a thoroughly reasonable and rational demand—on the part of the norm-subjects if not of the norm-authority—that permitted states of affairs can sometimes obtain, although the demand need not be that they can obtain always. If a state and its contradictory are both permitted, they cannot both *always* obtain—yet there is nothing irrational about both being allowed to obtain.

I shall say that a permissive norm is satisfiable if, and only if, it is possible that the permitted state of affairs obtains at *some* time in the history of the norm. And it is satisfied if, and only if, at some time in its history that which it permits actually is also the case.

---

[10] I owe this example to Professor Elizabeth Anscombe.

A norm (obligation or permission) which is satisfiable will also be said to be *normatively (self-)consistent*.

IX

For a finite set of co-existing norms I shall introduce the technical term a *corpus*.[11]

If the norms of a corpus are "historical", their histories may vary in length. By *the history of the corpus* I shall understand the overlapping portion of the histories of the norms which are members of the corpus. A long-lasting norm may thus be a member of a good many different corpora. The totality of norms which make up a legal order or system is normally a succession (family) of sets which are here called corpora.[12]

Since a corpus is a finite set of norms we can express its total content in the form of a conjunction of all the norm-formulations in the corpus. We thus form of the norm-formulations *one* (complex) norm-formulation.

A corpus of norms is satisfiable if, and only if, it is possible that all states which the norms of the corpus make obligatory obtain throughout the history of the corpus and all states which the norms permit obtain some time in this history.

A satisfiable corpus will be called *normatively consistent*; a corpus which is not satisfiable again normatively inconsistent.

I shall, furthermore, regard satisfiability as a criterion of *rationality* of a corpus of norms. A lawgiver may be said to envisage an ideal state which agrees with his wish or will, and in which everything obligatory is the case as long as the obligations exist and everything permitted is the case at some time or other in the history of the permissions. The lawgiver can be said to "will" that all obligations be satisfied or *fulfilled* and to "tolerate" that all permissions be satisfied or *used* at some time or other. For the sake of simplicity I shall in the sequel speak of his will or toleration as simply his "will".

If a norm, or corpus, is not satisfiable (normatively consistent) the lawgiver or supreme (sovereign) norm-authority cannot *rationally will* the ideal state envisaged in his norm-giving activity or legislation.

The condition of rationality which I have stated may be regarded as a necessary minimum condition. Further conditions may be laid down, for example that the obtaining of the various states which the norms make obligatory or permitted should also be physically possible, or humanly

---

[11] *Norm and Action*, p. 151.

[12] The conception of normative systems as a temporal succession of sets of norms has been emphasized and elaborated by Alchourrón and Bulygin. Cf. their book *Sobre la existencia de las normas jurídicas*, Oficina latinoamericana de investigaciones jurídicas y sociales, Valencia (Venezuela), 1979, Ch. XI.

possible, to achieve through action. But we shall not here discuss such additional requirements. Perhaps one could say that the condition as laid down above is the only one which is of relevance to a "logic" of norms.

Should it emerge, either from "theoretical deliberations" or from "legal practice", that a corpus does not satisfy the minimum condition of rationality, the lawgiver is likely to take various steps in order to "restore" rationality. He may, for example, *derogate* some norms, remove them from the corpus, or he may restrict their scope through some process of *conditionalization*. Both derogation and conditionalization of norms are interesting from a logical point of view. Derogation will not be further discussed in this essay;[13] but on the logical form of conditional norms remarks will be made in Part 2.

X

If the negation norm of a given norm is *not* satisfiable the norm itself will be called (*normatively*) *tautologous* or said to be a tautologous norm.

Consider, for example, the norm $O(p \lor \sim p)$. Its negation norm is $P(p \& \sim p)$. This is not satisfiable. At no time in the history of this "permission" could, for reasons of logic, its content be realized. Giving such a permission is not, on our adopted standard, rational.

That $O(p \lor \sim p)$ is a normative tautology does not *mean* that it is logically true, "a truth of deontic logic", that it is obligatory that p or not p. What it means is, simply, that one cannot "rationally will" the normative negation of $O(p \lor \sim p)$. And whether such willing is or is not possible depends upon what standards of rationality one adopts for norm-giving activity. Our adopted standards are not the only possible ones—and perhaps in *some* normative contexts not even the most reasonable ones.[14]

Consider next a corpus consisting of (or containing) the two norms Op and $O \sim p$. This corpus cannot be satisfied. The conjunction $Op \& O \sim p$ is normatively inconsistent. The normative negation of it is $Pp \lor P \sim p$. We shall call this too a normative tautology. But again it must be remembered that the tautological character of $Pp \lor P \sim p$ does not mean that it is "a truth of deontic logic" that either any given state of affairs is itself permitted or its negation is permitted. What it means is, strictly, that one cannot—on the adopted standards—"rationally will" that a certain state be and that it, at the same time, not be.

Let us assume that Op is a member of a normatively consistent corpus

---

[13] It is a merit of Alchourrón and Bulygin to have noted the peculiar logical problems connected with the concept of derogation (see above, pp. 137ff).

[14] These observations should remove the qualms which I have long felt about accepting, as a "truth" of a logic of norms, that tautologous states of affairs are "obligatory" (see above, p. 105).

of norms. If to this corpus we add $O \sim p$ it becomes normatively inconsistent. This we may regard as a reason for saying that the negation norm of $O \sim p$ which is Pp is *implicit* in the corpus, or that the conjunction of norms in the corpus *normatively entails* the norm Pp.

Op may be the only norm in the corpus. Then, by the above, Op entails Pp—assuming that Op itself is normatively (self)-consistent.

$Op \& O \sim p$ is the normative negation of $Op \rightarrow Pp$. The fact that $Op \& O \sim p$ is normatively inconsistent is our ground for calling $Op \rightarrow Pp$ a normative tautology. Does this tautology "mean" or "show" that an obligation *entails* a corresponding permission or that it is a truth of deontic logic that what is obligatory is also permitted? Saying this would be obscuring, not to say false. The right thing to say is this: If something has been ordered, it would be irrational also to forbid it. Therefore, if one has made something obligatory, one is "tacitly committed" to permit this thing too. But this commitment is not "logical". It is a commitment which one has only in so far as one aspires to be rational.

We could lay down the following *Rule of Rational Commitment* as I shall call it: *If the conjunction corresponding to a given corpus of norms is normatively consistent as it stands but becomes inconsistent when a new norm is added to the corpus, then the negation-norm of the added norm was "implicit" in the corpus.*

XI

We can apply this rule for obtaining equivalents of many of the well-known theorems of deontic logic:

(*i*) $O (p \& q) \& P \sim p$ is normatively inconsistent. Hence a corpus of norms containing $O (p \& q)$ also contains implicitly, in the sense of our Rule of Commitment, the negation-norm of $P \sim p$, i.e. Op—and, of course, Oq too.

(*ii*) $Op \& Oq \& P (\sim p \vee \sim q)$ is likewise normatively inconsistent. Hence, if a corpus contains the two norms Op and Oq it also implicitly contains $O (p \& q)$.

(*i*) and (*ii*) jointly constitute the formula $O (p \& q) \leftrightarrow Op \& Oq$ of traditional deontic logic. This formula is thus a normative tautology.[15]

(*iii*) $O (p \vee q) \& O \sim p \& O \sim q$ is another normative inconsistency. Thus a corpus is irrational in which there is a norm which makes it obligatory that the one or the other of two states of affairs obtain, but also norms prohibiting the obtaining of both states individually. If the lawgiver

---

[15] There is no conflict between this and the non-validity of the "corresponding" equivalence formula in more finely structured systems of deontic logic (cf. above, pp. 125f, and below, p. 190).

wishes to retain the two prohibitions he is, in the name of rationality, committed to permit the obtaining of the conjunction of the negation of both the prohibited states too ($P(p \& q)$). If again he is keen on the disjunctive obligation he will have to cancel at least one of the two prohibitions.

This last may be said to be a reflection of the deontic formula $Op \& O(p \to q) \to Pq$, sometimes rendered in words by saying that what is obligatory can commit only to something which is permitted. Since, in fact, also $O(p \lor q) \& O \sim p \& P \sim q$ is inconsistent, we can strengthen this to a principle which is sometimes expressed in words by saying that the obligatory commits only to things which are themselves obligatory. This is reflected in the formula $Op \& O(p \to q) \to Oq$ of deontic logic.

(*iv*) $P(p \lor q) \& O \sim p \& O \sim q$ is a normative inconsistency. What deontic commitments would follow from this?

One commitment is obvious: an authority which prohibits both of two states cannot rationally allow that one of them sometimes obtains. But assume that he is keen on allowing that either of them sometimes obtains. Then he cannot rationally prohibit them both. He must allow at least one of them. But which one? This is open to his choice. Shall we therefore say that, if a corpus contains a disjunctive permission, it implicitly contains also a disjunction of two permissions? This sounds strange. A corpus contains norms. Is a disjunction of norms a norm? The question can also be put as follows: Has "or" a *prescriptive* use for joining norm-formulations? We have already raised the questions once (above, p. 134). I feel tempted to answer No to the first and Yes to the second—but I think we should be liberal here. The agent who is being told that it is permitted that *p or* permitted that *q* may feel at a loss and complain that he has not been given any rule for his acting (for what he may do). The norm-authority, on the other hand, could say to himself "I cannot rationally prohibit both states, so I must allow at least one of them"—and this soliloquy could perhaps be called "prescriptive".

When we abandon talk about norms "entailing" each other, the puzzle dissolves in a natural manner. The situation with regard to the "normative tautology" $P(p \lor q) \leftrightarrow Pp \lor Pq$ is simply this: if the norm-authority permits a disjunctive state of affairs, he is "rationally committed" to permit at least one of the disjuncts. If he prohibits both, his norm-giving activity is "irrational". And this is all we have to say.

It is worth making here the following observation on the *prescriptive* use of *permissive* norm-formulations: A prescription permitting a disjunctive state of affairs to obtain is normally understood to permit every one of the disjuncts individually. This does not make $P(p \lor q) \to Pp \& Pq$ a "normative tautology" as defined by us. But it may be taken to suggest that one should exclude, as being "incorrect" or "ungrammatical", a combined use of a prescriptive "it is permitted" and a prescriptive "it is forbidden" for permitting a disjunction of some states and, at the same time, prohibiting one or several of the disjuncts. "It is permitted that *p or q* but forbidden that *p*" may be a true statement about the deontic status of some states of affairs. But as a prescription this would either be unintelligible or understood as an "odd" way of permitting that *q* while prohibiting that *p*. (Cf. above, pp. 104f and p. 124 on the notion of "free choice permission".)

XII

There have been endless discussions among deontic logicians of some "paradoxes". In elementary deontic logic they are essentially variations of one and the same, *viz.* the so-called Ross Paradox. It arises, as well known, from the fact that the norm Op is alleged to "entail" the norm $O(p \lor q)$.

Let us see how this is reflected at the level of rational norm-giving activity. $Op \& P(\sim p \& \sim q)$ is normatively inconsistent. Hence, if a corpus contains a norm to the effect that it ought to be the case that *p*, it cannot "rationally" also contain the negation-norm of the norm that it ought to be the case that *p* or *q*. The negation-norm would permit that neither of these two states obtains and *a fortiori* that the first of them does not obtain either. Hence what the Ross Paradox amounts to is simply that a lawgiver cannot rationally *both* make a state obligatory *and* at the same time permit that this state, together with some other arbitrary state, does not obtain. This is obvious and not in the least "paradoxical". It appears paradoxical only when one speaks about it as an "entailment" between a norm Op and a norm $O(p \lor q)$. There *is* no such thing—and the Ross Paradox makes us aware of the absurdity of talking as though it existed. Let it be said here in tribute to the memory of the eminent Danish jurist that Alf Ross was right when he offered his paradox as a proof that, properly understood, there could not be such a thing as a logic of norms. But then one must also lay special emphasis on the words "properly understood".

XIII

When considering norms of the first order we need not pay attention to possible restrictions on the time during which the norms exist. It suffices to assume that the norms of a corpus are co-existent. The norms may even be "eternal" ("ahistorical"), existing "from the dawn of creation" to "the end of time".

When we proceed to consider norms of higher order the situation is different.

Consider, for example, the expression POp, "it may be the case that it ought to be the case that *p*". When would this form of words be used? Perhaps for saying that a superior legal (or moral) authority permits a subordinate norm-giving authority to issue a norm to the effect that a certain thing ought to be the case. This would be a descriptive use for stating the norm-proposition that a certain permissive norm has been issued, exists. This norm permits the state of affairs that a certain thing is obligatory. Whether this state exists or not depends upon whether the subordinate authority has availed himself of the permission or not.

Assume that the sub-authority avails himself of the permission. This he need not do "at once", as soon as the permission is given. He may do it when the permission has already existed, been "in force", some time. The permission may then be withdrawn or otherwise cease to exist. Does it follow that the obligation too then ceases? Not necessarily. It may have acquired an existence "independent" of the permission. But this part of its life, if there is such a part, will not interest us here.

It may also happen that the sub-authority avails himself of the permission and makes a certain thing obligatory (for some norm-subjects) but then withdraws the norm while the permission to issue it is still in force. He may do so repeatedly. This is not at all unrealistic. A sub-authority may, for example, be permitted (entitled, have a right) to order a curfew in the case of emergency. From time to time he may avail himself of this right.

The satisfaction of a given norm may thus require the coming into existence of other (subordinate) norms. The norms thus coming into existence may outlast the life-span (history) of the superior norm, but such parts of their life are immaterial to the satisfaction of the superior norm.

Let the norm be OOp. If this norm is satisfied then, throughout its duration, there exists a norm—issued maybe by a sub-authority—making it obligatory that p. Assume that this is the case but that the state of affairs that p does not obtain throughout the duration of the norm or norms making it obligatory. Then some norm of lower order is *not* satisfied. Shall we say that the higher-order norm *is* satisfied, or not?

The answer is not immediately clear. We could answer the question by Yes or by No. If we give the first answer then the higher authority "does not care", one could say, whether what the lower authority makes obligatory is or is not. His "will" is only that there always be such an obligating norm. But why should he "will" this unless he is anxious that the state of affairs itself, which is made obligatory, obtains? At least in normal cases, an authority who orders that something be made obligatory wants the obligation satisfied. He, as it were, "transmits" his will through the intermediary of a lower authority. Therefore his will is not fulfilled unless the norms which are its immediate objects are themselves satisfied.

If we do not add (some) such Principle of Transmission of Will, as I shall call it, to the notion of rational willing (norm-giving) the theory of higher-order norms becomes "uninteresting". That is: it would not then contain any deontic tautologies over and above those already familiar from first-order deontic logic.

Accepting this principle, an obligation norm of higher order is satisfied if, and only if, the state of affairs which it makes obligatory exists throughout its history *and* all norms the existence of which is a constituent part of this state of affairs are themselves satisfied.

If instead of "throughout its history" we say "some time in the course of its history" we obtain the criterion of satisfaction for permissive norms of higher order.

With this extension of the notions of satisfaction and satisfiability, or of our criterion of rational norm-giving, one can also apply to norm-formulations of higher order and their molecular compounds our previously defined notions of normative consistency, tautology, and entailment.

Consider $Op \to OOp$. Its normative negation is $Op \ \& \ PP \sim p$. Why cannot an authority rationally issue two norms, one ordering it to be the case that p and another permitting it to be permitted that it is not the case that p? The answer is not obvious. The two norms rationally conflict only if we assume that an authority who permits (to some sub-authority to give) a permission that it be not the case that p is bound in consistency to tolerate that it is not the case that p. Only if we assume this is there a conflict with the norm, issued by that authority, that it ought to be the case that p. But it is at least highly natural, even if not compelling, to accept this as a criterion of rational norm-giving.

Assume that Op is normatively consistent. Since adding $PP \sim p$ to a consistent corpus containing Op would then make the corpus inconsistent, we can also say that the higher-order norm OOp is implicit in this corpus. But no such norm need have been given. Its "implicit existence" consists only in the fact that issuing its negation-norm would be an act of "irrational legislation". The legislator could not rationally permit anybody (himself included) to permit that it be the case that $\sim p$ since he has made it obligatory that p.

This is the sense in which $Op \to OOp$ may be regarded as a "law of deontic logic".

A formula which has been much discussed as a plausible candidate for a higher-order truth of "deontic logic" is the formula $O\,(Op \to p)$.[16] "It ought to be the case that if it ought to be the case that p then it is the case that p." This sounds intuitively plausible. That which ought to be the case is, as everyone knows, not necessarily the case—but it ought to be the case, since it is obligatory. The formula $O\,(Op \to p)$ is indeed a normative tautology. This means that its negation norm $P\,(\sim p \ \& \ Op)$, if ever given or issued, could not possibly be satisfied. A lawgiver who enacted such a norm would surely undermine his own authority. He could also be said to

---

[16] Introduced into the literature by Arthur N. Prior in his book *Formal Logic*, 2nd edn, Oxford University Press, London, 1962.

be irrational, or not fully to understand what obligations and permissions are.

Assume that a lawgiver actually ordained that it ought to be the case that that which (according to his will) ought to be the case also is the case. What would we think of such a "law"? Perhaps not that to enact it is "irrational"—but maybe a little ridiculous. Perhaps its enactment would be a way of emphasizing that the lawgiver wants his (other) laws to be taken seriously. Like his saying, with emphasis, "if something *ought to be* the case it ought to *be the case*". Be it observed in passing, that ordaining $O(Op \rightarrow p)$ does not "entail" that Op had been ordained. As regards the state of affairs that p the norm is conditional. It only says that should this state be made obligatory, now or in some future time, then it ought to obtain.

The question may be raised how we should understand the idea of the sovereign authority "transmitting his will" to sub-authorities if we had opted for a weaker conception of the notion of a "negation-norm" not allowing the shift from $\sim O$ to $P \sim$ or from $\sim P$ to $O \sim$ within the scope of a higher-order deontic operator (cf. above, p. 136). Assume, for example, that the normative negation of OOp were $O \sim Pp$ (and not $OO \sim p$). The sovereign wants that the sub-authority does *not* permit the state that p. Does he then want this state to be prohibited, i.e. does he want the norm-subjects to behave in such a way that the state that p does not obtain? Possibly this is what he wants, but not necessarily, it seems. But he may be said to want to "reserve room", logically speaking, for such a prohibition. If the prohibition were issued it must also be possible that it is observed, i.e. it must be (logically) possible that the state of affairs that $\sim p$ never obtains within the existence-span of this prohibition. But this is precisely what ought also to be possible if he had wanted a sub-authority to issue the prohibition. Hence from the point of view of a Transmission-of-Will Principle the two norms $O \sim Pp$ and $OO \sim p$ have the same conditions of satisfiability. Whether one could define satisfiability in such a way that the difference between the two norms becomes perceptible (at the level of satisfiability) is a question into which I shall not here inquire. Be it observed, however, that I do not claim that the two norms are "identical". They obviously are not.

XIV

Under the name "deontic logic" one may understand an axiomatized logical calculus the theorems of which are all the normative tautologies. What counts as a normative tautology, however, depends upon how the notion of satisfiability of norms is defined—and this again depends upon our choice of criteria for rational norm-giving and/or rationality in norms.

The system of deontic logic for norms of the first order has the following axioms:

A0. All tautologies of PL when for the variables are substituted norm-formulations.

A1. $P(p \lor q) \leftrightarrow Pp \lor Pq$

A2. $P(p \lor \sim p)$

A3. $O(p \lor \sim p)$

A4. $Op \leftrightarrow \sim P \sim p$.

The rules of inference are:

R1. For a variable may be substituted another variable or a molecular compound of variables.

R2. The usual Rule of Detachment.

R3. Formulas which are probably equivalent in PL are intersubstitutable in DL.

If we extend R1 by allowing substitution of formulas of DL for variables, and extend R3 to formulas provably equivalent in DL, we obtain a system of deontic logic under a restricted definition of the notion of satisfiability.

If we extend the notion of satisfiability in accordance with the "Transmission of Will"-Principle we may add to the system the axioms

A5. $Op \rightarrow OOp$

and

A6. $O(Op \rightarrow p)$

The system of deontic logic thus obtained may be said to be S4-like.

If the system admitted the principle $POp \rightarrow Op$ it would be S5-like. This formula says that if it is permitted that something is obligatory then this thing *is* obligatory. In our view of rational norm-giving this is not a deontic tautology. Its normative negation is $POp \,\&\, P \sim p$. The sovereign permits that it is not the case that p but also that a sub-authority forbids this. This corpus would be satisfied if, for some time, the sub-authority does not avail himself of his permission and during that time, or a part of that time, it is not the case that p. The following illustration shows that the negation of $POp \rightarrow Op$ is satisfiable:

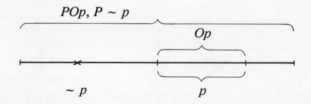

The satisfiability of the corpus consisting of POp and $P \sim p$ essentially depends upon the fact that the sub-norm Op may have a shorter existence-span (history) than the corpus itself. If, however, norms were not historical entities but had infinite duration (were eternal) then the sub-norm would have to be coexisting with the superior norms of the corpus. And then no occurrence of $\sim p$ could be allowed. The addition of $P \sim p$ to POp would result in an inconsistency and the principle $POp \rightarrow Op$ would be a "normative tautology". Hence we may conclude that the deontic logic of eternal norms is S5-like.

It is also of some interest to note that (our) deontic logic is not even S4.3-like. This is shown by the fact that $Pp \,\&\, Pq \rightarrow P(p \,\&\, q) \vee P(p \,\&\, Pq) \vee P(q \,\&\, Pp)$ is not a deontic tautology. Its normative negation is $Pp \,\&\, Pq \,\&\, O(\sim p \vee \sim q) \,\&\, O(\sim p \vee O \sim q) \,\&\, O(\sim q \vee O \sim p)$. The following illustration shows that this conjunction is satisfiable:

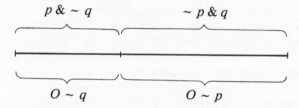

If things are as in the picture then, in the history of this corpus of five norms, it is sometimes the case that p and sometimes the case that q, always the case that it is either the case that not p or that not q (in other words, never the case that both states obtain), always the case that not q when it is the case that p and, finally, always the case that not p when it is the case that q. This means that the five norms are all satisfied.

XV

It is one of the traditional views of the nature of norms that norms are expressions of a norm-giving authority's will. What is said here about the laws of deontic logic as "principles of rational norm-giving" must not be taken as an endorsement of the said view. It is nevertheless a useful fiction, it seems to me, to think of a set of norms belonging to the same code, or normative order, or system as emanating from a "will" that certain things be the case and certain other things tolerated. It is natural to make it a criterion of the *rationality* of such a "will" that the "willed" total state of affairs be (at least) logically possible. On the basis of this criterion one can then determine the analogical meanings of contradiction and entailment also for norms, although norms have no truth-value.

If there existed no source, *like* a will, for the unity of a set of norms there would be no reason, it seems, why the contents of norms should be mutually consistent rather than contradict each other.

One could, however, drop the fiction of a "will" behind the norms and speak *only* of the *ideal* state of things envisaged in a normative order. It is a natural requirement that an ideal should picture a logically possible state of affairs. Ideals which do not satisfy this requirement are like crying for the moon; to entertain such ideals is "irrational" just as it is "irrational" to demand (to "will") that the world should live up to them.

2. CONDITIONAL NORMS AND HYPOTHETICAL IMPERATIVES

I

A good many, perhaps a majority, of (genuine) norms which actually are issued are *conditional* or *hypothetical*. The standard way of formulating them in language is to say that *if* something or other is the case (or is done), *then* something else ought (may) also (not to) be (or be done).

As we shall see this standard way of formulating conditional norms is not altogether happy and can easily lead to (serious) confusion.

Let us ask: How shall conditional norms be adequately expressed in the symbolic language of a "deontic logic"? The question has aroused much discussion and many different answers have been suggested.

In my first paper on deontic logic (1951) I did not discuss explicitly conditional norms but made some remarks on the related notion of (a) *commitment*. I used for this the symbol $O(p \rightarrow q)$. It may be read "it ought to be the case that, if p, then q", or, more accurately, "it ought to be the case that either not-p or q".

Against this it has been objected that the suggested formalization runs into the difficulties caused by the so-called Paradoxes of Implication.[17] If it is prohibited that it be the case that p, then *if*—notwithstanding the prohibition—it *is* the case that p, there is a "commitment" that it be the case that q too. This is thought to be so because in a deontic logic of the traditional type $O \sim p$ "entails" $O(p \rightarrow q)$. Similarly, if it is obligatory that q then whatever is the case "commits" to its being the case that q. Oq too "entails" $O(p \rightarrow q)$.

As easily seen, these "paradoxes" are but variations of the Ross Paradox. By substituting "$\sim p$" for "p" and replacing "$p \rightarrow q$" by "$\sim p \vee q$" in $O \sim p \rightarrow O(p \rightarrow q)$ and cancelling double negations we obtain the Ross Paradox formula $Op \rightarrow O(p \vee q)$. Similarly, $Oq \rightarrow O(p \rightarrow q)$ is but an equivalent form of $Op \rightarrow O(p \vee q)$.

It was, among other things, in order to avoid such "paradoxes" that I set out to develop a theory of *dyadic* modalities in the early 1950s.[18] The

---

[17] The first to point out this was A. N. Prior in a note "The Paradoxes of Derived Obligation" in *Mind*, **63**, 1954.

[18] First in a congress report "A New System of Modal Logic" in *Proceedings of the 11th International Congress of Philosophy*, Vol. 5, Amsterdam-Louvain, 1953; and then, in

idea was to let a dyadic functor $N(p/q)$ symbolize the *relative necessity* of one proposition given another. Similarly, one could have a symbol $M(p/q)$ for relative possibility, connected with the symbol for necessity through the (defining) equivalences $M(p/q) \leftrightarrow \sim N(\sim p/q)$ or $N(p/q) \leftrightarrow \sim M(\sim p/q)$.

In a note in *Mind*[19] I made a first attempt to apply these ideas about dyadic modalities to deontic concepts and propositions. The attempts were continued, with variations in several directions, in my writings on the logic of norms through the 1960s. The fullest statements of them were in *Norm and Action* (1963) and in *An Essay in Deontic Logic and the General Theory of Action* (1968).

It is not clear to me yet what the interest and merits are of a theory of dyadic modalities in general and of dyadic deontic operators in particular. But as I see things now, the logical problems connected with the formulation of conditional norms can be satisfactorily coped with *without* resort to a dyadic theory. This I would regard as an advantage.

Consider the form $p \rightarrow Oq$. It has been one of the candidates for the logical form of a conditional norm. We shall then have to think of "p" as representing a closed sentence expressing a (true or false) individual proposition. "q" may represent a closed or open sentence. The expression Oq, we know, has two interpretations, *viz.* a prescriptive and a descriptive (existential) one. How do these interpretations "match" the form $p \rightarrow Oq$?

On the descriptive interpretation of Oq, the implication formula says that it is either the case that it is not the case that p *or* it is the case that (there is a norm to the effect that) it ought to be the case that q. So therefore, *if* it *is* the case that p, it is also the case that there is a norm to the said effect. This is a factual statement, true or false as the case may be. It would be wrong or at least highly misleading to call this the expression of a conditional norm.

On the interpretation of Oq as a prescription (norm), the expression $p \rightarrow Oq$ would consist of a descriptive and a prescriptive ingredient joined by a sentential connective. Does such an expression "make sense"? The question is not really easy to answer. It seems to me clear, however, that if the sentential connective in question is a *truth*-connective, then this "linguistic hybrid" is a monster with no place in meaningful discourse. Since I wish to stick to the truth-functional understanding of the implication sign ("$\rightarrow$" meaning "*not – or –* "), my answer to the above question is in the negative.

One could, however, give to $p \rightarrow Oq$ a prescriptive interpretation by regarding it as an elliptic formulation with a concealed or suppressed

---

much greater detail, in an essay with the same title, published in my book *Logical Studies* (1957).

[19] "A Note on Deontic Logic and Derived Obligation", *Mind*, **65**, 1956.

second-order deontic operator. The words "if *p* then it ought to be that *q*" might very well be used for giving someone to understand that this is how things ought to (or may) be. A higher authority could thus address a subordinate authority. The full expression would then be $O(p \rightarrow Oq)$ where the second-order O is prescriptive and the first-order O is descriptive (cf. above, p. 135).

To say that $O(p \rightarrow Oq)$, when prescriptively interpreted, expresses a conditional norm seems to me correct. And the same is true of the first-order expression $O(p \rightarrow q)$. Indeed this last is what I should regard myself as the *prototype* logical form of a conditional (obligation) norm.

But how then shall we deal with the "paradoxes"? Does not $O \sim p$ "entail" $O(p \rightarrow q)$ and does this not mean that doing the forbidden "commits" the agent to doing just anything? The fault here is with the use of the words "entailment" and "commit". The fact that $O \sim p \rightarrow O(p \rightarrow q)$ is what I have called a "deontic tautology" only means that in a normative code in which it is (categorically) forbidden that it is the case that *p* it cannot "consistently" be permitted that that *p* is the case in conjunction with something else. This, moreover, is "consistency" in the sense of "rational norm-giving", not in the sense of "formal logic".

Similarly, there is no question of a categorical obligation "entailing" a(n infinity of) hypothetical norm(s) to the effect that something or other by being the case would "commit" one to doing the obligatory thing. The fact that $Oq \rightarrow O(p \rightarrow q)$ is a "deontic tautology" only means that, if something is obligatory, then it cannot consistently with this (in the sense of "rational norm-giving") be the case that the negation of this thing, under some circumstances, is permitted.

The Paradoxes of Commitment and of Derived Obligation are thus harmless. The air of paradox originates through an unwarranted *reading* of such formulas as $O \sim p \rightarrow O(p \rightarrow q)$ or $Oq \rightarrow O(p \rightarrow q)$, which are valid in any sound system of deontic logic. These formulas constitute as such no obstacle to regarding the form $O(p \rightarrow q)$ as the prototype form of a conditional norm.

Let there be a conditional norm $O(p \rightarrow q)$. Assume now that, on some particular occasion *o*, it is the case that *p*. Is it then not absolutely natural to say that, on this occasion, it also ought to be the case that *q*?

This looks like an inference, *modo ponente*, from $O(p \rightarrow q)$ and p_o to Oq_o. This, of course, is not in ordinary logic a valid schema. Formally valid would be an inference from $p_o \rightarrow Oq_o$ and p_o to Oq_o or from $(o)(p_o \rightarrow Oq_o)$ and p_o to Oq_o. Shall we conclude then that, after all, the correct expression for the conditional norm is $p \rightarrow Oq$ and not $O(p \rightarrow q)$? I think the solution to the puzzle is as follows:

When from the norm to the effect that it ought to be the case that, if *p* then *q*, in combination with the fact that it is the case that *p* we "infer" that it ought to be the case that *q*, we are actually using "ought" here in two senses. The first is the ought of a (genuine) norm or a "deontic Ought" as I shall also call it. The second is what I propose to call the ought of a "practical necessity" or a "technical Ought". For the second, "must" is perhaps a better word than "ought".[20]

The technical Ought is not properly a normative concept. It expresses that something or other has to be (done) in order that something else is (attained or secured). Unless the first is, the second will not be. In the case of our hypothetical norm $O(p \rightarrow q)$ above, Oq_o says that unless in a situation o when it is the case that p it is not also the case that q, the norm will not be satisfied. Something it prohibits will be the case.

Since the two oughts are (very) different, we should distinguish them also in the symbolism—for example as O_d and O_t.

A technical ought-statement is, nearly always, *elliptic* in the sense that it contains implicit reference to something which will not be if that which, in the technical sense, ought to be is not. There are a great many things which can be referred to thus. A common characteristic of them seems to be that they are actual or potential *ends* of human action, something we may intend, or want, or wish to attain. The thing of which a technical ought is predicated usually has the character of a *means* to this end.

When a technical ought-statement is supplemented with mention of the (actual or potential) end, we have a statement of the type often called a *hypothetical* norm or imperative. In ordinary language such norms are formulated, sometimes as if-then-statements ("If you want − − −, you must (ought to, have to) − − −"), sometimes as in-order-to-statements ("In order to attain − it is necessary that −"), sometimes as "Unless"-statements ("Unless − − −, − − − will (not) be").

Hypothetical norms in this "technical" sense must not be confused with conditional norms in the "deontic" sense—even though the latter too may, not inappropriately, be called "hypothetical", and the former "conditional". I myself prefer to call the former *technical norms*.[21]

As seen, one can from the deontic Ought $O_d(p \rightarrow q)$ "extract" a conditional technical Ought $p \rightarrow O_t q$ where the latter formula is an elliptic way of saying that, if it is the case that p then it must also be the case that q in order that the norm $O_d(p \rightarrow q)$ be satisfied, the requirement which it imposes fulfilled. But we could also "extract" from it a conditional $\sim q \rightarrow O_t \sim p$ which says that if it is not the case that q then, in order that the norm $O_d(p \rightarrow q)$ be satisfied, it must also not be the case that p. Or we could co-ordinate to $O_d(p \rightarrow q)$ a technical Ought $O_t(p \rightarrow q)$ which then says, elliptically, i.e. without explicit mention of the end in view, that, in

---

[20] Cf. the discussion of practical necessity, the "must", and what is here called "technical norms" in the first essay in this volume, above, pp. 1−17. On the two senses of Ought, see also above p. 74 and 96.

[21] Cf. *Norm and Action*, p. 9f.

order that $O_d(p \rightarrow q)$ be satisfied, it must be the case either that not p or that q.[22]

The agent who is under the obligation $O_d(p \rightarrow q)$, or another agent who is anxious to "enforce" this obligation, may from the technical $p \rightarrow O_t q$ (and correspondingly from $\sim q \rightarrow O_t \sim p$) "extract" a *new* norm or order in the particular situation when the state that p (or that $\sim q$) happens to obtain. This would be a norm $O_d q$ (or $O_d \sim p$), the existence-span of which ranges over this or that particular situation o when it is the case that p (or $\sim q$) (cf. below, p. 165f).

II

What is the logic of the technical Ought, O_t? Answer: it is the same logical structure as the logic of the deontic Ought, O_d. This is a reason, I presume, why we naturally use the same word "Ought" in both cases—but also a reason why one is inclined to confuse the two.

The identity of logical structure referred to is not a triviality. It is a fact which emerges from what has been termed "a reduction of deontic logic to alethic modal logic".

The technical Ought, as we know, is "elliptic". It refers to a necessary condition of some state of affairs—for example the attainment of some good (end) or the avoidance of some evil. Call this state S. The technical Ought, in relation to this state, can then be defined as follows: $O_t p =_{df} N(S \rightarrow p)$, where "$N$" is the conventional symbol for necessity.

We now stipulate that the state that S is possible (its contradictory state not necessary). If then the definition of the technical Ought is used for translating the axioms A1–A4 of the standard system of first-order deontic logic we obtain a fragment of a system of alethic (ordinary) modal logic known as the System M or T. This is the (non-trivial) sense in which deontic logic may be said to be reducible to standard modal logic and also the sense in which the logic of the technical and the deontic Oughts are the same formal structure.

The *locus classicus* of this reduction is Alan Anderson's note in *Mind*, **67**, 1958 entitled "A Reduction of Deontic Logic to Alethic Modal Logic".[23] Later, the idea was taken up by myself and further developed in

---

[22] Cf. the discussion of "derived obligations" in the essay "Practical Inference", above pp. 14ff. See also above p. 70f on the foundation of normative statements in technical rules.

[23] The idea is already found in an earlier, mimeographed paper by Anderson, "The Formal Analysis of Normative Systems", Technical Report No. 2, Office of Naval Research, Group Psychology Branch, New Haven, 1956. Essentially the same "reductivist" idea also occurs in a mimeographed paper by Stig Kanger, "New Foundations for Ethical Theory", Stockholm, 1957, reprinted in *Deontic Logic: Introductory and Systematic Readings*, ed. by Risto Hilpinen; D. Reidel, Dordrecht, 1971.

several papers.[24] My (and Anderson's) mistake, as I see things now, was not to have realized that the "reduction" actually was, *not* of the *deontic*, but of the *technical* Ought.

Note on a Paradox of Åqvist

The difference between deontic and technical Oughts can be nicely illustrated by considering a "paradox" invented by Lennart Åqvist.

Let it be the case that OKp where "Kp" is read: "it is known that p". In any standard system of epistemic logic it is assumed that if something is known it is also true, $Kp \rightarrow p$. In a deontic logic which accepts the traditional distribution principle for the O-operator and a Rule of Extensionality to the effect that logically equivalent formulas are intersubstitutable (in formulas of deontic logic) one then immediately proves $OKp \rightarrow Op$. The formula says, roughly, that that which ought to be *known* also ought to *be*.

This, as such, is hardly a "paradox". But a suitable choice of instantiations of p may make it appear paradoxical. For example: Let "p" say that some disaster has occurred. Assume that this ought to be known (at least to some person concerned). Then it ought also to be the case that the disaster has occurred. *This* has a ring of paradox.

The appearance of paradox is at once mitigated, I think, by the observation that a duty to know, normally, is *conditional*. This is surely so in the example we have just given. *Since* or *if* a disaster has occurred somewhere, it may be the duty of so-and-so to take cognizance of this fact. It may also be his duty to be alert to the possibility. But it cannot very well be anybody's duty to know this *simpliciter*. If it unconditionally ought to be the case that something is known then this thing surely also ought to be. If this sounds paradoxical it is only because the oddity inherent in *unconditional* demands that something be known.

A duty to know something, should this thing be the case, answers to a conditional norm $O_d \ (p \rightarrow Kp)$. It says that the following ought to be: either it is not the case that p or (if this be the case) it is also known to be the case. No logically permissible argument will from this lead to $O_d p$, i.e. to the conclusion that it ought to be the case that p.

From the conditional norm one can "extract", we have said, a conditioned technical Ought, $p \rightarrow O_t Kp$. This is elliptic and may refer to the fact that, if it happens to be the case that p, then, unless it is also the case that Kp, the norm $O_d \ (p \rightarrow Kp)$ is not satisfied. If it can be made the case that Kp, it *must* be thus made—or else the norm is violated.

That Kp entails that p. Does not the conditional $p \rightarrow O_t Kp$ then entail $p \rightarrow O_t p$ or, for that matter, $O_t Kp$ by itself entail $O_t p$?

The answer is Yes. Assume that it is the case that p. Then, by virtue of

---

[24] Mainly in "Deontic Logic and the Theory of Conditions", *Critica*, **6**, 1968, reprinted in the anthology *Deontic Logic*, ed. by R. Hilpinen (see note 23, above).

the technical norm involved, it is required that this fact (that p) be known (that Kp). This is a genuine requirement which may or may not be satisfied. But to say that, if it is the case that p then it ought, in the "technical" sense, to be the case that p is not to state any "requirement" at all. Unless one extends the term "requirement" so as to include, as a "limiting case", also the statement "in order for it to be the case that p, it is required that it be the case that p".

But can one not argue as follows: By the norm $O_d \, (p \rightarrow Kp)$ it is a *deontic* requirement that, if it be the case that p, this be also known. And since, if it is known that p, it is also the case that p, is not this last a deontic requirement too? Consider the following transformations: $O_d \, (p \rightarrow Kp)$ entails $O_d \, (p \rightarrow p \, \& \, Kp)$, since that Kp is logically equivalent with that $p \, \& \, Kp$. But $p \rightarrow p \, \& \, Kp$ is logically equivalent with $(p \rightarrow p) \, \& \, (p \rightarrow Kp)$. Therefore, in a deontic logic with the normal distribution law for the O-operator, $O_d (p \rightarrow Kp)$ (normatively) entails $O_d (p \rightarrow p)$. This is true but completely harmless and trivial. It does not mean that it ought to be the case that p.

Let the conditional norm be $O_d \, (p \rightarrow Kq)$. For example: It ought to be the case that, if the tyre bursts, it is *known* that there is a spare wheel under the bottom of the car. Then, by the same type of argument as above, we deduce $O_d \, (p \rightarrow q)$ or that it ought to be the case that, if a tyre bursts, there *is* a spare wheel under the car. This is no paradox. When the two norms are spelt out so that it is seen to whom they are addressed, it would normally turn out that they have different addressees. The driver should know where the spare wheel is, and the manufacturer of the car should see to it that the wheel is installed in its proper place.

Consider, finally, the conditional sentence $p \rightarrow O_d Kp$. From it we infer $p \rightarrow O_d p$. Here the deontic consequent must be interpreted descriptively. $p \rightarrow O_d Kp$ is now a (true or false) statement to the effect that either it is not the case that p or there is (exists) a norm to the effect that it ought to be known that p. A norm to this effect "normatively entails" that it ought to be the case that p. But these inferences and relationships do not show that from the fact that one ought to know that a certain thing is the case, *should this thing be the case*, one can infer that this thing ought to be the case *simpliciter*.

Note on Contrary-to-Duty Imperatives

I have argued that the implication paradoxes do not constitute an objection to regarding $O \, (p \rightarrow q)$ as the prototype form of a conditional norm. But they may be said to point to another problem which is serious. It concerns the status of those norms which Professor Chisholm has called Contrary-to-Duty Imperatives.[25] This peculiar category of norms can be described as follows:

---

[25] R. M. Chisholm, "Contrary-to-Duty Imperatives and Deontic Logic", *Analysis*, **24**, 1963.

Let there be a norm of the form *O*- and another norm of the same form which prescribes what ought to be the case if the first norm has been violated and thus cannot be satisfied. If, for example, the first says that it ought to be the case that *p*, the second says that it ought to be the case that *q* if not-*p*. The first is *Op* and the second *O* (~ *p* → *q*). The second is a Contrary-to-Duty Imperative.

We introduce the following defining characterization: A Contrary-to-Duty Imperative is a conditional norm which coexists in a corpus together with an obligation norm the content of which is the contradictory of the antecedent of the first. (Or, considering the possibility of contraposition, we could also say "the content of which is identical with the consequent of the first".) When therefore the obligation norm is violated, the satisfaction of the Contrary-to-Duty Imperative requires that the consequent (or, with contraposition, the contradictory of the antecedent) in its content comes true. This requirement is a "technical" Ought.

Assume now that there is a norm *O* ~ *p*, prohibiting that *p*, and correlated with or corresponding to it also a Contrary-to-Duty Imperative *O* (*p* → *q*). As we know, the first norm "normatively entails" the second. This "entailment" is independent of the "value" of "*q*". *O* ~ *p* equally "entails" *O* (*p* → *r*). These "entailments", moreover, are valid quite independently of whether the conditional norms (Contrary-to-Duty Imperatives) actually *exist*, or not. (It should be remembered what "entailment" here *means*; *viz.* that the negation norms of the conditional norms in question are "rationally inconsistent" with the given prohibition.)

Assume next that the two Contrary-to-Duty Imperatives *O* (*p* → *q*) and *O* (*p* → *r*) actually coexist with *O* ~ *p* in a corpus. This in itself need not lead to trouble. It only means that, if the prohibition is violated, the co-ordinated Contrary-to-Duty Imperatives require, for their satisfaction, that both that *q* and that *r* come true. This requirement is satisfiable provided that both states are logically compatible.

But what if the two states are incompatible? For example, *O* (*p* → *q*) stipulates at most five years of imprisonment and *O* (*p* → *r*) at least ten years of imprisonment consequent upon the prohibited state coming true. The conjunction of the two states that *q* and that *r* is a logical impossibility— and so is the conjunction of the two technical Oughts O_tq and O_tr.

If a case like this occurred "in real life", the legislator would presumably take steps to remove the conflict—say by derogating one of the conditional norms or by making them, somehow, consonant. (That *q* may be made consequent upon that *p* & *s* comes true and that *r* upon that *p* & ~ *s*.) But this is a problem for the legislator and not for the logician.

What is the logical problem here? *Is* there a logical problem at all?

The trouble is *not* that the two norms *O* (*p* → *q*) and *O* (*p* → *r*) could not form a "rationally consistent" corpus with the norm *O* ~ *p*. Provided that " ~ *p*" describes a logically possible state of affairs, a corpus consisting of the three norms is consistent—and satisfied if, and only if, it is always the case that *p*, "the crime never committed".

But in real life crimes are sometimes committed, prohibited states of affairs sometimes come to obtain. Assume that this happens with the state that *p*. If the norm-subjects, call them "judges", who are the addressees of the Contrary-to-Duty Imperatives, are anxious to do *their* duty, what shall they do? Sentence the criminal to at most five years imprisonment or to at least ten years? Perhaps it is logically possible to pass "contradictory" sentences. But it is not logically possible that a man suffer both at most five years and at least ten years imprisonment on the same occasion for punishment. Therefore those whose duty it is to satisfy the two Contrary-to-Duty Imperatives will necessarily "sin" at least against one of the two.

It is certainly right to say that the two norms *conflict*. One may even wish to say that they "contradict" each other. But "contradiction" does not mean here that the two norms were rationally inconsistent, as for example Op and $O \sim p$ are. That the two norms "contradict" each other only means that, if the norm to which they are co-ordinated as Contrary-to-Duty Imperatives is violated, then their satisfaction imposes contradictory (in the strict logical sense) requirements on the norm-subjects.

Such contradictions cannot be "solved" in logic, only in the practice of norm-giving. It is an *illusion* to think there is a logical problem here. The illusion originates from thinking that normative entailment is an existential relationship between norms. If this were the case, *any* obligation norm would give rise to conflicting ("contradictory") Contrary-to-Duty Imperatives. This would be so because Op "entails" $O (\sim p \rightarrow q)$ and also $O (\sim p \rightarrow \sim q)$. But this does not mean that if the first exists, the other two coexist with it. Whether they do this or not depends upon which norms have been enacted (or otherwise come to be). If the conflicting norms exist, which they may do, the legislator is well advised to amend legislation. The *logician* cannot help him.

One could call the obligation-norm to which a Contrary-to-Duty Imperative has been correlated *primary* and the correlated norm *secondary*. When the Contrary-to-Duty Imperative stipulates some punishment or sanction to be consequent upon something it may, without further statement, be taken for granted that the thing in question is prohibited. A penal code can be and, it seems, often is, written in the terms of formulations of secondary norms only. These secondary norms can be said to "criminalize" certain actions or states of affairs without expressly prohibiting them. The law may stipulate that murder be punished in such and such a way, but it need not say "Murder prohibited!". Shall we nevertheless say that the law prohibits murder? The answer is not a matter of deontic logic but depends on further considerations of the meaning of *punishment*.

A distinction between primary and secondary norms corresponding to our distinction above was made by John Austin. Austin speaks of primary and secondary duties and rights.[26] The primary duties prescribe the conduct which the lawgiver "wills" that the citizens observe, and the secondary duties the sanction which ought to be applied to those who do not observe their primary duties.

The same distinction, but with a reversal of terminology, is found with another classic of jurisprudence, Hans Kelsen. Kelsen called norms stipulating sanctions for a delict *primary* and the "underlying" prohibitions (obligations) *secondary*. He says:[27] "Law is the primary norm, which stipulates the sanction ... It is only if one makes use of the concept of secondary norms in the presentation of law that the subject 'ought' to avoid the delict and perform the legal duty ... Only the organ can, strictly speaking, 'obey' or 'disobey' the legal norm, by executing or not executing the legal sanction." The formulation of secondary norms, Kelsen continues:[28] "undoubtedly facilitates the exposition of law. But such a procedure is justifiable only if it is kept in mind that the only genuine legal norm is the sanctioning norm." One could—using Professor Chisholm's terminology—say that, on Kelsen's view, law is a system of Contrary-to-Duty Imperatives addressed to the state organs. It is an interesting question in its own right whether this view can (for reasons of logic) be consistently carried through for the totality of norms constituting a legal order. The answer is presumably negative.

Kelsen's use of the terms "primary" and "secondary" may be thought awkward since it is obvious that the notion of a sanction (punishment) presupposes the notion of a delict which in its turn can be said to presuppose the notion of a prohibition ("primary norm" in our terminology). This is so notwithstanding the fact that the prohibition need not be "expressly stated" but may remain "tacitly understood".

3. NORMS WITH TEMPORAL QUANTIFIERS

I

The norm Op, we have said, is satisfied if, and only if, the state that p obtains throughout the existence span of the norm. We took, in other words, the view that what the norm demands is that something *always* be the case (as long as the demand persists).

Similarly, we took the view that a permissive norm Pp allows the permitted state to obtain *sometime* as long as the permission is there.

---

[26] *Lectures on Jurisprudence*, Lecture XLV.

[27] *General Theory of Law and State*, Harvard University Press, 1949, p. 61.

[28] *Op. cit.*, p. 63.

We introduce the symbol ∧ for "always" and ∨ for "sometime(s)". The second may also be regarded as an abbreviation for ~ ∧ ~ ; and the first as an abbreviation for ~ ∨ ~ .

The notions of "sometime(s)" and "always" I shall call *temporal quantifiers*. The scope of these quantifiers can also be relativized to a time-span of limited duration. Then "∧ *p*" says that the state that *p* obtains always throughout this span. The span can be, for example, the time during which a certain norm *exists*.

There are also, however, other possibilities to be considered. The requirement expressed in an obligation norm might be that a certain state of affairs should obtain sometime(s) in the existence span of the norm. And a permission might say that the permitted state may obtain always as long as the permission holds. A symbolic expression for the obligation norm would be *O* ∨ *p* and for the permission norm *P* ∧ *p*.

The variable "*p*" in "*Op*" or "*Pp*", we have said, is a schematic representation for an *open* sentence expressing a *generic* proposition, e.g. "*p*" = "it is raining" (see above, p. 132). Generic propositions are not "by themselves" true or false; but "∨ *p*" and "∧ *p*" are *closed* sentences expressing true or false individual propositions—for example that it sometime(s) is raining or is always raining respectively.

When the norm content is generic it is certainly most natural to understand an obligation norm with this content as requiring that the content be realized "always", i.e. throughout the existence of that obligation. Thus the "natural meaning" of "*Op*" might be said to be "*O* ∧ *p*". With regard to permissions the situation is less clear. If it is permitted that *p*, does this not "mean" that it may be the case that *p* throughout the time when the permission is "in force"? Or does it only mean that this state may come to obtain during the time of the permission—but not necessarily that it may be there the whole time? I do not think that these questions have an answer which holds good for all permissive norms. "*Pp*" sometimes "means" "*P* ∧ *p*", sometimes "*P* ∨ *p*".

II

We next extend the notions of satisfaction and satisfiability to norms the contents of which are "bound" by temporal quantifiers. The norm *O* ∧ *p*, obviously, is satisfied if, and only if, throughout its history it is the case that *p*. But the same is true of the norm *P* ∧ *p*. Similarly, the norms *P* ∨ *p* and *O* ∨ *p* have identical conditions of satisfaction. Ordering something to be the case always, and permitting it to be the case always, is rational norm-giving (activity) if, and only if, it is *possible* that this thing is always the case (as long as the order or permission is "in force"). But whereas the order demands that its content be realized, the permission only "tolerates" this.

It is of some interest to see that the above results can also be obtained by applying to the norms the criteria of satisfiability which we originally (Part 1, Section VIII) gave for norms with generic norm-contents. Applying the given criterion to $O \vee p$, for example, we should have to say that the norm is satisfied if, and only if, throughout its existence it is sometime(s) the case that p. But to say that it is always the case that it is sometimes the case that p is tantamount to saying that it is sometimes the case that p. "Always sometime" reduces to "sometime", the combination of symbols $\wedge \vee$ to $\vee$, when "time" means "all time", past, present, and future—either unrestrictedly, from an infinitely remote past to an infinitely remote future, or restricted to the finite span of time during which a certain norm exists.

Analogously, the satisfaction condition for $P \vee p$ is $\vee \vee p$ which also reduces to $\vee p$; that for $O \wedge p$ is $\wedge \wedge p$ which reduces to $\wedge p$; and that for $P \wedge p$ is $\vee \wedge p$ which also reduces to $\wedge p$. This is so because the tense-logic for "all time" is S5-like. But one could also express these same findings by saying that the iteration of the temporal quantifiers *makes no sense* in application to a *closed* sentence.

The situation would be different if "$\vee p$" had been taken to mean "it *will* sometime be the case that p" or "it *was* sometime the case that p"— and correspondingly for "$\wedge p$". Then the sentences in question would have been *open*. The proposition that it will sometime be the case that p is true or false depending upon from which moment the future is counted. To say that it will always be the case that it will sometime be the case that p is not the same as saying *simpliciter* that it will sometime be the case that p. Now $\wedge \vee p$ makes sense and expresses a stronger proposition than $\vee p$. The S5-reduction no longer holds true.

Such "forward-looking" temporal quantifiers also have a place in normative discourse. One may, for example, wish to say that something or other ought to be the case, not necessarily all the time, but always "from time to time". The expression for the norm would then be $O \wedge \vee p$ where "$\wedge$" stands for "now and in all the future" and "$\vee$" for "now or in some future"; and this expression would have a different meaning both from $O \vee p$ and from $O \wedge p$—*also* when, in the last two expressions, "$\wedge$" simply means "always" and "$\vee$" "sometime".

Norms with forward-looking temporal quantifiers deserve a special study. This study will not be undertaken here.

III

We next consider the following example: $O(p \vee \vee q)$. The formula says that it ought to be the case that p or sometime q. This is a rather "unperspicuous" formulation. What does the "part" of the norm's requirement that it be the case that p amount to? That this always be the case? Then the norm could be better expressed $O (\wedge p \vee \vee q)$. Or is the demand that it always, i.e. as long as the norm is in force, be the case that either p or sometime q? This demand could also be expressed $O \wedge (p \vee \vee q)$. But note that $\wedge (p \vee \vee q)$ is, on our adopted criterion, also the statement of the satisfaction condition for $O (p \vee \vee q)$.

Consider now the expression $\wedge (p \vee \vee q)$. It says that it is always the case that it is the case either that p or sometime q. This obviously means the same as that if it never is the case that q then it is always the case that p. In the S5-like temporal logic of "always" and "sometimes" $\wedge (p \vee \vee q)$ reduces to $\wedge p \vee \vee q$. And similarly $\wedge \wedge (p \vee \vee q)$.

The two suggested answers to our initial question concerning the meaning of $O (p \vee \vee q)$ thus turn out to amount to the same. $O (p \vee \vee q)$ and $O (\wedge p \vee \vee q)$ and $O \wedge (p \vee \vee q)$ are three, from the point of view of their satisfiability, alternative ways of formulating the same norm.

IV

We now proceed to formulas of any degree of complexity formed of variables p, q, ..., truth connectives, temporal quantifiers, and deontic operators. By an atomic norm-formulation we shall understand a formula to which has been prefixed the operator O or P.

Let there be a set of atomic norm-formulations. To it answers what we have called a *corpus* of norms. The atomic members of a corpus are thought of as coexisting and, moreover, coexisting over the same time-span or history.

The deontic operators which do not themselves stand within the scope of any deontic operator, i.e. the operators in front of the atomic norm-formulations themselves, will be said to be (operators) of the first order. Deontic operators which stand within the scope of just one deontic operator will be said to be of the second order. And so forth up to an nth order.

Atomic norm-formulations with only a first-order deontic operator express norms of the first order. An atomic norm-formulation within which there is a deontic operator of order n but none of higher order expresses a norm of the nth order, or of degree n.

In a similar manner we can arrange the temporal quantifiers according to degrees or orders. An operator $\wedge$ or $\vee$ which occurs in the scope of a deontic operator or the first order but not in the scope of any *deontic* operator of higher order will be said to be a temporal quantifier of the first order. Temporal quantifiers in the scope of a deontic operator of order n but not of any deontic operator of higher order than n are temporal quantifiers of degree or order n.

The definition of the orders allows for the possibility that temporal quantifiers of the same order occur within the scope of each other. This is a "luxury" with which we could also have dispensed. Because of the S5-like character of the tense-logic of "all time", an expression involving temporal quantifiers of the same order within the scope of one and the same deontic operator is logically equivalent with an expression in which no temporal quantifier of this order stands in the scope of another temporal quantifier of the same order.

We next perform the following change in the atomic norm-formulations in our initially given set (corpus): We replace every occurrence of a deontic or temporal operator by the same operator to which has been attached an index showing its degree.

Some examples: The atomic formulas POp and Op become P_1O_2p and O_1p respectively. In them there is no temporal quantifier. Our formula above (p. 161) $O(p \vee \vee q)$ becomes $O_1(p \vee \vee_1 q)$. The formula $O \wedge (p \vee \vee q)$ becomes $O_1\wedge_1 (p \vee \vee_1 q)$. In it a temporal quantifier of degree 1 occurs in the scope of another temporal quantifier of the same degree. The expression $\wedge_1 (p \vee \vee_1 q)$, however, is equivalent with $\wedge_1 p \vee \vee_1 q$ in which no temporal quantifier occurs within the scope of another. Compare this with the formula $O \wedge (p \vee P \vee q)$. Indexing the operators, it becomes $O_1\wedge_1 (p \vee P_2\vee_2 q)$. Here neither a distribution nor a reduction corresponding to that in the formula $O_1\wedge_1 (p \vee \vee_1 q)$ is allowed.

Finally, we replace every occurrence in the norm-formulations of the operator O by the temporal quantifier $\wedge$ and every occurrence of P by $\vee$, retaining the indices. To mention an example: the penultimate formula above now becomes $\wedge_1\wedge_1 (p \vee \vee_2\vee_2 q)$.

The norm expressed by an atomic norm-formulation is satisfiable if, and only if, the formula resulting from the described transformations expresses a logically possible proposition. And a corpus of norms is satisfiable if, and only if, the conjunction of the norm-formulations for its members, after transformation, is logically consistent.

This definition of the notion of satisfiability embodies in tense-logical terms the idea which was previously (above, p. 145) referred to as the Transformation-of-Will Principle (of higher-order deontic logic).

As seen from the example given above, in a formula transformed there may again occur temporal quantifiers in the scope of other temporal quantifiers of the same degree.

Such clusters of quantifiers can be eliminated in accordance with the rules for S5-reductions. After these reductions, one quantifier in the scope of another is always one degree higher than the second. For example: the above formula reduces to $\wedge_1 (p \vee \vee_2 q)$.

Are reductions possible when a temporal quantifier appears in the scope of another of lower degree? The answer to this question is not as obvious as the answer to the same question when quantifiers of the same degree are concerned. In order to give an answer we must consider inclusionship relations between existence spans of possibly different length of norms and the relation between individual occasions and spans of time.

The temporal quantifiers of degree 1 all span over the entire history of the initially given corpus of norms. The temporal quantifiers of degree 2 span over a part (in the limiting case the whole) of the history of the corpus; but these parts need not coincide. The quantifiers of degree 3 which occur inside a given quantifier of degree 2 span over a part (or the whole) of the span covered by that quantifier of degree 2; these parts need not coincide just as the spans of the different quantifiers of degree 2 need not coincide. And so forth. A span which falls inside another span (or possibly coincides with it) is called a sub-span.

It follows that, if something is true of *all* occasions in a span, then this same thing is also true of all occasions in any given sub-span of that span, but not necessarily vice-versa. Moreover, if something holds good of *some* occasion in a given sub-span it also holds good of *some* occasion in the span itself, though not necessarily vice-versa.

To the principle $O\,(Op \rightarrow p)$ of higher-order deontic logic discussed above (pp. 146f) corresponds the tense-logical formula $\Lambda_1\,(\Lambda_2 p \rightarrow p)$. It says that it is true of every occasion in the span of the higher-order norm that this occasion either falls in a sub-span in which on some occasion it is *not* the case that *p or* is an occasion on which it is true that p. ($\Lambda_2 p \rightarrow p$ is logically equivalent with $V_2 \sim p \vee p$.) What the formula says is logically true.

A weakened form of the above formula is $\Lambda_1 \Lambda_2 p \rightarrow \Lambda_1 p$. It says that if something is true of every occasion which falls within any sub-span of a given span then this same thing is true of every occasion in the span itself. This tense-logical truth reflects in our interpretation the higher-order deontic formula $OOp \rightarrow Op$.

Moreover, if something is true of every occasion which falls within a given span, then it is also true of every occasion in the span that it falls within a sub-span such that the thing in question is true of every occasion in the sub-span. This tense-logical truth, $\Lambda_1 p \rightarrow \Lambda_1 \Lambda_2 p$ reflects the deontic formula $Op \rightarrow OOp$ (cf. above, p. 146).

If some occasions fall within a sub-span of a span such that a certain thing is true of every occasion in that sub-span, it does *not* follow that this thing is true of every occasion in the span itself. $V_1 \Lambda_2 p \rightarrow \Lambda_1 p$ is not a tense-logical truth and therefore, under the interpretation under consideration, $POp \rightarrow Op$ is not a deontic tautology either (cf. above, pp. 148f).

4. Norms for Individual Occasions

I

The variables p, q, etc. which occur in deontic formulas are, we have said, schematic representations for *open* sentences describing *generic* states of affairs or processes. Such states obtain, or do not obtain, on what I have called individual *occasions*. An occasion, roughly speaking, is a location in space and time. The notion is connected with many problems some of which will be briefly hinted at in subsequent chapters. Throughout this study we pay attention only to the temporal component of occasions. It is sometimes convenient to refer to this component as a *moment* in time.

As symbols for occasions I shall use o, o', o'', etc. That the state of affairs that p obtains on the occasion o will be symbolized by "p_o" (cf. above, p. 152). The formula represents an open or a closed sentence depending upon whether "o" is regarded as a variable standing for a "random" occasion or as a name of an individual occasion.

The atomic components of a molecular compound of variables may be associated with different occasions. For example: p_o & $q_{o'}$. The sentence says that on o it is the case that p and on o' that q. The atomic component "p" will be said to be (specified) *for* the occasion o or to *refer to* the occasion o. Of the molecular compound itself we shall say that it is (specified) for the two occasions o and o', or for the pair of occasions o, o'.

II

A norm, obligating or permissive, may be issued for an individual occasion or for a set of individually specified occasions. An obligation-norm which is given for an individual occasion is often also called a *command* or an *order*.[29]

Here we shall consider only norms of the *first* order which are for individual occasions. We begin with the simple case when all norm-contents are propositions referring to one and the same occasion o.

A corpus consisting of orders, prohibitions, and permissions for one occasion o is satisfiable if, and only if, it is logically possible that, on this occasion, *all* the things ordered and *none* of the things prohibited obtain together with *every one* of the things permitted.

When satisfiability is defined in this way, special attention must be paid to the case when the contents of some of the *permissions* (if there are several) are logically incompatible. Normally, if something is permitted without also being obligatory, the contradictory of this thing is permitted too. The occurrence of both a norm Pp and a norm $P \sim p$ in a corpus of norms which exists over a certain period of time, and not just for one

---

[29] One could *distinguish* norms from commands by stipulating that the former are "general rules". But at least for our purposes such a separation seems unwarranted. Cf. Kelsen in *General Theory of Law and State*, p. 38: "... law does not consist of general norms only. Law includes individual norms, i.e. norms which determine the behavior of one individual in one non-recurring situation and which therefore are valid only for one particular case and may be obeyed or applied only once."

occasion (instant, moment) o, presents no problem from the point of view of satisfiability. There may then exist enough "logical space" within the time-span of the corpus both for it some time being the case that p and some time the case that $\sim p$. But if the norms are strictly individual and for the same occasion, the situation is different. A corpus which consists of (or contains) Pp_o and $P \sim p_o$ is not, on the given definition, satisfiable— since $p_o \& \sim p_o$ is a logical contradiction. And from this it follows that $Op_o \vee O \sim p_o$ is what we have called a "normative tautology".

That $Op_o \vee O \sim p_o$ is a deontic tautology does *not* mean that there exists, for any given occasion o, either a norm ordering the obtaining of the state that p (on that occasion) or a norm prohibiting this. It means only that a corpus containing both Pp_o and $P \sim p_o$ is not satisfiable. This, as such, is no cause for alarm.

However, it is obviously possible (indeed often the case) that both the obtaining and the not-obtaining of a given state is allowed on a given occasion. The question is how to express this correctly in prescriptive language. I think the answer is $P(p_o \vee \sim p_o)$. The formula is, as we know, another normative tautology. That such is the case means that its normative negation $O(p_o \& \sim p_o)$ cannot be satisfied and hence its content not "rationally willed", required to obtain. But this does not prevent the formula $P(p_o \vee \sim p_o)$ from having a genuine *prescriptive* use in a situation *when neither disjunct is obligatory or prohibited*. Saying "it is permitted that p or that $\sim p$ obtains on this occasion o" would be naturally understood to express a Free Choice Permission (cf. above, p. 105 and pp. 143f) to the effect that the tautologous state that $p_o \vee \sim p_o$ may obtain either in the "form" of the state that p or in the "form" of its contradictory. Since it will necessarily obtain in either form and cannot possibly obtain in both, what is *permitted* in this case is the (free) *choice* between the two alternatives. The prescriptive "$Pp_o \& P \sim p_o$" means "$P(p_o \vee \sim p_o)$".

(Similar observations apply to permissions of the type $P \wedge p$, the satisfaction of which would "consume" the entire time-span of a corpus of norms.)

There is also another way of dealing with the problem of satisfiability here. On this other way, a corpus of orders, prohibitions, and permissions for an individual occasion is satisfiable if, and only if, it is logically possible that, on this occasion, all the things ordered and none of the things prohibited obtain together with every one of the things permitted *taken separately* (individually). Speaking in the terms of an agent and his actions, a corpus of this kind is satisfiable if the agent can avail himself of any one of the things he is allowed without violating any one of his obligations. This definition of satisfiability corresponds to the criterion of consistency of a set of norms which I gave in *Norm and Action* (Ch. I, Sect. 4). It would also correspond to a treatment of the problem with the tools of "possible world semantics". This treatment seems to me now less satisfactory since it by-passes the special problem caused by the application of deontic (and modal) formulae to individual occasions. The problem is related to an idea known from the history of modal logic according to which "everything which is is necessary *when it is*", and related to problems concerning diachronic and synchronic attributions of modality. This, however, is not the place for a more detailed discussion of these questions.

III

We next consider the case when all deontic formulae are of the first order but the norm-contents are propositions referring to a set of different occasions $o_1, \ldots, o_n$. This case presents no special difficulties.

That the norms for the different occasions make up *one* corpus means that they are all already there (exist, have been given) on the first of the n occasions and that none of them has ceased to be (exist, has been cancelled, withdrawn or derogated) before or on the last of the n occasions. This definition of the unity of the corpus calls for a comment.

A command or prohibition or permission which is for one specified occasion may come into existence either before this occasion or on the occasion. But what happens to the norm when the occasion is past? Does it still "exist", or has it ceased to be? (If the norm was not satisfied it will often be re-issued for a new occasion—but this possibility does not affect our question.) One can answer Yes or No. The above definition of the unity of the corpus presupposes that the answer is Yes. If the answer is No, one must replace the phrase "before or on the last of the n occasions" by the phrase "before or on the occasion to which it(s content) refers".

IV

Consider the norm (command) Op_o. It says that it ought to be the case that it is the case that p on o. But *when* ought this to be the case, *viz.* that it is the case that p on o? The question sounds strange. Does it even make sense?

Assume that the order that it ought to be the case that p on o was issued on an earlier occasion o', but then cancelled on some occasion o'' between o' and o. Surely it was then the case on o', but no longer the case at o'', that it ought to be the case that p on o. The norm (command, order) that it ought to be the case that p on o *can* exist before o and *need not* exist on o. (The question of its existence after o is uninteresting; cf. above.)

The existence of a norm is a state of affairs, and like any other state of affairs it may be understood both in a generic and an individual sense. This is so, independently of whether the state of affairs which is the content of the norm is understood in the generic or the individual sense. We can distinguish the following four cases:

$O_{o'}p_o$ which says that, on o' it ought to be the case that, on o, it is the case that p;

Op_o which says that, without specifying when, it ought to be the case that, on o, it is the case that p;

O_op which says that, on o, it ought to be the case that, without specifying when, it is the case that p; and

Op which says that it ought to be the case that p, without saying when the norm is supposed to hold and when its content is supposed to obtain.

In the first case the proposition is "fully" individual(ized) and in the fourth "fully" generic. In the second it is generic with regard to the existence of the norm but individual with regard to the occasion for its satisfaction—in the third the roles of the generic and the individual compound are reversed.

When shall we say that the obligation $O_{o'}p_o$ is satisfied? When it is the case on o that p? But assume that the order has been cancelled in the meantime—maybe even replaced by an order to the effect that it must *not* be the case that p on o. It seems nonsensical to speak about satisfaction here at all, unless it is assumed that the obligation that it be the case on o that p *lasts* (at least) throughout the interval from o' to o. The obligation $O_{o'}p_o$, in other words, must be thought of as an "instantiation" of an obligation norm which spans (at least) from the time of the individuation of the obligation to the individuation of the obligatory state of affairs. In a primary sense it is this norm, call it O_sp_o, where "s" denotes a span of time which includes the occasion o, which is satisfied if, and only if, it is the case that p on o. Only in a *secondary* sense can one then also say that the individual obligation norm $O_{o'}p_o$ is satisfied—o' being a moment in the span which includes o. But it seems better not to speak of the satisfaction at all of such individuated norms as the one exemplified by $O_{o'}p_o$.

We return to our example above of which we said that at o' but no longer at o'' it was the case that it ought to be the case that p on o, the earlier obligation having been cancelled. What this meant, more strictly speaking, is that at o' there existed a norm the span of which was (then) intended or understood to also include the occasion o although this norm was later cancelled.

The individuation of norms is primarily to *spans* of time and not to occasions. The logic of deontic expressions thus individuated we shall not subject to a further study in this paper.

When the norms are rules of action they impose obligations on and give permissions to agents. When no agent is indicated the expression $O \sim$ or $P \sim$ is *open* (the norm expressed generic) in the sense that it may apply to one agent a but not to another agent b. Another way of individuating obligations and permissions is therefore by reference to agents or to groups of agents or to all or some agents of a group. Such individuations of norms will be considered in Part 7 of this study.

5. ACTION LOGIC AS A BASIS FOR DEONTIC LOGIC

I

A great many human actions are such that they cannot truthfully be said to have been (successfully) performed unless, when they are accomplished, a certain state of affairs obtains in the world. I shall call such actions *achievements*, and the states the obtaining of which is a logical prerequisite of their performance I shall call their *results*. For example: the actions of opening a window or of stealing someone else's belongings or of killing a person are achievements. They result in that a certain window is open, that a thing is no longer in the possession of its owner, and that a man is dead respectively.

The fact that a certain state of affairs obtains can be the result of two different types of action. Some agent may have *produced* this state, i.e. changed the contradictory state into the one which obtains; or the agent may have *sustained* it, i.e. prevented it from vanishing, from ceasing to obtain. The opening of a door would be an example of a productive action; the keeping of a door open which would otherwise close is a sustaining action.

The "reverse" of a productive action is a destructive one, and the "reverse" of a sustaining action is a suppressing one. An agent who changes a state into its contradictory *destroys* this state—and an agent who sustains the contradictory of a state *suppresses* the state itself, i.e. prevents it from coming to obtain.

For schematic representations of sentences describing generic states of affairs I shall, as before, use lower case letters p, q, ... As a symbol of a random agent I shall use "a", and as a symbol for a random occasion "o".

The letter "B" is an operator signifying production (or destruction), "S" an operator signifying sustaining (or suppressing). $B_{a,o}p$ may be read: (an agent) a on (an occasion) o produces the state that p. Instead of "produces the state that" we can also say "brings it about that" or "makes it so that". $S_{a,o}p$ accordingly says that a on o sustains the state that p, prevents it from vanishing.

Since we shall here, on the whole, ignore reference to agents and occasions in the symbolic formulas, we shall simplify the above expressions to Bp and Sp. We can also give to the expressions, thus simplified, an "impersonal" reading: "the state that p is brought about" for Bp, and "the state that p is being sustained" for Sp.

Later, in the concluding part of the present essay, I shall also use the same symbols *B* and *S* for the verb-phrases "to produce the state of affairs that" and "to sustain the state that" respectively (see below, pp. 205ff).

It is important to note that $B_a,\ _op$, $S_a,\ _op$ and their abbreviated forms *Bp*, *Sp*, etc. are *open* (schematic) sentences expressing *generic* propositions which are not true or false unless the "values" of the variables *a* and *o* are specified. In this respect *Bp*, *Sp*, etc. are like *p*, *q*, etc.

II

Actions of the achievement type are performed by *agents* on *occasions* which afford *opportunities* for performing the actions.

What is an "occasion"? Roughly speaking, it is the spatio-temporal location, the When and Where of the performance of an action (cf. above, p. 165).

What is an "opportunity"? Roughly speaking, a condition which has to be satisfied in order that it is possible to perform the action on a given occasion. For example: It is not possible to open a window on a given occasion unless the window is then closed and does not open "of itself", i.e. independently of the interference of an agent with the prevailing state of affairs.

I shall define the following types of opportunity for action:

The productive action *Bp* can be performed by a given agent on a given occasion only on condition that the state of affairs that *p* is absent and remains absent unless some agent interferes and produces it.

The sustaining action *Sp* can be performed only on condition that the state *p* is present on the occasion but ceases to exist unless some agent interferes and destroys it.

The destructive action $B \sim p$ can be performed only on condition that the state that *p* is present on the occasion and remains present unless an agent interferes and destroys it.

The suppressing action $S \sim p$ can be performed only on condition that the state that *p* is absent on the occasion but comes into existence unless an agent interferes and prevents this.

Assume that an occasion affords an opportunity for performing a certain action. Shall we then say that an agent who is not *present* on that occasion, and therefore does not perform the action, thereby *omits* to perform it? This is not an easy question to answer. If the agent could not have *known* of the opportunity or could not have been present on the occasion, one might say that the occasion did not afford an opportunity *for him* to perform the action then. In most situations when the agent could have known but did not know, or could have been but was not present, one would probably also say that there was no opportunity *for him* to perform the action and that therefore he did not "properly" *omit* to perform it either. But in all cases we should not say this. If the agent, because of some moral or legal or other commitment of his, *ought* to have known about the opportunity or *ought* to have been "on the spot" we should probably count his not-doing the action as an omission—and blame him for it.

As we notice, one can make a distinction between an occasion offering an opportunity for action *simpliciter* and offering an opportunity *for a specified agent*. The types of opportunity which we defined above were opportunities in the first and broader sense. I shall not here inquire into the further conditions which occasions have to satisfy in order to constitute opportunities for action in the second and more restricted sense. But it is of some importance that we should have noted the distinction (cf. below, p. 174).

III

By *omission in the widest sense* I shall understand the not-doing of an action by an agent on an occasion when there is an opportunity (*simpliciter*) for performing this action.[30] Thus a on o omits, in this widest sense, to produce the state that p if o affords an opportunity for producing this state but a does not produce it; and similarly for sustaining, destroying, or suppressing a state.

In this notion of omission no attention is paid to the *ability* of the agent. Also when an agent is not able to produce a certain state, e.g. because he has not learnt to do this or in one way or another is disabled or incapacitated, his failure to produce this state on an occasion when there is an opportunity counts as omission. This includes the case when he *tried* but did not succeed.

One could make ability a "presupposition" of omission. Then an agent can omit only actions which he *can* (is able) to perform. The *can do* which implies ability must be distinguished from the *can do* which implies that there is an opportunity on a given occasion.

So far no attention is being paid to the *intentions* of the agent. One could make intentionality a condition or presupposition of an even stronger notion of omission. Then an agent who does not perform an action which he is able to perform and for the performance of which the occasion affords an opportunity omits this only on condition that his not performing the action is intentional. Intentional not-doing is often also called *forbearance*. A stronger form of forbearance is *abstention*. A forbearance is an absten-

---

[30] This definition of "omission in the widest sense" is slightly wider than the definition which was given in the essay "On the Logic of Norms and Actions", above pp. 109f. There, in addition to *opportunity*, *ability* was also made a requirement for omission.

tion, roughly speaking, when the agent wanted to perform the action but has some overriding motive or reason against performing it.

In what follows I shall ignore these stronger forms of omission. "Omission" is thus here understood in what I called above "the widest sense".

For omission (in the widest sense) I introduce the symbol $\daleth$. $\daleth B_{a, o}p$ thus says that a on o does not produce the state that p which, on o, does not obtain and does not come to obtain unless someone produces it.

We henceforth omit "a" and "o" from the formulas. It should be remembered, however, that in any molecular compound *all* components of the form B- or S- with or without the sign $\daleth$ in front of them must be understood as referring to the same (unspecified) agent and the same (unspecified) occasion.

IV

I have in former publications distinguished between the *results* and the *consequences* of actions.[31] It is worth saying here some words about how these concepts apply to omissions.

The action of producing the state that p has not been performed by anybody on o unless, on that occasion, the absence of this state has given place to its presence. So, if somebody produces the state in question, the change in question necessarily takes place. The action results in the change and therewith in the obtaining (at least for some short time) of the state that p.

Similarly, the action of sustaining the state that p has not been performed by anybody on o unless, on that occasion, the presence of this state is a fact. The sustaining action results in that the sustained state continues present.

That a on o omits to produce a certain state of affairs presupposes, we have said, an opportunity for producing it. Then it may happen that another agent b "seizes the opportunity" and produces the state on the occasion in question. Therefore, from the fact that a on o omits to produce the state that p it does not follow logically that this state on that occasion will not change from absent to present. The omission logically presupposes that the state *is* absent but not that it *stays* absent. It may, or may not, come to be present depending upon what other agents, beside a, do on the occasion in question.

Similarly, if a on o omits to sustain a certain state of affairs somebody else may do this and prevent that state from vanishing. Therefore, from the fact that a on o omits to sustain the state that p it does not follow

---

[31] *Norm and Action*, pp. 39f. See also above p. 107.

logically that this state on that occasion will change from present to absent. It may or may not change, depending upon what other agents do. "As far as *a* is concerned it will (would have) change(d)", one could say.

Thus whereas the *performance* of a productive or sustaining action logically entails the occurrence and non-occurrence respectively of a certain change ("in the world"), the *omission* of such action, by some agent on some occasion, does *not* entail the non-occurrence and occurrence respectively of corresponding changes. This is a noteworthy logical asymmetry between action and omission—and I shall make it a reason for saying that *omissions* of actions, as opposed to performances of actions, *have no results*.

By the *consequences* of an action I have understood (subsequent) changes and non-changes which are *causally connected* with the result of the action. The notion has a direct application to performances—but not to omissions.

One talks about the consequences of omissions; the notion obviously makes good sense—but its definition is connected with certain complications.

If a change occurs *because* some agent omitted to produce a certain other change or to prevent a certain other change, i.e. to sustain a certain state, then the change which occurred was a consequence of the omission in question. Similarly, if a change does not occur because some agent omitted to produce or prevent a certain other change, the non-occurrence of the first change is a consequence of his omission. The complication here is with the meaning of "because". It does not signify simply causal connectedness between changes or non-changes. That something happens because of an omission presupposes (entails) that the action which the agent omitted on the occasion in question was not performed by some other agent on that same occasion. Hence the consequence of *his* omission is equally a consequence of *any other agent's* omission who on that occasion had an opportunity for doing the omitted action. But it does not follow that all agents who omitted the action are equally *responsible* for the consequences of their omission. Responsibility for omission is a (partly) *normative* notion; it depends upon what the agents are expected or obliged to do.

V

A state of affairs can obtain, be present, as a result of two different types of action, i.e. because it has been produced or sustained. And it can fail to obtain, be absent, as a result of two different types of action, i.e. because it has been destroyed or suppressed. To each of these four types of action answer four corresponding types of omission (in the widest sense).

The eight cases just mentioned I propose to call the eight atomic or elementary modes or types of achievement action. They are enumerated below:

1. Bp producing a given state of affairs
2. $\daleth\, Bp$ leaving the state to continue absent
3. Sp sustaining the state
4. $\daleth\, Sp$ letting the state cease to obtain
5. $B \sim p$ destroying the state
6. $\daleth\, B \sim p$ leaving the state to continue present
7. $S \sim p$ suppressing the state
8. $\daleth\, S \sim p$ letting the state come to obtain.

For the sake of convenience I shall also refer to these eight cases with the abbreviations $p_1, \ldots, p_8$.

As seen, p_2 is the omission corresponding to productive action, p_4 to sustaining, p_6 to destructive, and p_8 to suppressive action.

Any two of the eight cases are mutually exclusive of one another. But whereas the members of the pairs p_1 and p_2, p_3 and p_4, p_5 and p_6, p_7 and p_8 exclude each other as action and (corresponding) omission, any two members of different pairs exclude each other because the actions (omissions) answer to different opportunities. For example: p_1 and p_3 are exclusive because there is, for reasons of logic, no occasion which would afford an opportunity both for producing and for sustaining one and the same state of affairs.

I shall regard it as a logically necessary truth that, given an occasion o and a state of affairs that p, the state of affairs in question either obtains (is present), or comes to be, or ceases to be, or does not obtain (is absent) on that occasion. In the cases when the state either comes to be or ceases to be it is presupposed that the "occasion" has a certain duration, beginning with a "phase" when the state of affairs is absent (present) and ending in a "phase" when the state is present (absent) (cf. below, pp. 195f).

With this presupposition or stipulation regarding the occasions, any given occasion will constitute an opportunity for one and only one of the four actions p_1, p_3, p_5, and p_7 and the correlated omissions p_2, p_4, p_6, and p_8. On any given occasion, the agent either performs or omits to perform the action for which there is an opportunity. It is then presupposed that the opportunity qualifies as an opportunity *for that agent* (cf. above, Section II).

The stipulations which make the eight cases of our table jointly exhaustive, in addition to being mutually exclusive, are not the only possible ones nor the only ones which might be of interest to study in a logic of action. The stipulations simplify the logic of the situations—for example by including under "omission" (in the widest sense) also the case of unsuccessful trying.

The disjunction $p_1 \lor p_2 \lor p_3 \lor p_4 \lor p_5 \lor p_6 \lor p_7 \lor p_8$ will thus be treated here as logically true.

Since, moreover, the disjuncts are mutually exclusive it follows that the negation of any one of them, or of any group of them, is logically equivalent with the disjunction of the rest. Thus, for example, $\sim p_1 \leftrightarrow p_2 \vee p_3 \vee p_4 \vee p_5 \vee p_6 \vee p_7 \vee p_8$. This gives us a means of eliminating negation signs $\sim$ which occur in front of symbols for the elementary modes of action.

It is important to distinguish between negation and omission. Omission too is "negation" of a kind, *viz.* the non-performance of a given action on an occasion when there is an opportunity for performing the action. Performance and omission are mutually exclusive and jointly exhaustive of the "logical space" constituted by an opportunity. But they are not jointly exhaustive of the "logical space" constituted by any given occasion. Of this latter space, however, performance and non-performance are exhaustive and, similarly, omission and non-omission.

VI

We shall now consider what happens to the expressions 1–8 for the elementary modes of achievement when for "*p*" we substitute a molecular compound of variables.

Consider $B(p \vee q)$. What is it to *produce* the state that p or (that) q? I do not think that the question can be answered univocally on the basis of considerations of ordinary language. We shall have to note alternative ways of interpreting the case—some of which may appear more, others less, natural. If we aim at univocity, we shall then have to make a decision.

Assume that neither of the two states is there on a given occasion, and that neither of them would come into being independently of action. If an agent then produces the one or the other of the two, or produces them both, he would surely rightly be said to have produced their disjunction. In this situation $B(p \vee q)$ is equivalent with $Bp \vee Bq$.

Assume next that one of the states is and remains absent independently of action but that the other is already there and remains unless interfered with. If the agent now produces the first state, it would indeed be odd, or perhaps even incorrect, to say that he had produced the state that p or q. What he did was *simply* that he produced the state that p.

But what if he had, on that same occasion when he produced the one state, destroyed the other which was already there? By his action he has "taken care" that one of the two states is still there. Is this "producing" their disjunction? If there had been an order (obligation, norm) to take care that at least one of the states obtains, he would have effected that order (obeyed the norm). The norm could have been simply $O(p \vee q)$: this is what *ought to be*. So if the first state is not there but the second is, the agent may destroy the second on condition that he produces the first. His acting on the occasion under consideration results in the state that $p \vee q$ being there. Has he not then "produced" this state? One *could* say this. The meaning of "produce" is not all that precise in ordinary talk about action. But one could also give a fuller description of the case and say that he produced one of the two states and destroyed the other, and since the one which he destroyed was already there it is in fact misleading to say that he *produced* the disjunction of the two.

Assume that the one state is absent and that the second would come into being unless prevented. Some agent *lets* it come. Has he then "produced" the disjunction? It seems unnatural to say that he has. But what if he prevents the state from originating, suppresses it, and produces the other (which could not have come independently)? Did he then "produce" their disjunction? This is a less clear case. His action would have conformed to a norm $O(p \vee q)$. But it does not strike me as natural to say that he produced the disjunctive state.

Assume that both states obtain but would vanish, unless there is interference. An agent sustains one of them. Thereby he "takes care" that the disjunction of the two states obtains. But it would surely be highly unnatural to say that he had "produced" the disjunctive state.

There are thus many possibilities of dealing with the expression $B(p \vee q)$. One could regard it as equivalent with $Bp \vee Bq$ and say that the agent produces a disjunction of two states if, and only if, he produces at least one of the two states *regardless of what happens to or what he does to the other*. I shall, however, here take a more restricted view and say that an agent produces a disjunction of two states if, and only if, he produces both of them or produces one of them letting the other remain absent. On this restrictive view, $B(p \vee q)$ distributes as follows: $Bp \& Bq \vee Bp \& \urcorner Bq \vee \urcorner Bp \& Bq$.

We now proceed to conjunctive states of affairs and the conditions of their "production". Let the expression under consideration be $B(p \& q)$. When can an agent be said to have produced the state that p and q? One case is obvious: If neither the one nor the other state is there and does not come into being unless some agent interferes, then the agent produces their conjunction if, and only if, he produces the two states individually, i.e. $Bp \& Bq$.

Assume, however, that one of the states already obtains and remains unless some agent destroys it—whereas the other state is absent and does not come into being unless some agent produces it. An agent now produces this second state, the first being left to continue. Has he then produced their conjunction? This much is certain: Through his productive action (in combination with an omission of his) he has achieved that the conjunction of the two states obtains, and not only one of the conjuncts. But is this "producing" the conjunction? The answer surely is a matter of decision. To me it seems not unnatural to answer the question in the affirmative. On the other hand, since the fact that the conjunction came to obtain is due to a combination of two elementary modes of action only one of which is productive, the other being an omission, one could also argue that the agent, strictly speaking, did not *produce* the conjunction. He would have done so only if he actually had produced *both* conjuncts.

What if one of the states obtains but vanishes unless the agent prevents its vanishing? He does this and, on the same occasion, produces the other state. Has he then produced their conjunction? My "linguistic intuitions" give me no guidance towards answering the question. An "arbitrary" ruling seems the only possibility if we wish to settle it. *My* ruling (here) is as follows: In the situation as described the agent does not "produce" the conjunctive state. What he does is correctly described by saying that he produces the one state *and* prevents the other from vanishing (and thereby "takes care", or "sees to it" that their conjunction obtains). He performs two actions, the one productive and the other preventive. If we call what he does producing a conjunction ("p & q"), we are equally justified in saying that he *prevents* a conjunction ("$\sim p$ & $\sim q$") from coming to obtain. For similar reasons, I shall not say that an agent who sustains two states thereby preventing them from vanishing, "produces" their conjunction. To say that he does would surely be contrary to "linguistic intuitions".

There are thus (at least) two rules which can claim plausibility for the distribution of the B-operator in front of conjunctions. One is quite simple: $B(p$ & $q) \leftrightarrow Bp$ & Bq. It says that a conjunctive state has been produced if, and only if, each conjunct in it results from productive action (by a certain agent on a certain occasion). The other rule is more complex. According to it a state which is a conjunction of two states has been produced if, and only if, either both component states have been produced or at least one of the components has been produced and the other, which already is there, has not been destroyed.

We next consider $\daleth B(p \lor q)$, i.e. the case when an agent omits (in the widest sense of "omit") to produce the disjunction-state of two states of affairs. Obviously, the *action* which he then omits to perform is the action described by $B(p \lor q)$. The omission therefore requires an opportunity for performing that action. On the view which we have taken, such an opportunity is there on an occasion when both states are absent and remain absent unless an agent interferes. That, on an occasion of this character, an agent omits to produce the disjunction in question clearly must mean that he omits to produce the one as well as the other of the two states. Therefore, what $\daleth B(p \lor q)$ "means" is $\daleth Bp$ & $\daleth Bq$.

What is the meaning of $\daleth B(p$ & $q)$? The agent omits to produce the conjunction of two states. As in the previous case, the omission must be relative to an opportunity for producing the conjunction. But the definition of "opportunity" is now less clear than in the case of a disjunction of states. It depends on which distribution rule for $B(p$ & $q)$ we adopt. If we opt for the simpler rule, there is an opportunity for producing a conjunction of two states only if both are and remain absent independently of action. If we opt for the more complex rule, then a situation when one of the two states is already there and stays present also counts as an opportunity for producing their conjunction.

On the first option, the agent fails (omits) to produce the conjunction if, and only if, he either produces neither state or produces only one of them. Thus $\daleth B(p \& q) \leftrightarrow \daleth Bp \& \daleth Bq \lor \daleth Bp \& Bq \lor Bp \& \daleth Bq$.

Now consider the second option. As already noted, if both states are and remain absent, the agent fails to produce their conjunction if he either produces neither or produces only one. If the state that p is already there, the agent obviously omits the production of the conjunction if he does not produce the state that q. But what shall we say of the case when the agent produces the second state but destroys the first? Or of the case when he simply destroys the first and lets the second remain absent? Has he then omitted to produce the conjunction of the two states? Here a ruling is needed. I think most of us would agree that it is natural to say that the agent also omitted to produce the conjunction in those two cases. The same ruling then also applies to the type of occasion when the state that q is already there (but the state that p is absent).

Accepting these rulings, the case when the agent omits to produce the conjunction of two states, $\daleth B(p \& q)$ covers *nine* different cases, *viz.* the three which answer to our first option and the following six: $\daleth B \sim p \& \daleth Bq \lor B \sim p \& \daleth Bq \lor B \sim p \& Bq \lor \daleth Bp \& \daleth B \sim q \lor \daleth Bp \& B \sim q \lor Bp \& B \sim q$.

It is indeed natural to say that if an agent does *not* perform an action on an occasion when there is opportunity for him to perform it, then he on that occasion *omits* to perform it (in the widest sense of "omit" which includes also the case when he is unable to perform the action and when he tries but fails). The two alternatives—performance and omission to perform—are then regarded as logically exhaustive of the given opportunity. The naturalness of this view is a strong motivation for defining omission to produce a conjunction of two states, if we opt for the second of the two alternatives, in such a way that the definition covers the nine cases enumerated above.

Using this criterion or condition of exhaustiveness of the two attitudes of performance and omission of an action, we can now easily state the distributive principles also for $S(p \lor q)$ and $S(p \& q)$ and for the corresponding omissions.

Consider first $S(p \lor q)$. When can an agent be said to sustain the disjunction of two states of affairs?

One case is clear. If the situation is such that both states are there but would cease to be unless some agent interferes, then the agent can be said to sustain their disjunction if, and only if, he sustains at least one of the states, i.e. prevents at least one of the two from vanishing. $S(p \lor q)$ then answers to the disjunction $Sp \& Sq \lor Sp \& \daleth Sq \lor \daleth Sp \& Sq$. And omission, $\daleth S(p \lor q)$, answers to the fourth possibility $\daleth Sp \& \daleth Sq$.

Assume, however, that the situation is such that only one of the two states is there and ceases to be unless some agent interferes. The other state is and stays absent. It would be right to say that their disjunction obtains, since the one state is there. Shall we say that the agent sustains the disjunction, if he sustains the obtaining state? And what if he lets the obtaining state disappear but "instead" produces the absent state? I do not think that "linguistic intuitions" provide us with clear answers to either of these questions. Perhaps some would say that sustaining the disjunction takes place in the first but not in the second of the two cases we envisaged. Or in both cases; or in neither case. This last will be our ruling. I shall take the view that only on an occasion when both states obtain but would vanish unless sustained is there an opportunity for sustaining their disjunction.

Consider, finally, $S(p \& q)$. What is it to sustain the conjunction of two states? When does an occasion afford an opportunity for this action?

A clear case is when both states are there but would both vanish unless sustained. Then sustaining means $Sp \& Sq$ and omission to sustain means $Sp \& \neg Sq \vee \neg Sp \& Sq \vee \neg Sp \& \neg Sq$.

Assume, however, that both states are there and that one of them stays on but the other vanishes unless there is interference. The agent sustains the state which otherwise would vanish and does not "touch" (destroy) the other state. Has he then sustained their conjunction? Again a ruling is needed.

My "linguistic intuitions" are that it would not be far-fetched or unnatural to regard also $Sp \& \neg B \sim q$ and $\neg B \sim p \& Sq$ as cases of sustaining the conjunction of the two states $p \& q$. To each one of the sustaining actions there would then answer three cases of omission.

Thus, in analogy with the case of producing and omitting to produce a conjunction of states, one can opt either for a simpler or a more complex rule for the distributivity of the operator S before a conjunction. On the simpler rule $S(p \& q)$ distributes to $Sp \& Sq$ and the corresponding omission is the three-termed disjunction $Sp \& \neg Sq \vee \neg Sp \& Sq \vee \neg Sp \& \neg Sq$. On the more complex view $S(p \& q)$ also covers the alternatives $Sp \& \neg B \sim q$ and $\neg B \sim p \& Sq$, and $\neg S(p \& q)$, also the three cases of omitting $Sp \& \neg B \sim q$ and the three cases of omitting $\neg B \sim p \& Sq$, i.e. in all nine cases.

It thus seems that no set of rules for the distribution of the action operators over molecular compounds of potential action results can claim to be *the* "correct" rules. The rules can be laid down in alternative ways—the alternatives answering to different "linguistic intuitions" which we may have in these matters. It seems, however, extremely natural, maybe even compelling, to take the view that the actions of producing and sustaining, and the corresponding omissions, should, when applied to molecular compounds of states of affairs, be dissolvable *some way or other* into molecular compounds of atomic or elementary cases of productive and sustaining actions and their omissions. Thus all complex actions of the achievement type may be viewed as molecular constructs of the eight simple cases which we distinguished in Section V above.

The simplest, and *perhaps* also most natural, distribution principles are the following ones:

(1) $\quad B(p \lor q) \quad \leftrightarrow Bp \,\&\, Bq \lor Bp \,\&\, \daleth Bq \lor \daleth Bp \,\&\, Bq$

(2) $\quad \daleth B(p \lor q) \leftrightarrow \daleth Bp \,\&\, \daleth Bq$

(3) $\quad B(p \,\&\, q) \leftrightarrow Bp \,\&\, Bq$

(4) $\quad \daleth B(p \,\&\, q) \leftrightarrow Bp \,\&\, \daleth Bq \lor \daleth Bp \,\&\, Bq \lor \daleth Bp \,\&\, \daleth Bq$

(5) $\quad S(p \lor q) \leftrightarrow Sp \,\&\, Sq \lor Sp \,\&\, \daleth Sq \lor \daleth Sp \,\&\, Sq$

(6) $\quad \daleth S(p \lor q) \leftrightarrow \daleth Sp \,\&\, \daleth Sq$

(7) $\quad S(p \,\&\, q) \leftrightarrow Sp \,\&\, Sq$

(8) $\quad \daleth S(p \,\&\, q) \leftrightarrow Sp \,\&\, \daleth Sq \lor \daleth Sp \,\&\, Sq \lor \daleth Sp \,\&\, \daleth Sq$

The four cases of omission (2), (4), (6), and (8) are obtained "mechanically" from the corresponding four cases of performance (1), (3), (5), and (7) respectively by observing the rule that performance and omission are logically exhaustive modes of action relative to the same opportunity.

In the following, when discussing the effects of the distribution of the operators B and S on molecular compounds of variables p, q, etc., it will throughout be assumed that the distribution laws involved are the principles (1)–(8) above.

VII

We shall next consider some special cases of action and omission.

Consider first $B(p \lor \sim p)$. Can one produce a tautological state of affairs? The idea seems odd and it can easily be shown to be a logical impossibility.

If we distribute $B(p \lor \sim p)$ according to (1) above, we get $Bp \,\&\, B \sim p \lor Bp \,\&\, \daleth B \sim p \lor \daleth Bp \,\&\, B \sim p$. Each one of the three disjuncts is a conjunction of two of the eight elementary modes of action which we have distinguished; and these modes of action (and omission) are mutually exclusive. Hence all three disjuncts are logically false—and therewith their disjunction, $B(p \lor \sim p)$, expresses a logical falsehood.

But the same is true of $\daleth Bp \,\&\, \daleth B \sim p$ which answers to the omission of the action $B(p \lor \sim p)$. It is logically impossible to produce a tautological state of affairs—but it is also logically impossible to "*omit*" the production of such a state. This, surely, is as we wish to have it in a reasonable action logic.

The reader can easily satisfy himself that $S(p \lor \sim p)$ and $\daleth S(p \lor \sim p)$ are also logically false. One cannot sustain or omit to sustain a tautological state of affairs.

What has been said here about producing and sustaining tautologous states must also hold for contradictions. Consider $B(p \& \sim p)$. After distribution by virtue of rule (3) above we obtain $Bp \& B \sim p$. Since the elementary modes of action are mutually exclusive, this is a contradiction. No agent can on any occasion both produce and destroy one and the same state of affairs. (Provided the notion of "occasion" is so defined that it presupposes the simultaneous performance of those two feats.)

It is easy to see that $S(p \& \sim p)$ too is a logical impossibility.

$\daleth B(p \& \sim p)$ too turns out to be a logical contradiction when distributed according to (4). Distribution and cancelling of double negations gives $Bp \& \daleth B \sim p \lor \daleth Bp \& B \sim p \lor \daleth Bp \& \daleth B \sim p$. Each one of the disjuncts is a contradiction and hence also the disjunction. Thus it is not logically possible to "omit" to produce a contradiction. Similarly, it is impossible to "omit" sustaining it.

VIII

Expressions formed of the operators B or S, with or without the sign for omission $\daleth$ in front of them and followed by a variable or molecular compound of variables will be called *atomic B-* or *S-expressions* or, for short, atomic *BS-expressions*. If the operator is followed by a single variable or by a variable preceded by the sign for negation $\sim$, the expression represents one of the eight elementary modes of action (or omission).

By *BS*-expressions generally we understand atomic *BS*-expressions and molecular compounds formed of atomic *BS*-expressions by means of the connectives $\sim$, $\&$, $\lor$, $\rightarrow$, or $\leftrightarrow$. (The sign for omission is not a "connective") (see below, pp. 193ff).

Let there be given a *BS*-expression. Such atomic components of it which do not represent elementary modes of action, we transform into molecular compounds of expressions for elementary modes of action in accordance with the distributive principles (1)–(8) described above in Section VI. The given *BS*-expression is then a compound of atomic components, all of which represent elementary modes of action. We transform it into its disjunctive normal form. It is then a disjunction of conjunctions of expressions for elementary modes of action with or without a negation sign in front.

Next we replace those expressions for elementary modes of action which are preceded by the sign for negation $\sim$ by the seven-termed disjunctions according to the principles explained in Section V. The conjunctions in the disjunctive normal form are then split into disjunctions of conjunctions of expressions for elementary modes of action which are such that none of the expressions has a negation sign in front of it. Some of these conjunctions may contain more than one expression for an elementary mode of action with the same variable (p or q or . . .). By what was said in

Section V, such conjunctions are contradictory; logically false. We omit all such conjunctions from the normal form. The remaining disjunction of conjunctions I shall call the *perfect* disjunctive normal form of the original *BS*-expression.

If the given *BS*-expression contains only one variable p, then its perfect disjunctive normal form will be a disjunction of some i of the eight elementary cases which we abbreviated (Section V) $p_1, \ldots, p_8$. (If $i = 0$, the expression is contradictory, i.e. it says that the agent a on the occasion o does something which, for reasons of logic, it is impossible to do—for example both produces and destroys the state of affairs that p.)

If the *BS*-expression contains two variables, p and q, its perfect normal form is an i-termed disjunction of some of the 8×8 or 64 non-contradictory conjunctions of one of the elementary p-cases with one of the elementary q-cases. If the expression has n variables, the maximum number of (non-contradictory) disjuncts in the normal form is 2^{3n}, each disjunct being an n-termed conjunction.

A *BS*-expression the normal form of which is maximal, i.e. 2^{3n}-termed, is "tautological", meaning that it says that an agent on some occasion does something which of logical necessity he will be doing then. ("Doing" here means "doing or omitting"; and omission, it should be remembered, means "omission in the widest sense", as explained earlier.)

If a given expression does *not* contain the variable p, one can introduce this variable vacuously into the expression by conjoining to it the disjunction $p_1 \vee \ldots \vee p_8$ which, as stipulated, is but an expanded form of the tautology $p_1 \vee \sim p_1$ (and $p_2 \vee \sim p_2$, etc.).

Be it observed, however, that a variable, say p, *cannot* be introduced vacuously into an atomic *BS*-expression by conjoining the tautology $p \vee \sim p$ to the variable or compound of variables which follows after the operator B or S in the expression. This "non-extensional" feature of our action logic is worth a further comment.

Consider Bp and $B(p \,\&\, (q \vee \sim q))$ or $B(p \,\&\, q \vee p \,\&\, \sim q)$. The last two are equivalent, but the first is not equivalent with either of them.

If $B(p \,\&\, (q \vee \sim q))$ is distributed in accordance with rule (3) we obtain $Bp \,\&\, B(q \vee \sim q)$. This is a contradiction since, as we know, the component $B(q \vee \sim q)$ is self-contradictory. It is logically impossible to produce a state *and* a tautological state. Therefore Bp is not equivalent with $B(p \,\&\, (q \vee \sim q))$.

We leave it as an exercise to the interested reader to satisfy himself that the expression $B(p \,\&\, q \vee p \,\&\, \sim q)$, when developed in accordance with the distribution rules, (1), (3), and (4), also yields a contradiction. Tautological transformations of molecular compounds in the scope of the operator B (or S) are allowed—but not the introduction of new variables into the compounds.

It may be considered "odd" that our action logic is, in the sense explained, intensional and not extensional. Does not "p & $(q \lor \sim q)$" describe the *same* state of affairs as "p"? Certainly it does. But "q" may describe a different state from "p". Therefore "$B(p \& (q \lor \sim q))$" describes a different action from "Bp" even though "$q \lor \sim q$" may be said not to describe any state of affairs at all. The identity of actions (as opposed to states of affairs) is in a characteristic sense "sensitive" to their descriptions.

IX

We now proceed to deontic logic. We add to the *BS*-calculus the symbols *O* and *P*. When we prefix them to *BS*-expressions (atomic or molecular) we get atomic *OP*-expressions of the first order. When we prefix them to atomic *OP*-expressions of the first order or their molecular compounds we get atomic *OP*-expressions of the second order. Molecular compounds of atomic *OP*-expressions of different orders are said to be of "mixed" order. If to them we prefix *O* or *P* we get atomic *OP*-expressions of mixed order. Every *OP*-expression is either atomic or a molecular compound of atomic *OP*-expressions.

Here I shall consider only atomic *OP*-expressions of the first order and their molecular compounds.

Given an atomic *OP*-expression. It is either of the form *O*- or of the form *P*- where the place of the blank is held by a *BS*-expression.

The *BS*-expression may be replaced by its (perfect) disjunctive normal form. To each disjunct in the normal form there answers an occasion which provides an opportunity for performing conjunctively (or omitting to perform) the actions described by the conjuncts of the disjunct in question. For example: $Bp \& \, \rceil \, Sq$ might be such a disjunct. It says that on some occasion (*o*) an agent (*a*) produces a certain state and omits to sustain another. The opportunity is thus a situation when the first state is and remains absent unless acted upon and the second state is absent but comes into being unless interference takes place. I shall call this a *type* of opportunity.

Given *n* states *p*, *q*, . . . there are 4^n different types of opportunity for action with regard to these states. On any given occasion *o* one and one only of these types of opportunity is there.

We next divide the set of disjuncts in the normal form of the *BS*-expression into groups. Disjuncts in the same group correspond to the same type of opportunity for action.

For example: $Bp \& Sq$ and $Bp \& \, \rceil \, Sq$ correspond to the same type of opportunity. If both occur in the same normal form they belong to the same group of disjuncts within it. $\rceil \, Bp \& Bq$, for example, corresponds to a different type of opportunity. Hence it belongs to a different group of disjuncts from $Bp \& Sq$ if both occur in the same normal form.

We rearrange the disjuncts in the normal form so that all disjuncts which belong to the same group stand in immediate succession of one another. For example: If the normal form is Bp & $Sq \lor \daleth Bp$ & $\daleth Sq \lor \daleth Bp$ & Bq it satisfies this requirement of arrangements into groups. The two groups in it are Bp & $Sq \lor \daleth Bp$ & $\daleth Sq$ and $\daleth Bp$ & Bq.

Consider now an atomic *OP*-formula $O-$ or $P-$ where the dash stands for a *BS*-formula in the normal form with the proper arrangement of the disjuncts into groups. The different types of opportunity for action which correspond to the different groups I shall also call different types of *conditions of application* of the norm.

The norm, generally speaking, demands (or permits) that the agent to whom it is addressed do this or do that dependent upon which one of its conditions of application (if there are several) are satisfied on the given occasion. If the occasion is one when a certain condition of application of the norm is satisfied, the agent should (may) do *this*, if it is one when a certain other condition is satisfied he should (may) do *that*; on an occasion when none of the conditions is satisfied, the norm does not apply at all, i.e. it does not demand (permit) anything in particular.

It follows from this that a norm with a plurality of conditions of application may be resolved into a *conjunction* (set) of norms each one of which applies to just one type of opportunity for action.

For example: Let the norm be $O(Bp$ & $Sq \lor \daleth Bp$ & $\daleth Sq \lor \daleth Bp$ & $Bq)$. It can be dissolved, distributed into the two norms $O(Bp$ & $Sq \lor \daleth Bp$ & $\daleth Sq)$ and $O(\daleth Bp$ & $Bq)$. The first says that, if the first of the two states is absent and remains absent unless some agent interferes and the second is present but vanishes unless prevented, then the agent ought *either* to produce the first state and sustain the second, *or* let the second vanish but omit to produce the first. (The content of the norm thus is "disjunctive".) The other norm again says that, if the first and the second state are both absent and neither comes into existence independently of interference, then the agent ought to produce the second state but leave the first "untouched".

When a norm has several different conditions of application its demand on action cannot be stated univocally in terms of producing or sustaining (and the omission of such actions). If what has to or may be done on an occasion constituting one type of opportunity is, say, that a certain state ought to be produced, it will on an occasion of a different type be that this same state is, say, sustained (prevented from vanishing). The norms with multiple conditions of application cannot therefore generally be formulated simply as orders or permissions to perform or omit certain productive or sustaining actions. The natural way of formulating them is to the effect that something or other, which is not itself an action, ought to or may be the case. To this norm can be "appended", or from it "extracted", norms concerning that which ought (has) to or may be done under the various conditions when the original norm applies.

For example: Let the norm be that it ought *to be the case* that the state of affairs that p obtains. Assume that this norm is addressed to just one agent. What ought this agent then *to do*? The answer depends upon the prevailing situation with regard to the state in question. If the state obtains and remains unless interfered with, the agent has to let it continue. If it obtains but vanishes unless someone interferes, he has to prevent this, i.e. he has to sustain the state. If it does not obtain and remains absent he has to produce it—and if it is absent but comes to be independently of interference, he has to let it originate. Thus one can say that to the norm of the *Sein-Sollen* type Op there answer four norms of the *Tun-Sollen* type (cf. later, Part 7).

The *Tun-Sollen* norms, moreover, admit of two interpretations. They can either be genuine norms (prescriptions) issued by some norm-authority and "appended" to the *Sein-Sollen* norm addressed to the agent. Or they may be *technical norms* or rules concerning that which the agent must (has to) do in order to satisfy the *Sein-Sollen* norm (cf. above, pp. 152ff). In the second case they are probably "extracted" by the agent himself from the originally given norm.

An order or permission to do something which has several conditions of application is often given in the form of a *disjunction*. For example: "open the window *or* leave it open (as the case may be)". But this order could also be made more explicit, as follows: "open the window, if it is closed, *and* leave it open, if it is (already) open". The *Sein-Sollen* norm corresponding to the first form would be $O(Bp \vee \neg B \sim p)$, the norm corresponding to the second form $OBp \& O \neg B \sim p$. Logically, the two expressions are equivalent.

Let us still consider the following example: $O(Bp \vee Sq)$ or an order, addressed to an agent a, that one state of affairs be produced or another state sustained.

We first rewrite it in the form $O(Bp \& Sq \vee Bp \& \sim Sq \vee \sim Bp \& Sq)$. The negated atomic expressions in the disjuncts may be replaced by seven-termed disjunctions of unnegated expressions. We shall use the abbreviations introduced for the atomic cases. Then we can write the expression in the form $O(p_1 \& q_1 \vee p_1 \& (q_2 \vee q_3 \vee q_4 \vee q_5 \vee q_6 \vee q_7 \vee q_8) \vee (p_2 \vee p_3 \vee p_4 \vee p_5 \vee p_6 \vee p_7 \vee p_8) \& q_1)$. By "multiplying up" we get from here a 15-termed disjunction of two-termed conjunctions after the operator O.

The disjunction can be divided into seven groups answering to different types of opportunity for doing the action in question. We distribute the O-operator and obtain a seven-termed conjunction of O-norms. The first is $O(Bp \& Sq \vee Bp \& \neg Sq \vee \neg Bp \& Sq)$. This norm applies to situations when there is an opportunity both for producing the one and sustaining the other state. The agent can now satisfy his obligation on any given situation of this type either by both producing the one and sustaining the other state or by producing the one letting the other disappear or by letting the first remain absent and sustaining the second.

The second norm is $O(Bp \,\&\, Bq \vee Bp \,\&\, \neg B \sim q)$. This applies to situations when the first state can be produced but the second *cannot* be sustained because it is and remains absent (and may thus either be produced or left to remain absent). The agent can now satisfy an obligation either to produce the first state or sustain the second *only* by producing the first. What he does to the second is immaterial. Trivially, he *will* either produce it or let it continue absent. $Bq \vee \neg B \sim q$ is, one could say, a tautology "under the given circumstances". In the case which we are considering, the obligation $O(Bp \vee Sq)$ thus "reduces" to OBp. But this, of course, does not mean that the first "logically entails" the second.

There are two other O-norms in the conjunction which are such that only by producing the first state can the agent satisfy an obligation to produce the one or sustain the second. And similarly there are three O-norms such that he can satisfy his obligation only by sustaining the second state.

Should the six cases when only one of the actions can be done count as cases when the norm $O(Bp \vee Sq)$ applies at all? The answer is: If one wanted to exclude them, one must give to the norm the more precise formulation $O(Bp \,\&\, Sq \vee Bp \,\&\, \neg Sq \vee \neg Bp \,\&\, Sq)$.

X

We shall now adapt the machinery of deontic logic developed in the first part of this paper to norms the contents of which are states of affairs (schematically) described by *BS*-expressions.

It is feasible to think that norms are "historical", i.e. that they come into being, exist over a period of time, and then pass away (cf. above, pp. 137f). Since, however, we are here considering only norms of the first order, considerations relating to the "historicity" of norms, i.e. to the fact that the norms of a given context may be of unequal "duration", need not concern us. We simply take it for granted or regard it as being presupposed that the norms under consideration last the same time. We may also think of them as "omnitemporal", everlasting.

A norm $O-$ is *satisfiable* if, and only if, it is possible that the actions and/or omissions which are the content of the norm take place on *all* occasions (in the history of the norm) which afford opportunities (for the agents concerned) for those actions and/or omissions, i.e. on all occasions when the conditions of application of the norm are fulfilled.

A norm $P-$ is satisfiable if, and only if, it is possible that the actions and/or omissions which are its content take place on *some* (at least one) occasion when the norm applies.

The phrase "it is possible" can be understood in several senses. It can mean "logically possible" or "physically possible" or "humanly possible". To the various meanings answer different concepts of satisfiability (cf.

above, pp. 140f). Here we understand possibility in the widest sense of *logical* possibility.

A norm which is satisfiable will be called (self-)consistent and a norm which is not satisfiable will be called (self-)contradictory or (self-)inconsistent.

Consider now a *corpus*, i.e. a finite set of norms. It is assumed that all norms of the corpus concern the same agents, e.g. all men, and are for the same occasions, e.g. for all occasions when the norms apply. Some of the norms may have several different conditions of application. These latter norms we distribute into conjunctions of norms with only one determinate condition of application. Thereupon we divide the corpus into as many sub-corpora as there are conditions of application of the norms, the norms of the same sub-corpus having the same conditions of application.

A sub-corpus of norms is satisfiable if, and only if, it is possible that no action and omission which the norms of the sub-corpus pronounce obligatory is neglected by any norm-subject on any occasion when the conditions of application of the norms are satisfied, and all actions and omissions which the norms pronounce permitted are such that every norm-subject does them on some occasion when the conditions of application are satisfied.

The corpus itself is satisfiable if, and only if, *all* its sub-corpora are satisfiable.

A corpus or sub-corpus which is satisfiable is also called consistent— and one which is not satisfiable, inconsistent or contradictory.

There are some special problems in this area arising from a possible plurality of agents to which the norms apply. If a permissive norm concerns the actions of several agents but covers a limited number of occasions it may happen that not every agent can (for reasons of logic) perform the permitted actions. In order that the norm be satisfiable the number of occasions must be "sufficient". If again an obligating norm concerns the actions of several agents then it may happen that they cannot *all* perform the duty-bound action(s) on any given occasion when the norm applies. In order that such a norm be satisfiable it is sufficient that all agents *for whom* the occasions when the norm applies afford opportunities can perform those actions. (Cf. what was said above in Section II on the notion of "opportunity for an agent".)

XI

We must next explain the notion of *normative negation*, or of a negation-norm, when the norm-contents are represented by *BS*-expressions.

Roughly speaking: the negation norm of an *obligating* norm *permits* the *omission* of the thing to which the obligating norm obliges—and the negation norm of a permissive norm makes obligatory the omission of the thing which the permissive norm permits. In a deontic logic in which the distinction between not-doing and omission is not observed or cannot be expressed, the negation norm of a norm $O-$ is the norm $P \sim -$, and the negation norm of $P-$ is $O \sim -$. In a deontic logic in which this distinction is noted things are a little more complex.

If the norm has several conditions of application we must first distribute it into a conjunction (*corpus*) of norms each one of which applies under uniquely specified circumstances.

Consider a norm with uniquely specified conditions of application. We transform the *BS*-expression following the deontic operator into its perfect disjunctive normal form. If the expression contains n variables p, q, etc., the normal form is a disjunction of some m of 2^n conjunctions of expressions for elementary modes of action and omission. We then obtain the negation norm of the given norm in the following way:

If the deontic operator was O we change it to P, and if it was P we change it to O. After the operator follows the disjunction of those $2^n - m$ conjunctions which do *not* appear in the normal form of the original *BS*-expression. (In the limiting case $m = 2^n$ the disjunction "vanishes", is zero-termed.)

For example: Let the norm be $O(Bp \,\&\, Bq \lor \daleth Bp \,\&\, \daleth Bq)$, decreeing that some agent(s) either produce both of two states or not produce either of them. The negation norm is then $P(Bp \,\&\, \daleth Bq \lor \daleth Bp \,\&\, Bq)$ permitting that the agent(s) produce only one of the states, letting the other continue absent.

The negation-norm of a norm with several conditions of application is the conjunction (*corpus*) of the negation-norms of the norms in the conjunction into which the original norm has been split up.

The normative negation of a compound of O- and P-norms is obtained as follows:

Let the compound in question be C. We transform the expression $\sim C$ according to the rules of ordinary propositional logic (PL) so that the negation-sign occurs immediately before the symbols O and P (and possibly inside the scope of the deontic operators). Thereupon we replace each one of the negated O-norms by their negation-norms, and similarly each negated P-norm. The expression obtained after these transformations is the normative negation of C.

We can now also (re-)define the notions of a normative tautology and of normative entailment in conformity with the definitions given in the first part of this essay.

If a *corpus* of norms is inconsistent, i.e. not satisfiable, we shall say that its normative negation is a normative *tautology*.

If a corpus of norms is consistent but the addition to it of a further norm makes the enlarged corpus inconsistent, then we say that the negation-norm of the added norm is *entailed* by, or is implicit in, the original corpus.

XII

Consider *OBp* or *PBp*, or abbreviated Op_1 and Pp_1. $q_1 \vee \ldots \vee q_8$ is logically true. Hence, if an agent produces the state that p he will also, on that same occasion, "react" in one of the elementary modes to the state that q.

Consider now $O(p_1 \& (q_1 \vee \ldots q_8))$. We "multiply" up and distribute the expression so as to get a conjunction of four norms $O(p_1 \& q_1 \vee p_1 \& q_2) \& O(p_1 \& q_3 \vee p_1 \& q_4) \& O(p_1 \& q_5 \vee p_1 \& q_6) \& O(p_1 \& q_7 \vee p_1 \& q_8)$. The first says that the agent(s) ought to produce the state that p and either produce or omit to produce the state that q. This norm applies only to situations in which the second state *can* be produced, i.e. is and remains absent independently of action. Whatever an agent does in a situation of that kind he will "tautologously" either produce or omit to produce the state that q. The only "real" obligation then is that the state that p is produced. And similarly in the three remaining cases.

If we had also considered a third state, say that r, the norm *OBp* would have been distributable into a 16-termed conjunction of norms with different conditions of application. But the only "real" obligation would be as before, *viz.* that the state that p is produced.

The *OP*-calculus thus is "extensional" in the sense that it allows the vacuous introduction of new variables into its expressions by virtue of the (agreed upon) tautological character of the disjunction of the eight elementary modes of action with regard to any state of affairs. In this the *OP*-calculus differs from the *BS*-calculus which does not admit of the vacuous introduction of new variables through *PL*-tautologies of the type "$p \vee \sim p$" (cf. above, Section VIII).

XIII

Some observations on special cases will next be made.

Consider $O(Bp \vee \neg Bp)$. This norm is necessarily satisfied on all occasions which afford an opportunity for producing the state that p. To other occasions it does not apply. Its negation-norm is expressed by P followed by a zero-termed disjunction, corresponding to the disjunctive normal form of the self-contradictory expression $Bp \& \neg Bp$. This "norm" cannot be satisfied. It is self-inconsistent and on this ground we call the original norm "tautologous".

Consider $O(p_1 \vee \ldots \vee p_8)$. This norm is necessarily satisfied on all occasions. It may be dissolved into a conjunction (corpus) of four norms which are "tautologous" on the same grounds as $O(Bp \vee \neg Bp)$ above.

Consider next $O(Bp \& \neg Bp)$, $OB(p \& \sim p)$, and $O(Bp \& \sim Bp)$. They all "look" like contradictions; but there are some differences to be noted. The first norm applies on occasions when the state of affairs that p is absent and does not originate unless produced. Its negation-norm is

$P(Bp \lor \daleth Bp)$ which is of necessity satisfied. Hence $O(Bp \& \daleth Bp)$ is self-contradictory and $P(Bp \lor \daleth Bp)$ "tautologous" according to our definitions. The second and the third norm apply under no circumstances. The second, for example, would "apply" on occasions which afford an opportunity both for producing and for destroying the same state. Such occasions cannot exist, however. But the same holds true of the negation-norms of $OB(p \& \sim p)$ and $O(Bp \& \sim Bp)$ if we try to form them in accordance with the rules previously given. It is a matter of decision whether we shall say of a norm which never applies, i.e. the conditions of application of which are self-contradictory, that it is necessarily satisfied and "tautologous" or impossible to satisfy and self-contradictory; but it would seem far more natural to say the latter.

Consider now $O(Bp \& Bq)$. Does it entail OBp? The negation-norm of the second is $P \daleth Bp$. The conjunctive obligation applies to a situation when the two states are both absent but can be produced. The simple obligation and its "negation" apply to a situation when the first of the two states is absent but may be produced. The simple norm thus has a wider range of application. Hence the satisfaction of the conjunctive obligation does not entail the satisfaction of the simple one and is compatible with the satisfaction of the permissive norm, i.e. with the possibility that an agent on some occasion which is *not* an opportunity for producing both states but *is* an opportunity for producing the state that p omits the production of this state.

Thus $O(Bp \& Bq)$ does *not* entail OBp. This result is, I think, entirely agreeable to our intuitions—and in no conflict with the fact that in a deontic logic of the traditional type $O(p \& q)$ entails Op.

The entailment $OBp \& OBq \rightarrow O(Bp \& Bq)$, however, is valid, if we assume that the norms concern the actions of the same agent(s) and are for the same class of occasions. If the state that p ought to be produced whenever the occasion affords an opportunity and similarly the state that q, then whenever there is an opportunity for producing both states they must both be produced.[32]

In traditional deontic logic the "dual" of the conjunctive distribution formula for the O-operator is the disjunctive distribution formula for the P-operator. As can be expected, what has been said above in relation to the

---

[32] In the essay "On the Logic of Norms and Actions" I sketched a system of deontic logic in which the implication relation between a conjunction of obligation norms and a "corresponding" obligation norm with a conjunctive content was valid neither way (above, pp. 125f). There is, however, no contradiction between this and the system contemplated here, although both systems are based on action logic. In the previously developed logic, the content of a conjunctive obligation was so defined that it had to be realized through *one* action (by some agent on some occasion), whereas in the above formula Bp and Bq may be *two* separate actions (though performed by one agent on one and the same occasion). It may be thought that the view taken in the previous paper was too restrictive.

former holds "dually" for the latter. This means that whereas $P(Bp \lor Bq)$ entails $PBp \lor PBq$, the converse does not hold. This is most readily seen again from considerations pertaining to the conditions of application. The disjunctive permission applies only when the two states are both absent and remain absent unless produced. The single permissions apply when the one state is absent, regardless of what is the case with the other state.

These observations on distributivity are, I think, in good agreement with our intuitions—and explain why doubts have sometimes been expressed about the validity of the distribution laws in traditional deontic logic. The features of a logical nature which justified these doubts, however, cannot be reflected in systems of the traditional type. The deepest reason for this is that those systems fail to make a distinction between negation (of a proposition) and omission (of an action).

An obligation entails a "corresponding" permission. For example, OBp entails PBp. If we form a corpus of OBp and the negation norm of PBp which is $O \daleth Bp$, the corpus thus obtained is not satisfiable. Hence its normative negation which is $OBp \to PBp$ is "tautologous".

XIV

OBp entails, in our system, $OB(p \lor q)$. The negation-norm of the second is $P(\daleth Bp \& \daleth Bq)$ and the addition of this to OBp makes an inconsistent *corpus*. It is logically impossible that an agent should produce the state that p on all occasions which afford an opportunity and yet on some occasion, which also affords an opportunity for producing another state, omit the production of the state that p (and that of the other state).

But OBp does not entail $O(Bp \lor Bq)$. As we know, the normal form of $Bp \lor Bq$ is a 15-termed disjunction of two-termed conjunctions. To each one of the complex actions described by the conjunctions there are three cases of omission, also described by two-termed conjunctions. Thus the negation-norm of $O(Bp \lor Bq)$ is a permission covering 3 times 15 or 45 different conjunctive actions. Several of them are such that their performance on some occasion is fully compatible with the performance of the action Bp on all occasions when there is an opportunity.

(An example would be $Sp \& \daleth Bq$. It is left as an exercise to the interested reader to write out all the cases which are such that the agent does *not omit* to produce the state that p but *omits* to do something he would do if he either produced the state that p or produced the state that q.) Hence adding this permission to a corpus containing (or consisting of) OBp would not make the corpus inconsistent. Therefore OBp does not entail $O(Bp \lor Bq)$.

I think something can be learnt from this about Ross's Paradox. Take Ross's own famous example. Does an order to mail a letter entail an order to mail it or burn it? If we say that an order (obligation) to produce a state of affairs such that a certain letter is mailed entails an order to produce a state of affairs such that this letter is mailed or burnt, then the feeling of "paradox" is very mild, if there is any such feeling at all. It seems to me entirely acceptable that a reasonable deontic logic should contain a formula answering to this entailment among its theorems. This would be the formula $OBp \rightarrow OB(p \vee q)$. But if instead we say that an order (obligation) to produce a state of affairs such that a certain letter is mailed entails an order either to produce this state of affairs or to produce the state of affairs that this letter is burnt, we say something which sounds rather confusing and requires clarification before we can pronounce on its acceptability and truth at all. We must first make clear how a disjunction of two performances of action is to be understood and then what an omission of this complex performance amounts to. There may be more than one way of making this clear, i.e. assigning a meaning to it. The explication which I have attempted in this essay seems, at least to me, intuitively entirely acceptable; and accepting it, the entailment in question, *viz.* the formula $OBp \rightarrow O(Bp \vee Bq)$, simply does not hold true.

My suggestion therefore is that the appearance of "paradox" with Ross's example is due to a (easily understandable) confusion between saying something which is trivially true and not (very) "paradoxical" and saying something else which is in fact *not* true. If this second were true, there would indeed be something rotten with deontic logic. But fortunately it is not true.

XV

Bp, for example, is short for $B_{a,o}p$. In a molecular compound of B- and/or S-expressions it is assumed that all components refer to the same agent and the same occasion.

We might also want to consider cases when several agents and/or several occasions are involved. Then we would see that there are dependencies of a new kind demanding attention. For example, consider $B_{a,a}p$ and $S_{b,o}p$. Can, on one and the same occasion, one agent produce a state which another one sustains? Obviously not. But what of $B_{a,o}p$ and $B_{b,o}p$? Can two agents, on one and the same occasion, both produce the same state? The answer is not clear. One could argue that the action of the one agent destroys the opportunity for the other. But I incline to think that it is *better not* to say this—but to answer Yes to our question above.[33] What

---

[33] In previous publications I have relied upon a slightly different definition from the one adopted here of the notion of an opportunity for action. According to that other definition, one would say that an occasion o affords an opportunity for an agent a for producing the state of affairs that p if, and only if, this state does not obtain and does not originate unless produced by *the agent a* (cf. above, p. 170). Then the question whether two agents can

about $B_{a,o}p$ and $B_{a,u}p$? If a has produced a state, he cannot produce it again unless the state has first been destroyed or otherwise vanished. Whether this is the case cannot be decided in logic. But if o and u are "adjacent" occasions a cannot on both produce the same state—for reasons of logic. In a logic which considers the order of occasions one could study such dependencies between actions.

Consider $O(B_{a,o}p \ \& \ B_{b,o}q)$. Does this not entail $OB_{a,o}p$?

The answer to the question is No; because the obligation is for an occasion when a can produce a certain state *and* b can produce another. And if this is not the case the norm simply does not apply.

More will not be said here about the cases when several agents and/or several occasions are involved in the *BS*-sentences.

6. NOTE ON THE SYMBOL ⅂ FOR OMISSION AND ON HIGHER-ORDER ACTION

I

The sign ⅂ in front of the operator B or S denotes that the productive or sustaining action under consideration is *omitted* (by some agent on some occasion). That an action is omitted means that it is not performed although the occasion affords (the agent) with an opportunity for performing it. This, as we have observed, is a very *weak* notion of omission—but the only one which is considered by us here.

This weak notion of omission may be regarded as a *strong* form of negation. If an action is omitted it is not performed—but not necessarily the other way round. Thus a formula ⅂ $B-$ or ⅂ $S-$ entails a corresponding formula $\sim B-$ and $\sim S-$.

Such observations may suggest that ⅂ could be treated as a connective, formally on a level with $\sim$, $\&$, $\vee$, and the rest. This suggestion, however, leads to difficulties. For this reason the action logic which we have constructed does not allow iteration of the symbol nor prefixing it to molecular compounds of atomic *BS*-sentences. For example: neither ⅂ ⅂ Bp nor ⅂ $(Bp \vee Sq)$ are well-formed formulas in the action logic which we have considered here.

Can these restrictions be removed?

---

produce the same state on the same occasion has to be answered in the negative. Adopting this other definition, moreover, omissions would have definite results since that a on o omits to produce the state that p would then exclude the possibility that *some other agent* produces it. I think that one can argue in favour of either definition of the notion of an opportunity for action; but it seems to me that the definition which we have adopted here is in better agreement with actual discourse about actions and omissions.

What would it be to omit an omission? The phrase "omit to omit" is not very often used in ordinary language. If one wants the symbol ⅂⅂ in an action logic one will have to take a decision about its "meaning". It may seem natural to decide that *double omission equals performance*. When does an agent omit to omit to open a window? An answer could be that he omits this when, given that the window is closed so that there is an opportunity for him to omit to open it he (nevertheless) opens it thus "omitting the omission". This is stronger than merely *not* omitting to open the window. This last he will of necessity do whenever the window is already open—but the first he can do only when it is closed.

We discussed earlier what it is to omit to produce a disjunctive state of affairs. ⅂$B(p \lor q)$, we said, shall mean the same as ⅂Bp & ⅂Bq. But is this not also the meaning of ⅂$(Bp \lor Bq)$, i.e. of the omission to perform at least the one of two productive actions?

Before answering the question we should remind ourselves of the fact that the equivalence between ⅂$B(p \lor q)$ and ⅂Bp & ⅂Bq was no matter of course but resulted from a decision which seemed natural, not to say obvious, if we wanted to assign any meaning at all to the production of a disjunctive state of affairs and the omission of this action. Similarly, we have to argue concerning the possible meaning of ⅂$(Bp \lor Bq)$. It would not be at all unreasonable to take the view that the disjunction of two actions (productive or other) simply is something which one cannot omit. This is the view which I shall take here and which seems to me the soundest. In general terms: the symbol ⅂ for omission is *not* a sentential connective.

The question at stake is connected with another question: Can the action operators B and S be iterated? Does, for example, BSp make sense? Can one produce, bring about, the state of affairs that one suppresses a given state of affairs? This question we must, I think, answer in the affirmative. Generally speaking, BS-expressions, whether atomic or molecular, may occur inside the scope of the operators B and S themselves.

There are several ways in which actions which otherwise would not have occurred can be brought about. For example, by ordering people, or threatening or otherwise "compelling" them to do things which, on their own accord, they would not have done on the occasions in question. Similarly, actions which otherwise would have been done may be prevented or suppressed. Prohibition is a means to suppressing action. But when the action will, "in any case", be done (omitted), then there is no "opportunity" for bringing *it*, *viz.* the action, about (preventing it).

That one agent can "make another agent" do or forbear things seems obvious. Whether an agent can perform such feats on himself is perhaps problematic. It seems to me, however, that even in this case one can make sense of an iterated use of the operators B and S for describing in a symbolic language a situation when action takes place or is omitted. An agent can "force himself" to do something, perhaps out of a sense of duty, which he does not feel in the least inclined to do otherwise.[34] Or he can suppress in himself an action which he feels tempted to do.

II

We shall now return to our initial questions about omission and the "meaning" of the symbol $\daleth$. $\daleth(Bp \lor Bq)$ I said is not well-formed. But $B(Bp \lor Bq)$, I have argued, is well-formed. There is an action which consists in making an agent perform at least one of two actions; and this second-order action (like any other) may also be omitted. $\daleth B(Bp \lor Bq)$ also describes a mode of acting. The "monster" formula $\daleth(Bp \lor Bq)$, I would suggest, is an unsuccessful attempt to say what is correctly expressed either by $\daleth B(p \lor q)$ or by $\daleth B(Bp \lor Bq)$.

Something similar should be said, I think, about "omission of omission". There is no such thing, strictly speaking, as omitting to omit an action. But one can force oneself to omit it, e.g. in the face of a strong temptation to perform it. And this omission one can also fail (omit) to effect—for example by yielding to a temptation knowing that one should have resisted. But when no such second-order action is contemplated—either by the agent himself or by someone describing his conduct—there is not logically room for a second-order omission either.

III

I shall not here systematize and discuss the peculiarities of an action logic which allows an iterated use of the operators B and S. Only the following point will be briefly touched upon because it will serve to remind us of the *logical poverty* of the symbolism which we are using in this paper.

Are reductions between the orders of action possible? One may think, for example, that BBp entails Bp. If I bring it about that something is done (by me) then this thing is done. Certainly; but then by the same argument Bp entails p. If a state of affairs is produced then it comes to obtain, we have said. Why can nevertheless $Bp \rightarrow p$ (and *a fortiori* $BBp \rightarrow Bp$) not be accepted as a true formula of our action logic? The answer is this:

Actions correspond to *changes* (and non-changes). To produce a state of affairs is to make it come about on an occasion when it is absent and would not come about independently of action. A full expression of this in a logical symbolism would have to distinguish between two "phases" of an occasion o, call them o_1 and o_2, such that the second succeeds the first (cf. above, p. 174). If the state that p is to be produced it must be the case that: (i) the state is not there during the first phase, thus $\sim p_{o1}$; (ii) the state is there on the second phase, thus p_{o2}; (iii) if action had *not* taken

---

place the state would not have been there on the second phase, thus, counter-factually, $\sim p_{o2}$.

$Bp \rightarrow p$ would say that if a state is produced on some occasion then it *is* (already) there on this occasion. But this is logically false (or nonsense). If a state is produced on some occasion it *comes about* on that occasion. But to express this requires a more sophisticated symbolism than the one which we have provided in this essay.[35]

7. QUANTIFIERS IN DEONTIC LOGIC: *SEIN-SOLLEN* AND *TUN-SOLLEN*

I

I shall introduce a symbol "*BS(a, o)*". It shall represent an arbitrary, atomic or molecular, *BS*-sentence. If "*a*" or "*o*" or both are variables, the sentence is *open*.

An open *BS*-sentence may be closed by substituting constants for the variables—the name of an individual agent for "*a*" and the spatio-temporal specification of an individual occasion for "*o*".

An open *BS*-sentence may also be closed by quantifying it in the variables. There are six different ways of thus closing it, corresponding to the six combinations of quantifiers $(a)(o)$, $(Ea)(o)$, $(o)(Ea)$, $(a)(Eo)$, $(Eo)(a)$, $(Ea)(Eo)$. The combinations $(o)(a)$ and $(Eo)(Ea)$ I shall regard as identical with $(a)(o)$ and $(Ea)(Eo)$ respectively.

An open *BS*-sentence may, finally, be closed by a combination of quantification and substitution of constants for variables. There are four such cases. The name of an agent is substituted for "*a*" and the sentence asserted to be true either on all occasions or on some occasion. Or a spatio-temporal specification is substituted for "*o*" and the sentence asserted to hold good either for all agents or for some agent.

There are thus in all eleven different closed forms of an open sentence *BS(a, o)*. The closed sentences express true or false propositions. One can, in an extended sense, also say that they describe eleven different states of affairs. Of such sentences molecular compounds may be formed with the aid of truth-connectives.

We list the eleven cases below ("*a*" and "*o*" should be regarded as constants when they do not occur as apparent variables).

1. *BS(a, o)*   *a* on *o* does −, e.g. produces the state of affairs that *p* and omits to sustain the state that *q*.

---

[35] For a formally more elaborated treatment of these refinements cf. my *Essay in Deontic Logic and the General Theory of Action*, Ch. II.

2. $(a)BS(a, o)$ everybody on o does $-$.
3. $(Ea)BS(a, o)$ somebody on o does $-$.
4. $(o)BS(a, o)$ a always does $-$.
5. $(Eo)BS(a, o)$ a sometime does $-$.
6. $(a)(o)BS(a, o)$ everybody always does $-$.
7. $(Ea)(o)BS(a, o)$ somebody always does $-$; i.e. there is some one agent who on all occasions does $-$.
8. $(o)(Ea)BS(a, o)$ always somebody does $-$; i.e. on all occasions there is somebody who does $-$.
9. $(a)(Eo)BS(a, o)$ everybody sometime does $-$.
10. $(Eo)(a)BS(a, o)$ sometime everybody does $-$.
11. $(Ea)(Eo)BS(a, o)$ somebody sometime does $-$.

When productive action is concerned, some of these cases are obviously impossible for reasons of logic.

It is logically impossible for anybody to produce one and the same state of affairs always, i.e. on all occasions. This is so because an occasion affords an opportunity for producing a state of affairs only when this state is not there and does not come into being independently of action. In fact no two successive occasions can afford opportunities for the (generically) same productive action. At most, every second occasion can do this. These observations depend upon a certain conception of what constitutes an occasion and the generic identity of an action.

As far as sustaining (preventive) action is concerned, the eleven cases of the list do not encounter similar obstacles of a logical nature.

Can two or more agents on one and the same occasion perform the same, productive or sustaining, action? Can, for example, two agents on the same occasion open the same door? Perhaps. But the case is not logically transparent. If the answer to the general question is No, then cases 2, 6, and 10 in the list would have to be labelled logical impossibilities. How the question is answered depends upon how we conceive of the notion of an opportunity and the criteria of identity of actions.

I shall not here discuss further how considerations pertaining to the notions of occasion, opportunity, and (generic) identity of actions may affect the questions of logical consistency of the eleven cases of the list.

Not all the eleven cases are logically independent of one another. Thus the very strong case 6 may be held to entail all the other cases. Case 1 entails 3, 5, and 11. Case 2 entails 3, and 4 entails 5. Moreover, 7 entails 8, and 9 entails 10.

II

Do we not sometimes say of one agent or of several agents that he or they always perform, or maybe *ought to* perform, the same productive action, without implying a contradiction? Such locutions are certainly familiar.

The reason why they are not regarded as contradictory is that they are tacitly understood as referring (only) to occasions which afford opportunities for the action in question. What we wish to say is that he or they *always when there is an opportunity* do, or ought to do, the same thing.

It may be thought that in order to express in a symbolic language such statements as those above one would have, somehow, to restrict the scope of occasions covered by the quantifiers. But this is not necessary.

An occasion which affords an opportunity for an action is one on which this action is either performed or omitted. The condition that an occasion affords an opportunity can be expressed in our symbolism in the form of a disjunction, for example $B_{a,o}p \vee \daleth B_{a,o}p$. Thus one can also express that an agent performs a certain action whenever the occasion affords an opportunity, e.g. as follows: $(o)(B_{a,o}p \vee \daleth B_{a,o}p \rightarrow B_{a,o}p)$. Here the range of the apparent variable is not restricted, but covers *all* occasions.

The implication within brackets in the last formula can be simplified, however. It is, in our action logic, equivalent with $\sim \daleth B_{a,o}p$. This says that it is *not* the case that a on o *omits* to produce the state that p. If this is what a does on *all* occasions o, then he produces the state of affairs in question whenever there is an opportunity.

$\sim \daleth B_{a,o}p$, on the other hand, can be expanded into a seven-termed disjunction. Using the abbreviations which were previously introduced for the eight elementary modes of action and omission, $\sim \daleth B_{a,o}p$ is logically equivalent with the disjunction $p_1 \vee p_3 \vee \ldots \vee p_8$. If *this* is what a does on all occasions o, then he either produces the state that p or sustains or omits to sustain it or destroys or omits to destroy it or suppresses or omits to suppress it. This is but another and more involved way of saying that he produces the state in question *always when there is an opportunity*.

As the above considerations show, it is not necessary to restrict the scope of the quantifier over occasions in order to account for the fact that things can be done (or left undone) only on occasions which afford opportunities for doing them.

III

Expressions represented by the general form "$BS(a, o)$" will be called particular or *singular* BS-sentences. Expressions represented by the general forms 2–11 (on p. 197 above) will be called universal or *general* BS-sentences. The term "*BS*-sentence" shall henceforth cover both singular and general BS-sentences.

BS-sentences of the general forms 1–5 can be either open or closed; those of the general forms 6–11 are always closed.

The "contents" of BS-sentences may be pronounced obligatory, permitted or forbidden. Such pronouncements are symbolized by prefixing deontic operators, "*O*" or "*P*", to BS-sentences. The resulting symbols will be called atomic *OPBS*-sentences. Of them we can form molecular *OPBS*-sentences using sentential·connectives.

The correct reading of (atomic) *OPBS*-sentences, thus defined, is "it ought to (may, must not) be the case that —". For example: $O(Ea) \sim \neg B_{a,o}p$ says that it ought to be the case that someone does not fail to produce the state of affairs that p on the occasion o.

Is a pronouncement such as this last one a norm? Is it descriptive or prescriptive?

IV

Saying that something ought to be is often *elliptic*. Then it contains implicit reference to something else which would not be, or come to be, *unless* that which is said to ought to be is, was, or came to be, the case. That to which implicit reference is made is usually some *end* or *goal*, and that which ought to be is something which is (thought to be) required (needed, necessary) if the end is to be attained. The relation between the end and the thing needed for its attainment is usually *causal*. The required thing is often also called a *means* (to the end). The ought-sentence, when fully spelt out, then expresses what we have called a *technical norm* (cf. above, p. 153).

Should such an ought-sentence be called descriptive or prescriptive? It would be descriptive if we could, for example, regard it as logically equivalent with a ("correlated") causal means–end statement; but normally the two are not exactly the same. The elliptic saying that something ought to be usually also evinces a positive attitude ("pro-attitude") to the end in view. The end is something we value or wish for or are anxious to promote (attain)—and therefore we say of that which is required for the end that it *ought to* be or be done. This is not prescriptive in the same sense as a norm which is addressed to agents is prescriptive—but nor is it descriptive in the same sense as a true or false ("objective") statement is. Perhaps *evaluative* is the best term to use here. Technical norms advise us how to attain or secure *desired* ends.

The captain surveys the situation and says "Someone ought to leave the boat".[36] What does he mean? He has not (yet) ordered anybody to step ashore or overboard. He realizes that *unless* some passenger leaves, the boat will sink. This is the objective truth. But it is not the whole "meaning" of his pronouncement. The captain is also anxious that the disaster be avoided. He feels he must do something. But what? Perhaps throw the fat man sitting in the stern overboard. Or, since he is in a position of authority, order a passenger to leave. This he cannot very well do simply by shouting "Someone ought to leave the boat". But he may do it by pointing to someone and saying " *You* ought to leave the boat". If he does this, then it

---

[36] Cf. *Norm and Action*, pp. 78f.

is *in a new sense* objectively true that someone ought to leave the boat, *viz.* in the sense that someone has now been given the order, been put under an obligation, to leave the boat. In an extended sense, an order may be called a "norm" (cf. above, p. 165).

Yet the formulation "Someone ought to leave the boat" could also be used for giving an order. The captain might address one of the sailors with these words. The sailor understands that *he* has to see to it that someone leaves the boat. Whether he does this by issuing, in his turn, an order (to passengers) or simply by forcing one of the passengers to leave, may be immaterial. The captain wanted a certain state of affairs to obtain, *viz.* that the boat be less heavily loaded, and he decreed that this state be produced.

Orders and norms of action are quite frequently issued in the form "Such and such ought to be the case". The words are then addressed to some norm-subject or -subjects, who understand that they have to see to it that the decreed state of affairs comes about or is maintained. From this insight they will then have to extract some rule for their own action on the particular occasion or occasions. "The window ought to be (kept) closed." So, if it is closed, don't open it—and if it is open, close it (cf. above, p. 185).

V

But should not the captain, when he was still soliloquizing about the situation, have said "it ought to be the case that someone leaves the boat"— and not "someone ought to leave the boat"? It is no good moralizing about the correct use of language here. But it is a fact worth noticing that the second formulation is ambiguous in a way in which the first is not. Saying "someone ought to leave the boat" can mean *either* that the boat cannot carry its present load of passengers *or* that a certain passenger is under an obligation to leave. If they mean the first, the words allude to a technical norm; if they mean the second, they express a *norm-proposition* to the effect that a certain order or norm has been given or issued. This order may have been given with the words "You ought to leave the boat."

There is thus reason to distinguish the two formulations "it ought to be the case that −" and "so and so ought to −". Even when the dash in the first formulation is replaced by an action sentence it is not certain that the existence of a rule or order asking an agent to perform the described action is implied. "$OB_{a,o}p$" or "it ought to be the case that a on o produces the state that p" might very well be an elliptic way of stating that a certain action on a's part is required for some end or purpose. And this same thing might also be expressed by the words "a on o ought to produce the state of affairs that p". Just as the words "you ought to go for a walk" do not necessarily express an injunction or order. They might mean simply "going for a walk would do you good"—and using the words would be a mixture of a statement of fact and a piece of advice.

The distinction which I have in mind between the two forms of expression is sometimes referred to, in German, with the terms *Sein-Sollen* and *Tun-Sollen*. It would not be adequate, however, to say, in English, that the distinction is between what ought to *be* and what ought to be *done*. Because that which ought to be, e.g. for the sake of attaining an end, can very well be that something or other is done, by some agent or agents on some occasion or occasions. As we already noted, the blank in the form "it ought to be the case that − " can also be filled by a *BS*-sentence. *This* does not make the words express a *Tun-Sollen*. And it follows that the symbolic means so far at our disposal are of use only for a logic or theory of the *Sein-Sollen* (and *Sein-Dürfen*).

VI

Before tackling the question how to express the *Tun-Sollen* (*-Dürfen*) in an adequate symbolism we return to the question, raised at the end of Section III above.

In addition to the elliptic use of *OPBS*-sentences for stating what we have called technical norms, there is also a use of them for expressing genuine norms, thereby imposing obligations on, or giving permissions to, agents. This means that such sentences can be given both a prescriptive and a descriptive interpretation. Descriptively interpreted they state that norms exist to the effect that it ought to or may be the case that certain actions take place. But, be it observed, they do not say *to whom* the norms in question are addressed, i.e. who is obliged to see to it or to allow those actions to happen.

Consider an atomic *OPBS*-sentence in which the *BS*-component is a singular *BS*-sentence. An example would be the sentence $O \sim \daleth B_{a,o}p$.

Such a sentence may be quantified in one or in both the variables a and o. Counting the combinations of quantifiers $(a)(o)$ and $(o)(a)$ as identical, and also the combinations $(Ea)(Eo)$ and $(Eo)(Ea)$, there are in all ten different forms of quantified atomic *OPBS*-sentences, "corresponding" to the ten different forms of quantified singular *BS*-sentences.

Consider, for example, $(Ea)O \sim \daleth B_{a,o}p$. The sentence says that there is an agent a such that it ought to be the case that *he* on the occasion o does not omit to produce the state that p; i.e. that he produces it if there is an opportunity to do this on the occasion in question. But the sentence does not say *who* this agent is. For this reason it—unlike for example $O(Ea) \sim \daleth B_{a,o}p$—cannot be used prescriptively for enunciating a norm. Nor does it directly express a norm-proposition either, although it may be said to do so indirectly or obliquely since it entails that a norm exists to the effect that it ought to be the case that some named agent on the occasion o does not omit to produce the state that p.

Consider next $(a)O \sim \daleth B_{a,o}p$. It says that all agents are such that it ought to be the case that they on the occasion o do not omit to produce the state that p. Can this sentence be interpreted prescriptively? I think the answer is No. In order to see this, consider which state of affairs with regard to existing norms the sentence describes. It is the state when, for every agent, there is a norm of such and such content. The state of affairs which it describes is thus that of a plurality of norms, one for every agent. Which is the prescriptive, normative activity which created this state? Primarily it is the giving of the required number of norms, one for each agent separately. *Can* the same state be created collectively by giving a norm to all agents to the effect that it ought to be the case that they on the occasion in question do the stated thing?

It would indeed be possible through one act of norm-giving to put all agents under an obligation *to do* a certain thing. But the norm thus given is a norm of the *Tun-Sollen* type, i.e. a norm of the form "so and so ought to $-$", whereas the norm purportedly addressed to all agents is a *Sein-Sollen* norm, i.e. of the form "it ought to be the case that $-$". It would also be possible through one act of norm-giving to address a norm to all agents to the effect that it *ought to be the case that* they all do a certain thing. The norm thus given would be $O(a) \sim \daleth B_{a,o}p$ and *not* $(a)O \sim \daleth B_{a,o}p$. The apparent possibility of giving to the expression $(a)O \sim \daleth B_{a,o}p$ a prescriptive interpretation is due to a confusion, I would maintain, between the state described by this expression and the thing prescribed by "everyone ought not to omit to produce the state that p" or the (different) thing prescribed with "it ought to be the case that everyone does not omit to produce the state that p".

The conclusion is thus that quantified (atomic and molecular) *OPBS*-sentences must be interpreted descriptively and cannot be interpreted prescriptively. In this they differ characteristically from non-quantified *OPBS*-sentences. The latter have the same systematic ambiguity which is characteristic of sentences generally in which the deontic operator stands in front of descriptions for states of affairs—regardless of whether the *BS*-component of the sentence is singular or general.

VII

Is a quantifier-shift from outside a deontic operator to inside it, or vice-versa, allowed? "Allowed" here means that the expression on which the shift is made entails the expression which originates through the shift.

If quantified *OPBS*-sentences can only be interpreted descriptively, "entailment" here cannot be "normative entailment" but must mean (ordinary) "propositional entailment". The answer to the above question is, I think, that at the propositional level there are no entailments here.

We shall consider two sample cases.

The first deals with the expressions $(Ea)OBS(a, o)$ and $O(Ea)BS(a, o)$. A presumption in favour of thinking that the first entails the second but not vice-versa may exist. I shall abbreviate them to $(Ea)O$ and $O(Ea)$ respectively.

The first expression says that there is an agent such that it ought to be the case that *he* does this or that; the second that it ought to be the case that *some agent* does this thing. For all I can see, the two propositions are logically independent. What nevertheless may induce us to think that the first entails the second is this:

Assume that a norm-authority issued a norm to the effect that it ought to be the case that a certain named agent *a* does something. Then he could not consistently with this "rationally" permit that every agent does not do this (on the occasion under consideration). The permissive norm is the normative negation, $P(a)$, of the obligation norm $O(Ea)$. Hence the norm which makes it obligatory that *a* does the thing in question "normatively entails" the norm $O(Ea)$. Moreover, the norm-proposition that (there is a norm to the effect that) it ought to be the case that *a* does something entails (in the ordinary propositional sense) the proposition that there is an agent such that it ought to be the case that this agent does this thing. The entailed proposition is that $(Ea)O$. The fact that this proposition is entailed by a norm-proposition such that the norm corresponding to it "entails" the norm $O(Ea)$ is no proof, however, that the proposition that $(Ea)O$ entails the proposition that $O(Ea)$.

The second case concerns the expressions $(a)OBS(a, o)$ and $O(a)BS(a, o)$ or, for short, $(a)O$ and $O(a)$. There may be a presumption in favour of thinking that they mutually entail each other, are logically equivalent. In fact, they are logically independent.

The first expression says that every agent is such that (there is a norm to the effect that) it ought to be the case that he does a certain thing; the second that it ought to be the case that every agent does this thing. The truth of the first proposition is ensured by the existence of a plurality of norms, the truth of the second by the existence of one norm. These truth-conditions are independent. What may nevertheless induce us to think that there are entailments between them is, I think, the following facts at the level of *norms* (not norm-*propositions*):

Assume that a norm-authority decreed for every one of his norm-subjects that it ought to be the case that this subject does a certain thing. He could not then consistently with this "rationally" permit that some (un-named) subject does not do it. Thus a corpus which contains the norms for all subjects also implicitly contains the norm $O(o)$. This is "normative entailment". Conversely, if the authority decreed that it ought to be the case that all his subjects do a certain thing he could not consistently with this "rationally" exempt one named subject from this *onus*. Thus a corpus which contains the norm $O(o)$ also implicitly contains every single norm which decrees that it ought to be the case that a named agent does this thing. This again is "normative entailment". On the propositional level there is logical independence.

When a judge, for example, subsumes an individual case under a general norm and "concludes" that, since the law says that it ought to be the case that everybody – – – therefore it ought to be the case that this person too – – –, is he then performing a *logical inference*? The answer is that he is *not* making an inference, if "inference" means concluding from the existence of a certain (general) norm to the existence of another (individual) norm. What the judge does is that he issues (creates) *a new norm*, performs in fact a piece of legislation. But his action in so doing is "rationally consistent" with the will of the legislator who made the general law or norm. Had the judge's decision been that it may permittedly be the case that the agent *a* does not do the thing which everybody is presumed to do, he would have made the corpus of norms "rationally inconsistent". Rational willing, not logic, requires his subsumptive decision. One may *call* this "inference" if one wishes. But it should be noted that it is *not* an inference according to the rules of logic.

That judges make law in passing sentences "according to law" has, I think, often been noted.[37] But the first to have noted that, in so doing, they are not performing an operation of logic, i.e. that the subsumption of an individual case under a general law is not logical inference, was, to the best of my knowledge, Axel Hägerström.[38] To have understood this was, I think, a very considerable achievement which has still not been fully recognized.

VIII

We already (Section V) noted the distinction between the two formulations "it ought to be the case that – " and "so and so ought to – ". Also when the dash – in the first form is replaced by an action sentence, say "*a* on *o* produces the state that *p*", it is not clear *who*, if anybody, is under an obligation. Maybe the words allude to what we have called a technical norm which simply states the fact that unless *a* acts in a certain way

---

[37] Cf. Kelsen, *General Theory of Law and State*, p. 38: "The decision of the judge is a legal norm in the same sense and for the same reason as the general principle" (*sc.* the principle under which the individual case is subsumed by the decision).

[38] Hägerström's position as regards the nature of "practical inference" is perhaps most distinctly expressed in his study *Till frågan om den objektiva rättens begrepp*, I, 1917, included in English translation by C.D. Broad in Axel Hägerström, *Inquiries into the Nature of Law and Morals*, ed. by Karl Olivecrona, Almqvist & Wicksell, Uppsala, 1953. Discussing the judge's decision when he subsumes an individual case under a general law by virtue of a "syllogism", Hägerström says (Engl. transl., p. 114) that "all talk of a possible logical process in willing by practical syllogisms is idle". It seems that Hans Kelsen, too, towards the very end of his life came to a similar "expressivist" position on the nature of norms and "nihilist" view of the possibility of logical relations between norms. Cf. Ota Weinberger, "Kelsens These von der Unanwendbarkeit logischer Regeln auf Normen" in *Die Reine Rechtslehre in wissenschaftlicher Diskussion*, Manzsche Verlags- und Universitätsbuchhandlung, Wien, 1982.

something or other will not happen. Then no-one is as yet obliged to do anything. Or maybe the words express a genuine norm which, however, is not addressed to *a* but to somebody who has to see to it that *a* acts in a certain way. Then it is this other person who is placed under the obligation. (This case when somebody has to see to it that somebody else does something will be discussed later.) Of him we can now say that *he ought to* do something.

For "it ought to be the case that" we have the symbol O. For "*a* ought to" I introduce the symbol O_a. We could also have a symbol $O_{a,o}$ "*a* ought on *o* to" specifying the occasion when the agent is under the obligation; but I shall here restrict attention to the simpler symbol only.

In "$O-$" the place of the dash is occupied by a (descriptive) sentence, for example, "the window is open" or "*a* on *o* opens the window" or "someone opens the window". In "O_a-" the place of the dash is held by a *verb for action in the infinitive*, for example, "open the window".

In our action logic we have a symbol "$B_{a,o}-$" where the part "$B_{a,o}$" is read "*a* on *o* produces the state of affairs that" and the place of the dash is taken by a sentence describing the state in question. Omitting the indices "*a*" and "*o*" we used an abbreviated symbol "$B-$" which might also be read as an impersonal action sentence "the state that $-$ is produced" (see above, p. 169).

This last symbol, however, could also be used for the infinitive form of a verb-phrase signifying action. Then "$B-$" is read "to produce the state that $-$". Here, as in the original symbols "$B-$" and "$B_{a,o}-$", the place of the dash is held by a *sentence*.

Let the sentence be "the window is open". The new symbol "$B-$" then stands for the verb-phrase "to produce the state that the window is open". This is a clumsy way of saying "to open the window". Similarly, "$S-$" for "to sustain the state that the window is open" can be rendered more simply by "to prevent the window from closing".

One could build an action logic, dispensing with the symbols "B" and "S", in which the variables p, q, etc. represent verb-phrases and not sentences.[39] In this interpretation, too, the truth-connectives are applicable to the variables. "$p \& q$", for example, could be a schematic representation for "to open the window and (to) close the door". In an action logic thus simplified one cannot, however, without considerable complications distinguish between the productive (destructive) and the sustaining (preventing) modes of action, or between non-action and omission. For this reason I think it preferable to retain in an action logic for verbs the

---

[39] An action logic of this simple kind is sketched in my paper "Handlungslogik" in *Normenlogik*, ed. by H. Lenk; Verlag Dokumentation, Pullach bei München, 1974 (see also above, pp. 110f).

symbols "*B*" and "*S*" for producing and sustaining and let the variables, as in the action logic for sentences, stand for sentences.

A large part of the machinery of an action logic which we described in Part 5 can then, with a slight change in the reading of the formulas, be applied to a logic of action verbs.

There are some noteworthy differences, however. One is that iteration of the verb-symbols *B*— and *S*— seems not to make any sense, whereas the sentence-symbols $B_{a,o}$— and $S_{a,o}$— are iterable. Another difference has to do with quantification. Action sentences, as we know, can be quantified with regard to agents and occasions. In this way the form $B_{a,o}$— gives rise to ten different forms of, partly or totally, quantified action-sentence. This multiplication of forms has no immediate counterpart in a logic where "*B*" ("*S*") stands for "to produce (sustain) the state that".

IX

If an agent has an obligation to do something he is supposed to do this thing *himself*. This is in the nature of the case.

It is important to note, however, that the agent *whose action* is supposed to be obligatory (ought to be performed) is not necessarily identical with the agent *whose obligation* it is to make this action come about. The phrase "it ought to be the case that *a* on *o* does —" does not logically transform to "*a* ought to do — on *o*". The addressee of the norm to the effect that *a* ought to do this or that can perfectly well be some other agent *b* whose duty it is *to see to it* (as the phrase goes) that *a* does the prescribed action. This is quite commonly the case, not only in legal, but also in what may be termed "educational" contexts. The teacher has to see to it that his pupils — — —, the nurse that the children — — —.

What is it "to see to something"?[40] It surely is to *do* something, a mode of action. How does one see to it that another agent does a certain thing? For example, by ordering him or by requesting him to do the thing in question or, maybe, by compelling him to do it using a threat or even physical compulsion (coercion). As far as the result of the action of seeing to something is concerned, this action can be either productive or sustaining, destructive or suppressing. One can make a person do something which otherwise he would not have done, or one can make him continue something which he would otherwise have given up. In the first case one's action (seeing to it that the other person does something) is productive; in the second case it is sustaining. Parents very often see to it that their children do *not* do certain things which otherwise they would do. Then what the parents do is a "seeing to" of suppressive (preventive) nature.

Our previous symbols *B* and *S* can be used for expressing in an action

---

[40] Cf. the essay "Practical Inference", above, p. 11.

logic cases when an agent sees to it that an agent does something. One will then have to make an iterated use of the action operator since "seeing to" is a *second-order action*. $B_{b,o}B_{a,o}p$, for example, says that b on o sees to it that a produces the state that p then. The symbol shows, moreover, that also the "seeing to it"-action is productive, i.e. that had b not interfered with the behaviour of a the latter would *not*, on that occasion, have produced the state of affairs in question.

The state of affairs $B_{a,o}B_{b,o}$ can itself be the content of a norm. But the expression $OB_{a,o}B_{b,o}$ does not show to whom this norm is addressed, who the agent under an obligation is. It might be a third agent c whose duty it is to see to it that b sees to it that a produces the required state of affairs. That he performs his duty will then have to be expressed in an action sentence of the third degree or order.

In order to express that an agent, say b, is under an obligation to see to it that this or that happens we shall have to make use of the indexed symbol O_b. It is read "b ought to". Prefixing it to an action sentence does not yield a well-formed sentence in the English language (nor in the logical calculus). Instead of the symbol $B_{a,o}-$ which represents a sentence, we must use the symbol $B-$ which represents a verb-phrase "produce the state of affairs that $-$" where the place of the dash is held by a sentence (describing another state of affairs).

$O_bBB_{a,o}p$ says that b ought to produce the state of affairs consisting in that a on o produces the state that p. Or, in short—but omitting the piece of information that b's action is supposed to be productive and not sustaining: b ought to see to it that a on o produces that p.

Could b be identical with a? $O_aBB_{a,o}p$ says that a ought to see to it that he on o produces the state that p. Is that the same or not as $O_aB_{a,o}p$ which says that a ought to produce on o the state that p? If the answer were affirmative the second-order action of seeing to it that something is done would reduce to the first-order action of simply doing this thing when the two actions have the same agent. But this reductive step does not seem to me warranted. Surely there is something in our lives as agents which can be called "seeing to it that we do something" and which is different from just doing the thing. The first-order action may be something difficult or repulsive for us to do and we will have to make an effort ("of will") to make us go ahead with it. Then we see to it that we do something which, without that effort of ours, we would have left undone.[41]

X

It is characteristic of singular deontic sentences of the *Sein-Sollen* (-*Dürfen*)

---

[41] Cf. what was said earlier (pp. 194f) on "omitting to omit". The second-order omission can be regarded as a case of failing to see to it that something is omitted.

form that they can be interpreted both descriptively and prescriptively, whereas quantified sentences of this form must be understood descriptively. Is the same the case with deontic sentences of the *Tun-Sollen* (*-Dürfen*) type?

Consider the singular sentence O_aBp which says that a ought to perform a certain (productive) action. It obviously has both a descriptive and a prescriptive use. When used prescriptively in the presence of a the form of words employed would normally be "you ought to $-$". But also the form with the proper name can be thus used—for example for emitting a broadcast asking Mr so-and-so to report immediately to the police.

Consider next the quantified sentence $(Ea)O_aBp$. An instantiation could be our previous example "Someone ought to leave the boat". As we noted earlier these words might be used with the meaning of "It ought to be the case that someone leaves the boat". The "ought" in the last sentence can signify either a deontic or a technical Ought. If the former, the sentence can be understood descriptively or prescriptively. When interpreted prescriptively it does not mention the addressee of the norm. He need not be a person who ought (himself) to leave the boat. There may exist no such person at all. The addressee could be someone who ought to see to it that someone leaves the boat. It should now be obvious that it is a linguistic distortion to use the ought-to-do sentence with the meaning of the ought-to-be sentence. The meaning of $(Ea)O_aBp$ is strictly descriptive. The sentence states that someone is under a certain obligation without, however, saying who this person is.

Consider, finally, $(a)O_aBp$. Cannot the phrase "everybody ought to $-$" or "all people ought to $-$" be used prescriptively—for urging all agents to a certain mode of conduct? That the phrase has a prescriptive use seems undeniable. There is, moreover, no need here to construe the sentence "everybody ought to $-$" as another way of saying "it ought to be the case that everybody $-$" in order to warrant to the first a prescriptive use. The addressees of a norm "it ought to be the case that everybody $-$" would almost certainly not be the totality of agents. If this were the case, all agents would be urged not only to do a certain thing themselves but also to try to see to it that all other agents do it. This would presumably lead to a chaotic situation of people interfering with one another. It is more plausible to think of the addressee as some surveyor(s) of the public order who ought to shepherd the herd of people so that every member of the herd does a prescribed thing.

There is, however, another sense in which the form "$(a)O_a-$" seems "secondary" to a form "$O-$", the *Tun-Sollen* form to the *Sein-Sollen* form. How would one explicate the "meaning" of the form of words "everybody ought to $-$" if not by saying that a certain norm is addressed to all agents (or all agents of a certain category or class)? And similarly one would say that "somebody ought to $-$" means that a norm is addressed to some agent, but maybe we do not know who he is. And that "*a* ought to −" means that a norm is addressed to *a*.

If this is an acceptable explication of the *Tun-Sollen* form it should also be possible to say which *the norm* is which is thus being addressed to some agent or agents. We ought to be able to separate the norm from its addressee(s). How is this to be done? What *is* the norm?

The right answer, in my opinion, is as follows: The norm is *that* something or other ought to or may be done (by somebody on some occasion). The specification of the agent or agents to whom the norm is addressed, i.e. who ought to or may do certain things, is, so to say, "extraneous" to the norm itself.

Norms, also norms obliging to or permitting certain actions, are a *Sein-Sollen* (-*Dürfen*) which in their application to the world of facts become connected with agents who are then said to be under an obligation or to hold a permission. The nature of this connection is usually transient. Norms have a history, they come into being, exist for a limited time and then pass away. When they cease to exist, they have no longer any addressee. A not-existing norm can still be spoken of as a sort of "ideal entity" very much like the ideal entity philosophers call "proposition". Such talk, however, easily leads to mystification and should therefore better be avoided as unnecessary.

Subject Index

Index of Persons

Agazzi, E., ix
Ajdukiewicz, x
Alchourrón, C., 111, 120, 135, 140, 141
Anderson, A. R., 154–5
Anscombe, G. E. M., vii, 18, 19, 139
Åqvist, L. 155
Aristotle, 1, 5, 7, 15, 18, 27, 29, 100, 117
Austin, J.L., 158

Bentham, J., 100, 101, 102
Broad, C. D., 204
Bulygin, E., 120, 135, 140, 141

Chisholm, R. M., 156, 159

Davidson, D., 115
Dostoevsky, F., 76
Dubislav, W., 130

Fröström, L., 9

Hägerström, A., 204
Hansson, B., 103, 132
Hegel, G. W. F., 19
Hilpinen, R., ix, x, 100, 154, 155
Höfler, A., 101
Hume, D., 81, 83, 92, 96

Jørgensen, J., 130

Kanger, S., 154
Kant, I., viii, 9, 10, 17, 24, 82
Kelsen, H., 136, 159, 165, 204
Knuuttila, S., 100

Leibniz, G. W., 100–1, 102
Lenk, H., 105, 110, 205

Mally, E., 100, 101, 102, 130
Manninen, J., x, 19
Martino, A. A., x
Marx, K., 19

Olivecrona, K., 204

Paton, H. J., 9, 24
Perelman, Ch., 59
Plato, 15, 18
Prichard, H. A., 83–4, 93, 94
Prior, A. N., 146, 150

Rackham, H., 1
Ross, A., 130, 132, 144, 191–2

Stoutland, Fr., 38
Stranzinger, R., 104

Taylor, Ch., vii
Tuomela, R., x

Weinberger, O., 204